EatingWell®

FOR A
HEALTHY HEART
COOKBOOK

JOIN US AT **WWW.EATINGWELL.COM** FOR MORE DELICIOUS RECIPES AND THE INSPIRATION AND INFORMATION YOU NEED TO MAKE HEALTHY EATING A WAY OF LIFE.

Library of Congress Cataloging-in-Publication Data has been applied for.

ISBN 978-0-88150-724-9

Authors: Philip A. Ades, M.D., & the Editors of EATINGWELL | **Food Editor:** Jessie Price
Contributing Editor: James M. Lawrence | **Heart-Healthy Tips:** Cheryl Sternman Rule
Nutrition Editor: Joyce Hendley | **Associate Nutrition Editor:** Sylvia Geiger, M.S., R.D.

Managing Editor: Wendy S. Ruopp | **Assistant Managing Editor:** Alesia Depot
Production Manager: Jennifer B. Brown | **Research Editor:** Anne C. Treadwell
Test Kitchen: Stacy Fraser (Test Kitchen Manager), Carolyn Malcoun (Associate Editor),
Katie Webster (recipe developer, food stylist), Carolyn Casner (recipe tester), Hilary Meyer (recipe tester),
Patsy Jamieson (food stylist), Susan Herr (food stylist)
Indexer: Amy Novick, BackSpace Indexing

Art Director: Michael J. Balzano | **Production Designer:** Katherine Kenny
Photographer: Ken Burris | **Illustrator:** Daniel Chen/www.i2iart.com

EATINGWELL MEDIA GROUP **CEO:** Tom Witschi | **Editorial Director:** Lisa Gosselin

Front cover photograph: Classic Lasagna (*page 74*)

Published by
The Countryman Press, P.O. Box 748, Woodstock, Vermont 05091

Distributed by
W.W. Norton & Company, Inc., 500 Fifth Avenue, New York, New York 10110

Printed in China

10 9 8 7 6 5 4 3 2 1

CONTENTS

Foreword **7**

Introduction: Mysteries of the Heart **8**

PART I A HEALTHY HEART LIFESTYLE PLAN

1 The First Step: Know Your Heart
Understand the major health factors that
are at work in your life **14**

2 Reduce Your Risks, One by One
Time-tested, cardiologist-approved ways to confront
the warning signs.. **28**

3 The EATINGWELL Healthy Heart Plan
A science-based approach that celebrates good food
and personal tastes.. **44**

4 Movement as Medicine
Exercise can lower your risk of heart disease—and
energize your life **54**

5 Lifelong Strategies
Proven techniques for making sustainable changes in
your diet.. **60**

PART II EATINGWELL RECIPES FOR A HEALTHY HEART

Introduction to Heart-Healthy Cooking
Simple changes and makeover techniques for eating well
every day **69**

Recipes:

Recipe Guidelines **71**

Menus. **72**

Recipe Makeovers **73**

Breakfast **84**

Main-Dish Salads **100**

Soups. **114**

Vegetarian **128**

Chicken, Duck
& Turkey. **152**

Fish & Seafood **176**

Beef & Pork. **202**

Quick Sides **226**

Desserts. **237**

Resources **244**

Subject Index. **246**

Recipe Index **248**

DEDICATION

If this book helps anyone live longer or better, as is its goal, I dedicate those moments, months or years of time spent with family and friends to the memory of my father, Victor M. Ades (1918-1969).

This book is also dedicated to my wife, Deborah Rubin, M.D. (a radiation oncologist and a great cook), to our children, Rebecca, Jimmy and Anika, and to my mother, Vera. May their lives be long and healthy and filled with goodness and happiness. —P.A.

ABOUT THE AUTHORS

Philip Ades, M.D., has been a clinician, teacher and researcher at the University of Vermont's College of Medicine and Fletcher Allen Health Care since 1984. He is widely regarded as one of the leading cardiologists in the world in the field of cardiac rehabilitation and preventive cardiology and has authored a review in the *New England Journal of Medicine* on cardiac rehabilitation and secondary prevention of coronary heart disease.

His research has been funded continuously by the National Institutes of Health since 1988 and currently focuses on the benefits of weight loss, good nutrition and exercise for overweight patients with coronary heart disease. He is an active clinician and sees patients with recently diagnosed cardiac disease on a daily basis, helping them modify their lifestyles to improve the quality and quantity of their lives.

With his own family history of heart disease, he also personally practices what he preaches in terms of diet and exercise. He lives in Shelburne, Vermont, with his wife and three children.

Howard Dean, M.D., and Judith Steinberg, M.D., both graduates of Albert Einstein College of Medicine, shared a family medical practice in Shelburne, Vermont, prior to his becoming governor of the state from 1991 to 2003. Dr. Dean ran for President in 2004. Dr. Steinberg continues to practice internal medicine.

The **EatingWell Media Group's** mission is to deliver the information and inspiration people need to make healthy eating a way of life. EATINGWELL is a leading publisher of the award-winning EATINGWELL Magazine, whose tagline is "Where Good Taste Meets Good Health," as well as a series of cookbooks (most recently, *The EatingWell Diet* and *EatingWell Serves Two*) and a vibrant website, *www.eatingwell.com.*

This book could not be more timely. Despite enormous advances in the prevention and treatment of coronary heart disease, in North America we are winning small battles but losing the war.

As a society, we pay all too little attention to what and how much we eat. And as we engineer physical activity out of our lives, we have become amongst the most obese and least fit societies in the world. Childhood obesity is increasing to the point where we may well be the first generation to outlive our children.

The answer is not to insert more coronary stents, do more expensive, high-tech medical imaging or more bypass surgeries. Rather, we need a public policy agenda that emphasizes prevention over medical intervention. We need more walking paths, less time in our cars and more time on public transportation. To curtail spiraling healthcare costs and to improve the quality of our lives, we must provide people the motivation, facts and tools to lower their own risks. This book is just such a tool.

As physicians, my wife, Dr. Judith Steinberg, and I have had to give people the bad news about their cardiac test results. And we know firsthand how a diagnosis of heart disease can change lives overnight.

We can think of no one better suited to present a credible guide to heart-healthy living and eating than Dr. Phil Ades. We have had the pleasure of Phil Ades's friendship since our children were growing up together playing weekend hockey in Burlington, Vermont, in the early 1990s. We have also shared many patients over the years. His emphasis has always been one of prevention—maximizing the benefits of exercise and nutrition over costly and sometimes unnecessary medical interventions. We are extremely proud and pleased to support his healthy-heart eating plan with EATINGWELL. We know that Dr. Ades has a strong family history of premature heart disease and that he has spent his entire professional career learning the concepts he puts forth in this book. This is how he lives his life and if you have a need to prevent heart disease, this is how you should live yours.

Dr. Ades takes the reader through the risks, one by one, from genetics to unhealthy weight to high levels of LDL cholesterol, and offers concrete advice and understandable tactics for reducing or eliminating those levels of risk. Too often, we see patients who feel defeated and powerless against heart disease. Dr. Ades's approach empowers people to take charge of their own destiny.

Unlike so many who write about diet, Dr. Ades does not implore you to "eat his way" but rather, working closely with the food editors at EATINGWELL Magazine, gives you the skills to make over the foods you like and "eat your way." Since its founding in Vermont in 1990, EATINGWELL Magazine has worked very hard to dispel the myth that healthy food must be earnest, flavor-deficient and uninteresting. By gathering medical practitioners such as Dr. Ades, nutritionists and very creative cooks at the same table, EATINGWELL has brought healthy-cooking techniques and uniquely appealing recipes into hundreds of thousands of kitchens.

We urge readers to take heed of Dr. Ades's eminently practical program to prevent coronary heart disease. For anyone trying to prevent future heart problems, minimize a family predisposition to coronary artery disease or quell high risk factors in their health profile, this book and its wealth of appealing recipes is as illuminating and inspiring a guide as you will find.

We would love to put a copy of this book into the hands of everyone who wants to avoid heart disease.

—*Howard Dean, M.D., and Judith Steinberg, M.D.*

INTRODUCTION

MYSTERIES OF THE HEART

Coming face to face with the world's most prevalent disease and
discovering that you have the power to prevent and stop it

I was 17 and away at college. The priorities in my life were baseball, girls and schoolwork, roughly in that order. One day an unexpected call came from family friends and it was quickly arranged that I should hop on a plane that afternoon and head home. I was told that my father was sick.

I thought this was unusual, as I had just spoken with my parents the weekend before and my dad *never* got sick. I could not remember him missing a day from work in my entire lifetime, and he usually worked six days per week, trying to make ends meet. It was also unusual to put me on a plane, as we didn't have a lot of money and the Greyhound bus would have been a lot cheaper. As the cab pulled up to my house, I noticed the street was lined with parked cars. When I stepped from the taxi, friends and relatives rushed out to meet me and took me in their arms.

"There are risks and costs to a program of action. But they are far less than the long-range risks and costs of comfortable inaction."
JOHN F. KENNEDY (1917-1963)

My dad, only 50 years old, had died suddenly the day before. I would never see him again. I clearly remember my grandmother, my dad's mother, saying to no one in particular, "Why didn't they take me?"

Back then (this was 1969) you only saw a doctor if you had appendicitis or a broken leg. Heart disease and its causes were still cloaked in mystery. Knowing what I know now, my father was not an obvious candidate for a heart attack. He was thin, didn't smoke cigarettes and took pride in the fact that he could do 25 pushups and walk at a pretty fast pace for a man his age. But, he didn't know his cholesterol level, he didn't know his blood pressure and he smoked more than an occasional cigar. I remember him advising us at dinner: "Don't cut the fat off your steak, it's the best part." Butter was considered "wholesome" and we used a lot of it in our family.

My father's sudden death had a huge, lasting impact on me. Most painfully because I probably hadn't told my dad that I loved him since I was about four years old. I had been selfishly wrapped up in my own teenage life and he was usually tired after work. But it also gave me a first taste of my own mortality, a powerful feeling that I was *programmed to die* at age 50.

Fortunately, many of the mysteries of heart disease have been explained in recent decades. A lot has been discovered since 1969 about heart attacks, sudden cardiac death and the process of atherosclerosis that can lead to an early demise. One particularly important thing I have learned is that a family history of premature heart disease is not a death sentence but rather a "call to arms." Most of the impact of a family history of heart problems is carried by the company it keeps—high cholesterol, high blood pressure, a tendency toward obesity and diabetes—and these are all treatable or preventable. Pay attention to the risk factors, do something to keep them under control, and you prevent the disease. Simply put, we now have the knowledge—and the self-help strategies—for preventing the number one cause of premature death in men and women.

HEAL THYSELF

Whereas I once wanted to close my eyes to my future, thinking that my fate was sealed by genetics, I now look it squarely in the eye. After many misgivings, I finally embraced preventive cardiology as my calling. I spend my days as a cardiac rehabilitation/cardiac prevention specialist aware that knowledge is power. I am absolutely convinced that the heart disease information and personal prevention strategies I have gathered and developed are allowing me to live longer. They are all included in this book and I hope they will allow you to live longer as well.

These days we know much more about how diet and lifestyle can predispose modern humans to heart disease. Each day in my clinic, I meet with patients newly diagnosed with heart disease and all too often am tempted to say: "We were expecting you. You were smoking, overweight, sedentary and ignored the fact that heart disease runs in your family. It was just a question of time before you got here." Denial of heart risks, even among informed people who should know better, is commonplace.

As in my own case, people facing the reality of heart disease for the first time often have a sense of dread or doom. Fortunately, I have a message of hope for virtually all of them: "We can take this on and together we can markedly decrease your risk of having this happen again. Are you ready to change how you eat? Are you ready to change how you live? Are you ready to follow a program of diet, physical activity and, if necessary, medications that has been proven to make people like you live longer and live better? If so, let's work on this together."

For those who hesitate, I might add: "If there are barriers that hinder your ability to do this full-bore at this time, we'll work on those too. Without your life, you have nothing."

While it is true that medical therapies developed over the past 40 years, such as coronary bypass surgery, coronary angioplasty, coronary stents and statin medications, have improved the outlook for those with established disease or certain risk factors, coronary heart disease is not something fixed with the medical equivalent of fixing plumbing.

Coronary atherosclerosis is a lifestyle disease, a metabolic disease, and it is almost entirely preventable. My dad died at 50, but I am now 55, exercising regularly, keeping a normal weight and enjoying my family, my work and my life enormously. I don't plan to pack it in anytime soon. Yet, when I look at the constant influx of new patients in our inpatient

> "I will never have a heart attack. I give them."
> GEORGE STEINBRENNER,
> NEW YORK YANKEES OWNER

cardiology ward, it's difficult to think that our society, as affluent and well-informed as it is, is actually winning the war against coronary heart disease.

Despite myriad advances in treatment and prevention, heart disease remains the number one cause of premature deaths in both men and women, far outstripping cancer as a cause of death. It also contributes huge numbers of people to the ranks of the

MYTH: A family history of coronary heart disease (CHD) is a death sentence.

FACT: A family history of coronary heart disease is a "call to arms." Most of the risk of family history comes from treatable risk factors, such as high cholesterol and blood pressure, that can run in families. All family members, including children, should have their risk factors tested.

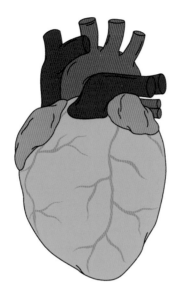

The Ultimate Pump

Ancient Greeks believed the heart held the human spirit, while the Chinese credited it as the font of happiness and the early Egyptians believed it was the seat of both emotions and intellect.

Although less romantic, the facts that have emerged about the human heart are no less awe-inspiring:

- The average human has about six quarts of blood, and this volume circulates completely through the body approximately three times per minute—so essentially the heart pumps 2,000 gallons per day.

- The adult human circulatory system, composed of arteries, veins and capillaries, is more than 60,000 miles in length—more than enough to travel twice around Earth's equator.

- By the age of 70, your heart will have beat some 2.5 billion times and pumped more than 50 million gallons of blood—enough to fill a swimming pool the size of a football field to a depth of more than 140 feet.

- The average lifespan of an American female is currently 80 years, a male 75 years. The estimated life of a modern industrial pump, by comparison to the human heart, is just 15 to 20 years.

prematurely disabled. An estimated 80 million Americans have one form of cardiovascular disease or another—coronary heart disease, high blood pressure or history of stroke. As the population ages and younger generations are growing up with increased risk factors, such as obesity, many observers believe that heart disease will become an ever-larger health issue in our society.

While we do not have all the answers, science has zeroed in on many of the causes of heart disease. We know the primary precursors—poor diet and a sedentary life—yet we, as a society, are fatter and less

"It's not that I'm afraid to die, I just don't want to be there when it happens."

WOODY ALLEN, FILMMAKER

fit than ever. The modern diet, dominated by processed foods high in empty calories and harmful fats and stripped of nutrients and fiber, is virtually a prescription for heart disease and the constellation of conditions that surround it. At the same time, we have had physical activity essentially engineered out of our daily lives. Time-saving and energy-saving devices that we have come to take for granted discourage walking, bending, lifting or even getting out of the car to do our banking or order lunch.

Who Needs This Book?

This book is intended both for individuals with recently diagnosed heart disease and for people who *want to avoid being diagnosed with heart disease*. In the latter category, in particular, are adults with a strong family history of coronary heart disease (CHD) at a young age. This identifies families and children with a genetic predisposition toward CHD and/or a family environment of lifestyle-related coronary risk factors, such as high cholesterol levels and high body weight, that lead to CHD.

In preparing this healthy-heart book and lifestyle plan, my goal is to combine my 25 years of clinical and research experience working with patients to minimize their risk of CHD, with the expertise of EATINGWELL's award-winning team of recipe developers and nutritionists. Thus, if you adopt the eating, cooking and lifestyle principles of this book, and follow your physician's advice, you can truly minimize your chance of developing CHD.

If you already have a diagnosis of CHD, this approach will minimize your chance of experiencing a second coronary event. It has been well demonstrated that cholesterol control and exercise can cut your risk of a second cardiac event by more than 50 percent. You will find that heart-healthy food can be tasty and completely satisfying. You won't miss fatty, salty, high-calorie fast-food chicken and burgers, deep-dish pizza, fat-laden prime rib and creamy desserts. Indeed, life tastes far better without the overdoses of heavy foods that are so clearly linked to the development of heart disease.

The good news is that we know what we can do, each of us, individually and with our families, to dramatically lower our risk of heart disease by as much as 90 percent. This is a lifestyle affliction that demands a lifestyle solution, and one that is within the reach of most people who are willing to make changes in the ways they shop, cook, eat and keep active.

CHD: WHAT IT IS

The underlying disease, termed *atherosclerosis* (from the Greek for "hardened paste"), is the buildup of cholesterol, calcium and plaque on the inner lining of the arteries. When it affects the coronary arteries that feed the heart, it can gradually, or abruptly (in a "heart attack"), choke off the supply of oxygen and nutrients to the heart. Individuals with multiple cardiac risk factors (high cholesterol, high blood pressure, smoking, obesity, diabetes and low fitness level) are at particularly increased risk for CHD and in many cases will need medication therapy, along with diet and exercise, to minimize their future risk.

In rare cases CHD is due just to genetics. However, more than 90 percent of cases in the U.S. are related to lifestyle. In other words, nine out of 10 cases of coronary artery disease could be prevented by eating well and by embracing a lifestyle that keeps your weight, your cholesterol, your blood pressure and your blood sugar down and your fitness level up. The well-described "obesity epidemic" has two-thirds of American adults measuring in as being overweight and more than a third as obese. It boggles the mind: One in three Americans is obese. One in three. The future consequences to millions of individuals, not to mention the cost to employers and taxpayers and the burden on the healthcare system, are difficult to contemplate.

Furthermore, more than 80 percent of newly diagnosed cardiac patients are overweight. It is partly what got them there, since being overweight is associated with high cholesterol, high blood pressure, type 2 diabetes and low fitness levels—the key factors that lead to coronary heart disease and heart attack.

What can we do about this? Do we need to prop open more arteries with coronary stents? Perform more bypass surgery operations? Is the answer more pills? Pills to lower cholesterol? Pills to lower blood pressure? Pills to lower blood sugar? The biggest developing field is pills to fight obesity itself. While there is a lot of money to be made in pills (the American pharmaceutical industry has the highest profit margin of any U.S. industry), it seems obvious that a lifestyle disease should have a lifestyle solution and a lifestyle plan to prevent it.

I am not pushing a diet. This is not the Ades Heart Diet or the EATINGWELL Heart Diet. There are no "etched in stone" recipe plans, no supplements to buy

"He who has health has hope, and he who has hope has everything."

ARABIAN PROVERB

from our website, no miracle treatments that falsely claim to "clear your arteries."

What you will find instead are my best efforts to tell you what foods you should eat less of, what foods you should eat more of, and how to protect your heart by getting more walking or other exercise into your life. Although there is no single "Best Heart-Healthy Diet," the foods and cooking methods we recommend owe a lot to the Mediterranean way of eating, which has been much studied as a model of good nutrition. Using the best of current knowledge about fats and other nutrients, we offer an array of truly delicious dishes that can be customized to suit your tastes and family preferences.

Right from the start I am here to say that, if you make your health a priority, healthy eating does not need to be complicated, it does not need to be expensive, but it does need to be consistent. A guiding principle of this book is that heart-healthy eating can be simple and straightforward and tasty and well worth the changes you will make in your shopping lists, cooking habits and favorite recipes.

Very likely, you have been motivated by the wake-up power of either a doctor's warning or a cardiac event—your own or a friend's or loved one's—and your inner voice is saying, "It is time!" I have seen thousands of people reach this point, a turning place in their lives, when they vow to make it a *priority* to eat well and live well.

If you have opened this book, you are probably thinking about making changes in how you have been living your life. Very likely, you have overcome the ambivalence you once had about taking on a healthy lifestyle and are ready to commit. I can assure you that the positive aspects of making a significant, permanent shift in diet and lifestyle will easily outweigh the loss of things you leave behind. Chances are very good that you will feel better, look better and enjoy life more, knowing that you have minimized your risks of heart disease and most likely extended your life by years, if not decades.

—*Philip Ades, M.D., Shelburne, Vermont*

CHAPTER 1

THE FIRST STEP: KNOW YOUR HEART

Understand the major health factors that are at work in your life

"This restaurant serves so much rich food they ought to give out Lipitor in place of after-dinner mints." Between stand-up comics with pharmaceutical jokes and daily headlines about medical breakthroughs, it is easy to understand why so many people assume that heart disease is being conquered by miracle drugs and ever more sophisticated treatment options. We hear it all too often: "By the time I need it, they will have a cure."

"Vitality shows in not only the ability to persist but the ability to start over."

F. SCOTT FITZGERALD
(1896-1940)

In fact, coronary heart disease leads the way as a cause of death in our society. Some 6 million Americans will suffer a heart attack this year and 16 million already have diagnosed coronary heart disease. Internationally, coronary heart disease, triggered by unhealthy modern diets and lifestyles, is rising ominously. "Coronary heart disease is now the leading cause of deaths worldwide," says a recent World Health Organization report. "It is on the rise and has become a true pandemic that respects no borders."

Here are the odds. In the U.S., a 40-year-old man has a one-in-two or approximately a 50 percent chance of developing coronary heart disease in his lifetime. A 40-year-old woman has a risk of greater than one in three or a 33 percent chance of developing coronary heart disease. This compares to a risk of one in eight women, or 12.5 percent, being diagnosed with breast cancer. Thus, a woman of 40 is more than twice as likely to develop heart disease as she is to develop breast cancer.

Unlike cancer, however, coronary heart disease is highly predictable. Anyone who takes the time to look can see it coming, or at least the likelihood of it entering his or her life.

Here are the major, well-documented factors that can put you at risk for coronary heart disease:

- Diabetes
- Cigarette smoking
- High blood pressure (Hypertension)
- Overweight/Obesity
- High cholesterol (Hyperlipidemia)
- Lack of regular exercise

The presence of these cardiac risk factors has a powerful effect on the subsequent development of coronary heart disease. One risk can lead to another, and interactions amongst these risk factors are important. For example, an overweight, physically inactive person is much more likely to develop high blood pressure, high cholesterol and diabetes. On the other hand, losing weight and/or taking up regular physical activity minimizes these same risk factors and can even treat a risky condition. As we will see, this is not all gloom and doom. You can change your whole risk assessment by making changes that we will explore.

Comics to Kings

Heart problems are great equalizers, afflicting rich and poor, famous and ordinary, young and old. Famous victims of premature heart attacks, with their ages at death:

John Candy, *comedian/actor* (Uncle Buck), 44

Gracie Allen, *comedian*, 62

Sergei Grinkov, *Olympic pairs skater* (Russia), 28

Cass Elliot, *singer* (The Mamas and the Papas), 32

Wolfman Jack, *disk jockey/actor* (American Graffiti), 57

Yolanda King, *daughter of Martin Luther King, Jr./
    actress* (King), 51

Jerry Garcia, *musician* (Grateful Dead), 53

Errol Flynn, *actor* (Robin Hood), 50

Peter Press "Pistol Pete" Maravich, *NCAA and
    National Basketball Association star*, 40

Robert Burns, *poet* ("Comin' Thro the Rye"), 37

Ted Demme, *film director* (Blow), 38

Mario Lanza, *opera tenor/actor* (The Great Caruso), 38

Jim Fixx, *author* (Complete Book of Running), 52

Darryl Kile, *baseball pitcher* (St. Louis Cardinals), 33

Brian Maxwell, *businessman and marathon runner*
    (PowerBar founder), 51

Rod Serling, *screenwriter* (The Twilight Zone), 51

Bart Giamatti, *baseball commissioner/university president*
    (Major League Baseball/Yale), 51

Robert Palmer, *singer* ("Simply Irresistible"), 54

Clark Gable, *actor* (Gone with the Wind), 59

John Spencer, *actor* (West Wing), 58

Roy Orbison, *singer* ("Only the Lonely"), 52

George VI, *King* (England), 56

WOMEN AND CORONARY HEART DISEASE

While it is commonly thought of as a disease of men, the number one cause of death in U.S. women is coronary heart disease. In fact, the number of women who die of heart disease exceeds that of those who die of the next 16 causes combined. In general, the onset of CHD is about 10 years later in women than in men. That said, a 40-year-old woman has a greater than one-in-three chance of dying of coronary heart disease and is eight times more likely to die of heart disease than of breast cancer. As in men, this risk is mostly preventable by lifestyle changes.

Information from an ongoing, large epidemiologic study called the Nurses' Health Study that followed more than 84,000 women has provided compelling evidence regarding the value of prevention in women. After studying these 84,000 women for 14 years, researchers found that more than 80 percent of the coronary events (heart attacks and cardiac death) experienced by these women were linked to a lack of practicing five healthy behaviors. Stated another way, *if women would follow these five healthy behaviors, they could prevent over 80 percent of major cardiac events.* These behaviors include:

1. Not smoking.
2. Keeping the body mass index below 25 (if 5'3" tall, less than 141 pounds).
3. Exercising (e.g., walking) for 3.5 hours per week (an average of 30 minutes per day).
4. Eating a healthy diet (high fiber, fish, leafy vegetables, high polyunsaturated fats, low saturated fats, low processed carbohydrates).
5. Moderate alcohol use (roughly 3.5 drinks per week).

Certain points that apply particularly to women, however, are well worth emphasizing:

1. A woman with diabetes (youth onset or adult onset) loses her premenopausal

Major Risk Factors Ranked

Relative increased risk of developing coronary heart disease (adapted from a 21-year observational study of 12,077 men and women, ages 30-79, in Copenhagen, Denmark).

Men's Increased Risk

Diabetes	+69%
High Blood Pressure	+ 46%
Smoking	+ 41%
Physical Inactivity	+ 28%
No Daily Alcohol Intake	+24%
High Cholesterol	+22%
Obesity	+ 20%
Low or Middle Income	+ 14%
High Triglycerides	+ 6%
Education (10 yrs. or less)	+ 1%

Women's Increased Risk

Diabetes	+ 174%
Smoking	+ 102%
High Blood Pressure	+ 42%
Physical Inactivity	+ 36%
High Triglycerides	+ 33%
Education (10 yrs. or less)	+ 28%
High Cholesterol	+ 23%
Low or Middle Income	+ 22%
Obesity	+ 19%
No Daily Alcohol Intake	- .01%

Results reported in "Coronary heart disease risk factors ranked by importance for the individual and community," *European Heart Journal* (2002) 23, 620-626.

hormonal protection and is more likely to develop CHD at a younger age and just as often as men who do not have diabetes.

2. Similarly, smoking markedly increases a woman's risk at any age, even if she's young.

3. The combination of smoking and use of birth control pills is particularly hazardous and should be avoided at all costs.

4. A woman's risk increases steadily after menopause so that by age 65 the number of new cases of heart disease (incidence) is equal between women and men.

Red flags go up when one individual has a cluster of risk factors. The presence of *multiple* cardiac risk factors *multiplies* your risk in a geometric fashion. For example, if you smoke, have high blood pressure or high cholesterol, any one of these risk factors doubles your likelihood of developing heart disease over the next six years. If, on the other hand, you have all three of these risk factors, you are eight times more likely to develop heart disease in the next six years.

The good news is that if you have all three risk factors and you effectively treat one of them with medications or lifestyle changes (in diet or exercise) you *cut in half* the likelihood of developing heart disease (from a factor of eight to a factor of four) compared with someone who has none of these factors. Again, coronary heart disease is a very preventable disease.

If you already have established coronary heart disease as manifested by a past heart attack, angina (chest pains with exercise) or past bypass surgery or stenting, controlling these same risk factors markedly decreases your risk of a second heart attack or need for repeat surgical intervention. In this category, you are more likely to need medications than a person who is trying to prevent his or her first manifestation of heart disease.

For someone who has not developed coronary heart disease, some sophisticated tables and tools allow you to do two things. First you can plug in

> "To see what is in front of one's nose needs a constant struggle."
>
> GEORGE ORWELL (1903-1950)

your own values for each of the risk factors and assess the likelihood that you will have a heart attack sometime in the next 10 years. Additionally, you can play with the numbers and assess the benefits of controlling your risk factors. This information is derived from the Framingham Heart Study that has been ongoing in Framingham, Massachusetts, since 1948.

So, using the Framingham Risk Calculator (*see the box below*), if you are a male, age 45, your father had a heart attack at age 50, you smoke a half pack of cigarettes per day, your total cholesterol is 220, your HDL cholesterol is 40 and your systolic blood pressure is 150, the risk that you will develop a heart attack in the next 10 years is 16 percent, which I would consider quite high.

If, however, you stop smoking, change the quality of your diet and lower your cholesterol to 200, you exercise and lose weight and your systolic blood pressure goes down to 120 and your HDL cholesterol goes up to 45, your risk is reduced to 3 percent. You have cut your risk by more than a factor of 5, from 16 percent to 3 percent—just for the cost of a pair of walking shoes. (Not to mention the savings on cigarettes!)

While the Framingham risk tables are enormously useful, they don't tell the whole story. They don't take into account several important factors, such as body weight, presence of diabetes, blood triglyceride levels, physical activity status and whether or not you are taking preventive medications, such as aspirin. Thus, by living well, you can have an even greater impact on your future risk than is predicted by the Framingham tables.

> **MYTH:** A family history of premature coronary heart disease, like your age or gender, is something that you cannot modify.
>
> **FACT:** Most of the predictive power of a positive family history works through its relationship with treatable risk factors. Thus, while high cholesterol levels or high blood pressure may well run in a family, once you identify them, you can treat them and nullify their risk to you.

Framingham Risk Calculator

The risk-assessment tool is available online at
http://hp2010.nhlbihin.net/atpiii/calculator.asp?usertype=prof

To use the online Framingham Risk Calculator, you need to enter the following information: your age, gender, total cholesterol, HDL cholesterol, systolic blood pressure, whether or not you are a smoker or take any medication to treat high blood pressure.

Most people don't have all of this information handy but it should be part of your medical records; simply call your doctor's office and ask for it.

1. High Cholesterol (Hyperlipidemia)

> **MYTH:** Your total cholesterol level is an accurate predictor of your risk of heart disease.
>
> **FACT:** Your total cholesterol is the least-accurate lipid marker of your risk compared with its components: LDL, HDL and triglycerides.

"High cholesterol" or hyperlipidemia includes a collection of several abnormalities of your blood cholesterol fractions that can lead to the development of coronary heart disease. While hyperlipidemia can certainly run in families, in North America it is most commonly related to a poor-quality diet. Having high levels of certain lipids in your blood increases your risk of having your arteries become narrowed with plaque formations. Other factors may be at work, including inflammation, but high cholesterol is strongly correlated with a risk of developing coronary artery disease. The United Nations attributes about a third of all cardiovascular disease worldwide to elevated cholesterol levels.

Your lipid or cholesterol numbers are measured with a blood sample after an overnight fast. Optimally, you should have fasted (nothing but water) for 12 hours and not have had alcohol within 24 hours. A single sample will give your physician a number of readings, not just total cholesterol.

Your total cholesterol is actually comprised of the three major lipid classes in your blood:

Total Cholesterol = High Density Cholesterol (HDL) + Low Density Cholesterol (LDL) + [Triglycerides ÷ 5]

Two of these subclasses are bad, and high levels of these predict a high risk for progressive coronary artery disease. These are the LDL (bad) cholesterol and the triglycerides.

On the other hand, HDL (good) cholesterol is highly protective, so high levels make you less likely to develop heart disease. An individual with a total cholesterol of 220 with an HDL of 60 is actually at a significantly lower risk than an individual with a total cholesterol of 200 but with an HDL of 40. More HDL is good.

What are your goals for your blood cholesterol levels? In reality your physician is guided not just by your lipid numbers, but by your overall cardiac risk.

For example, patients with established coronary heart disease have the most stringent goals and are essentially all considered at "very high risk." Their LDL cholesterol should generally be kept at or around 70 and the HDL should be as high as possible,

Your Cholesterol Test

To obtain an accurate lipid profile from a blood sample, it should be done after fasting overnight and with no alcohol ingestion for 24 hours. The total cholesterol, the triglycerides and the HDL cholesterol are directly measured and the LDL cholesterol is usually calculated using the following equation:

LDL CHOLESTEROL =
Total cholesterol – HDL – (triglycerides÷5)

- So, if your total cholesterol is 220 and your HDL is 60 and your triglycerides are 200, your LDL is

220 - 60 = 160 - (200÷5) = 120

- It is not useful just to get the total cholesterol measure because these *subfractions* are more important in predicting your risk.

"This was my life and I wanted more."

CL was 68 and had just moved with her semi-retired husband to Vermont to be closer to their grown children. She had been a history teacher and an accomplished cook and mom for her family of six. She and her physician had known that her cholesterol level was high but with a relative lack of other cardiac risk factors, they did not consider medications and did not discuss healthy eating to any significant degree. She made a mean quiche.

One evening she was working at her desk and had a sudden onset of chest pain and shortness of breath. She knew something was wrong and her husband, a psychiatrist, called for an ambulance. On arrival in the emergency room she was having a massive heart attack and received a clot-busting drug. Suffice it to say that she had every complication in the book, spent a week on a breathing machine and ultimately underwent high-risk bypass surgery by a skilled surgeon and survived. After a month in the hospital, she returned home. She was weak and frail and got short of breath with minimal activity.

On leaving the hospital it was made clear that her cholesterol level was a major issue: *the* major issue, if she wanted to live long. Her total cholesterol level had been as high as 325 before her heart attack. Since statins were only recently being developed, she started on niacin, obtained a healthy-heart recipe book and reduced her cholesterol level to 205. Soon thereafter she was started on a statin and her journey continued. She understood that diet and exercise were to be the cornerstone of her therapy and she entered cardiac rehabilitation.

As for the motivation to change her eating habits, to live without butter, cheese, eggs and fatty meats, she says: "If certain foods were making me sick, why would I eat them? Since I was in charge of food at home, it wasn't difficult. This was my life and I wanted more."

CL gradually became adept at eating well with healthy substitutions and she retained her pride in her cooking. She had the full support of her husband and family who adored her. She committed to long-term exercise as a high priority in her life. She has had a bump or two in the road over the past years, but CL just turned 90.

You have cut your risk by more than a factor of five, from 16 percent to 3 percent—just for the cost of a pair of walking shoes.

over 50 ideally. For most patients with diagnosed coronary heart disease, cholesterol medications, particularly statin medications, are prescribed.

Individuals with diabetes, or those with chronic kidney disease or disease of the blood vessels, particularly in the legs or the carotid arteries of the neck, are considered at "high risk." For these individuals, the target would be LDL cholesterol below 100 and HDL as high as possible, preferably over 50. Most patients in this category will need a cholesterol medication, but some will be able to get there with dietary and lifestyle modifications, such as exercise.

Individuals at moderate risk, such as postmenopausal women with other risk factors like high blood pressure or a family history, and men with other risk factors, will have a goal of getting the LDL below 130 and the HDL as high as possible. Doctors tend to be a bit more casual with these individuals, working on lifestyle-changing efforts over a period of months before prescribing medications.

Finally, individuals at fairly low risk, with few risk factors and parents who lived to an old age, will rarely need medications to control cholesterol and in general would only consider medications if their LDL remains over 160 despite long-term attempts at diet and exercise.

Abnormalities of blood triglyceride levels also predict risk of heart disease but are often ignored. Why? One reason is that they are often tied to metabolic problems, such as poorly treated diabetes, obesity, hypothyroidism, alcohol use and pancreatitis. Treating the underlying problem will treat the elevated triglyceride levels. On the other hand, high triglyceride levels (from whatever cause) clearly predict increased risk of heart disease and should not be ignored. More than with LDL cholesterol, treatment involves lifestyle and dietary changes (see the next chapter), although effective over-the-counter supplements and prescription medications are also available. A triglyceride level that is consistently over 200 is abnormally high.

More than with LDL and HDL, triglycerides are very much affected by what you have eaten and done over the past 24 hours, so to accurately gauge them, they should be measured several times. Ingesting alcohol within 24 hours will elevate them.

2. Overweight/Obesity

We are currently in the midst of an obesity epidemic hitherto unseen in the history of the world. While scholars are researching and arguing the societal, philosophic and scientific causes of this phenomenon, the basic issue is straightforward. Overweight/obesity is due to either too much food, too little exercise, or a combination of the two. Resulting directly from this are higher rates of diabetes, high blood pressure, hyperlipidemia and physical inactivity as obesity leads to each of these. No one in our society is immune—obesity rates have skyrocketed in children, men, women and the elderly. While it is more prevalent among lower-income people, recent statistics have found that obesity is growing fastest among higher-income men and women.

Some people complain that the BMI can be incorrect if you are very muscular or "large-boned." This is true in rare cases. To correct for this, you proceed to what I call the **"Ades-ocular"** test. To perform the Ades-ocular test you strip down to your underwear (do this at home). Stand sideways in front of a full-length mirror and focus on your abdomen. If it droops or sticks out, the BMI is correct, particularly if your bottom is also drooping. If your abdomen does not droop or stick out, but rather is flat and firm, indeed, your BMI may be incorrect.

Obesity Calculator

There are two ways to determine if you are obese. The first is to calculate your body mass index. The second is called the "Ades-ocular" test (*page 20*).

Body mass index (BMI) is calculated from your body weight (in kilograms, or kg) and your height (in meters).

The equation is:

Body Mass Index = Body Weight ÷ (height)^2

You can calculate your weight in kilograms by dividing your weight in pounds by 2.2.

You can calculate your height in meters by multiplying your height in inches by 0.0254. Then you multiply the resulting number by itself to get meters squared.

Here's how a woman who weighs 145 pounds can calculate her weight in kilograms:

145 ÷ 2.2 = 66 kg

If she is 5'7" tall, 67" x .0254 = 1.70 meters. To square that, multiply 1.7 x 1.7 = 2.89. Thus, her BMI is:

66 ÷ 2.89 = 22.9

A normal BMI is 18.5 to 24.9. A BMI of 25 to 29.9 is considered overweight, and a BMI of 30 and above is considered obese.

For a quick BMI calculation, log on to http://www.nhlbisupport.com/bmi/

THE SHAPE YOU'RE IN: APPLE OR PEAR?

Body fat distribution also plays a role in whether a given person has medical consequences for his/her obesity. By this, I mean whether body fat is deposited primarily in the abdomen or in the butt and hips. The former is called an "android" pattern and the latter is called a "gynoid" fat pattern. In common parlance, these are also known as the "apples" and the "pears." An abdominal fat pattern (apple) is much more likely to be associated with adverse medical effects, such as type 2 diabetes, hyperlipidemia, high blood pressure and a condition called "metabolic syndrome" (*see page 23*). Each of these factors markedly increases your likelihood of developing coronary heart disease.

> *"You can't talk of the dangers of snake poisoning and not mention snakes."*
>
> C. EVERETT KOOP, M.D., FORMER U.S. SURGEON GENERAL

A simple way to measure body fat distribution is to measure your waist circumference. Your waist circumference is not the same as your pants size, as many individuals wear their pants very low in the presence of a large abdomen. Your waist should be measured either of two ways. The easier is to measure it at the level of your belly button. The more scientific way is to measure it halfway between your lowest rib (at your side, below your arm) down to your iliac crest, which is the top level of your pelvic bone, again at the level of your arm. A waist measurement of greater than 40 inches in men or greater than 35 inches in women is considered unhealthy. This measure, however, is a continuum where higher levels are more associated with medical problems and lower measures are more favorable both above and below the cutoff levels cited. Thus, it is better for a man to have a waist circumference of 35 inches rather than 38 inches even though both are below the cutoff value of 40 inches.

3. Lack of Physical Activity/Physical Fitness

A lack of physical activity is probably the most underrated of the cardiac risk factors. It is also the most prevalent, with 70 percent of Americans getting little to no regular exercise. Additionally, it is not only an independent risk factor (meaning that it has a direct effect on preventing coronary heart disease), but it also has important interactions with other risk factors. People who exercise are also less likely to be overweight, diabetic or hypertensive and are also less likely to smoke. A physically active lifestyle is commonly described as one where the individual gets aerobic exercise (such as walking, cycling, swimming or jogging) most days of the week, for at least 30 minutes per session. While it is preferable that some of this exercise be at an intensity high enough to make you sweat, more important is that it be regular: winter, spring, fall and summer. Your body doesn't

"Every human being is the author of his own health or disease."

BUDDHA

know excuses but it does know the droopy, flabby, low feeling of not having been taken out for a walk. Furthermore, exercise does not have to occur only during a "bout" of devoted exercise. It is just as effective, and more convenient in many cases, to fit it into your day by walking for the bus, walking in from the far reaches of the parking lot or taking the stairs at work rather than the elevator.

Physical fitness is generally the result of having a regular program of exercise but there is also a definite genetic component. Higher levels of fitness in a given subset of individuals—whether it be healthy men in their forties, healthy women in their fifties or cardiac patients in their sixties—will predict a longer life, more free of medical problems.

4. High Blood Pressure (Hypertension)

High blood pressure has long been known as the "silent killer"—a major risk factor for developing coronary heart disease, kidney problems, strokes and a condition known as chronic heart failure. You cannot feel your blood pressure; it needs to be measured. It has also long been known that controlling high blood pressure prevents many health complications.

Overall, a blood pressure above 140/90 is generally considered elevated, but optimally the measures should be at 120/80 or lower. The first number, the systolic pressure, is measured as your heart pumps blood, whereas the second number, the diastolic blood pressure, is measured as your heart rests between beats. Your blood pressure should be measured in the seated position after 5 minutes of rest. If not, it may be falsely high.

Many people think they have "white coat hypertension," meaning they feel it is only high when they see the doctor and are nervous. Most people in this category have an intermediately high blood pressure

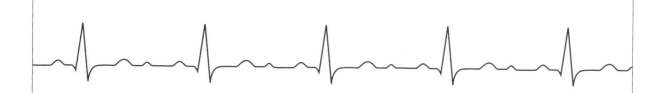

The Metabolic Syndrome

Metabolic syndrome is a collection of risk factors that are directly related to the presence of abdominal obesity. It is characterized by "insulin resistance," which is a prediabetic state and markedly increases the chance that you will develop coronary heart disease and/or diabetes. *It is a very significant risk factor and calls for emergency preventive measures.*

A diagnosis of metabolic syndrome requires the presence of any three of the following five factors:

- Abdominal obesity. Waist 40 inches or greater in men, 35 inches or greater in women
- Blood pressure over 130 systolic (first number) or 85 diastolic (second number)
- Fasting blood triglycerides over 150
- HDL cholesterol under 40 in men, 50 in women
- Fasting blood sugar of 100 or higher (over 126 signifies diabetes)

The presence of metabolic syndrome can increase the risk of someone developing heart disease by five to ten times compared with that of individuals who have none of these characteristics. It also signifies an extremely high risk of developing diabetes. Diabetes not only makes developing CHD more likely, but also is associated with the development of eye problems, kidney problems, sexual dysfunction, neurological pain and poor circulation to the legs and brain. You want to prevent it, or reverse it if you can.

Rates of metabolic syndrome have been climbing rapidly, driven by the obesity epidemic. In 2002, the prevalence of metabolic syndrome in all American adults was 24 percent, but there was a powerful effect of age. Men and women in their sixties and seventies had a nearly 45 percent rate of metabolic syndrome. So, not only is 66 percent of the U.S. population overweight, but by the age of 60, almost half will likely have a "toxic" form of obesity that is very closely linked with diabetes and coronary heart disease.

Still, if you or someone you know has metabolic syndrome, there is no reason to give up. Bad outcomes in individuals with metabolic syndrome or "prediabetes" can be prevented. In a three-year study sponsored by the National Institutes of Health in adults with obesity and prediabetes, with a simple program of exercise (30 minutes, 5 days a week) and weight loss (5 to 7 percent or roughly 10 to 15 pounds), participants' likelihood of developing diabetes dropped 58 percent over the course of the study. Whereas 29 percent of participants who did not exercise or lose weight developed diabetes over the three years, only 14 percent of those in the exercise group did.

that reacts to minor stress with an elevation. One solution is to take many blood pressure readings at home at different times of the day (not just when you are relaxed) using a portable blood pressure monitor and taking an average of these readings. It is the average blood pressure that matters the most and predicts problems.

In some clinical categories a lower blood pressure is considered abnormal. For example, people with diabetes or those with chronic kidney problems are considered to have high blood pressure if their pressure is over 130 or 80. This is because for these individuals even minor elevations in these categories have been associated with the development of severe kidney problems. There is ongoing debate as to whether patients with coronary heart disease should lower their goal to less than 130/80, though they probably should.

5. Diabetes

As you likely know, there are two types of diabetes. Type 1 diabetes generally has its onset in childhood, is related to a near total deficiency of insulin, always requires insulin supplementation and is not brought on by obesity. It is, however, associated with the development of coronary heart disease and complications of kidney problems, eye problems and nerve problems later in life. Its prevalence is not changing and many promising therapies are in the offing including nasally applied insulin and stem-cell therapies.

Type 2 diabetes is by far the more common type, accounting for 90 to 95 percent of diabetes cases in the U.S. From 1980 to 2005 the number of Americans with diabetes nearly tripled. This is due primarily to increases in overweight and obesity in the U.S. but it is also due to the increased percentage of senior citizens in the U.S. population. More than 20 percent of people over age 60 have type 2 diabetes compared with an overall American prevalence of 7 percent. Type 2 diabetes is also associated with premature development of coronary heart disease, kidney problems, eye problems, stroke and other nervous system disorders.

In type 2 diabetes blood insulin levels are actually elevated; it is more a disorder of insulin resistance than of insulin deficiency. An insulin-resistant state ("prediabetes") almost always precedes the diagnosis of full-blown diabetes. At this earlier stage, a program of weight loss and exercise can really make a difference: it has been associated with a greater than 50 percent reduction in the development of type 2 diabetes over a three-year period. Once diabetes has developed, many options of pharmacologic therapy can help improve glucose control and reduce complications of the heart, kidney and eyes. Optimal care can be provided by a diabetologist or endocrinologist.

6. Cigarette Smoking

Any amount of cigarette smoking, cigar smoking, pipe smoking or tobacco chewing substantially increases your risk of developing coronary heart disease, not to mention an array of cancers including lung and head and neck cancers, along with chronic lung disease. Smoking just one to four cigarettes a day almost triples the likelihood that you will develop heart disease compared with a nonsmoker. Non-smokers live an average of 14 years longer than smokers and have far lower healthcare costs.

Whatever your array of cardiac risk factors, stopping smoking should be your number one priority. Two years after quitting, your risk of developing heart disease falls to a level no different from that of someone who never smoked—*and* you will have saved thousands of dollars to spend on more healthful pleasures. While several approaches to quitting are available, the most successful include setting a clear quit date. Prepare for the quit date by tapering the amount you smoke, throwing away smoking para-phernalia, such as ashtrays, using a nicotine replace-ment therapy, such as nicotine gum, and enlisting the support of your spouse and friends. Other pharmaco-logic aids, such as bupropion and varenicline, may also help, but these are prescription drugs so you will need to discuss them with your physician. Most successful quitters have had to try several times, so if you do not succeed, gather yourself for another quit attempt when you are ready. Quitting is difficult but if you set your mind to it, you absolutely can do it.

YOUR PERSONAL RISK PICTURE

You can get a pretty good handle on your risk of developing coronary heart disease, or on your risk of having a second cardiac event, by assessing your overall risk factor profile. Essentially all of your con-trollable risk factors should be at the target goals. These include your cholesterol profile, your blood pressure and your body weight. You should not be smoking and you should be exercising regularly.

In selected situations, physicians may use even more sophisticated ways to fine-tune your risk of developing heart disease than those presented by the Framingham tables. In some situations, particularly if you are having symptoms, such as chest pains or

"If I Were King": The Ades Smoking Edict

If I were king (or president), I would give the tobacco companies 10 years to close up shop and diversify their business. Each year they would have to cut production by 10 percent and prices would go up accord-ing to the laws of supply and demand. Kids would stop smoking first, as they are most sensitive to price, and by year 10 only the rich and the truly addicted would still smoke. The nation's healthcare costs would plummet, life would be good. For heart attack survivors, quitting smoking literally cuts in half the likelihood of having a second heart attack, or of dying, in the two years following the baseline heart attack.

shortness of breath, an exercise stress test might be ordered. It could involve electrocardiographic moni-toring and in some cases will also involve cardiac ultrasound or injection of a nuclear tracer, each of which can pinpoint any narrowing of the blood vessels to your heart. Additional blood tests can also focus your level of risk.

These might include a C-reactive protein test, which assesses your overall level of inflammation. A

Personal Risk Targets

Risk Factor	Target		
SMOKING	Zero Cigarette Use		

BLOOD PRESSURE		Systolic (1st number)	Diastolic (2nd number)
	Target:	120	80
	Borderline High:	120-139	80-89
	High:	140 and higher	90 and higher

CHOLESTEROL (fasting levels in blood)

Total Cholesterol	Target: Less than 200 mg/dL
	Borderline High: Up to 239 mg/dL
	High Risk: Over 240 mg/dL
LDL Cholesterol	Target: Less than 100 mg/dL
	(less than 70 if you have heart disease)
	Borderline High: 130-159 mg/dL
	High Risk: Over 160 mg/dL
HDL Cholesterol	Target: 60 mg/dL (higher is better)
	At-Risk Men: Less than 40 mg/dL
	At-Risk Women: Less than 50 mg/dL
Triglycerides (fasting levels in blood—lower is better)	
	Target: Less than 150 mg/dL
	Borderline High: 150-199 mg/dL
	High Risk: Over 200 mg/dL

BODY WEIGHT

Body Mass Index*	Target: Under 25 (and over 18.5)
	Overweight: 25-29.9
	Obese: 30 and above
Waist Size – Males**	40 inches or less
Waist Size – Females**	35 inches or less

EXERCISE	Target:	Aerobic exercise daily (walk, jog, bike, row, climb stairs, etc.)

DIABETES

Fasting Blood Sugar Level	
Target:	Less than 100 mg/dL
Borderline High:	100-125 mg/dL
Diabetes:	126 and higher mg/dL

Notes: *Body Mass Index Calculator/BMI (online): *http://www.nhlbisupport.com/bmi/*

**Waist Size: Circumference, measured around navel, not belt size.

high level has been tied to an increased risk of CHD. Furthermore, increased levels of more sophisticated lipid subfractions, such as lipoprotein (a), or a direct measure of your LDL cholesterol, can be helpful. Finally, cardiac CT angiography is a noninvasive way to directly visualize your coronary arteries. If significant blockages are found and cardiac symptoms are present, an invasive cardiac angiogram, or cardiac catheterization, may be needed. During this procedure, if blockages are found, cardiac stents can be placed to prop open a blocked artery. In some cases bypass surgery may be necessary; in other cases medication therapy will suffice along with aggressive preventive approaches.

If your risk profile tells you that you are on a path to heart disease, you might want to heed the words of baseball philosopher Yogi Berra: "If you come to a fork in the road, take it." You can use the following chapter to find the right fork for each risk factor that may be of concern to you.

CHAPTER 2

REDUCE YOUR RISKS, ONE BY ONE

Time-tested, cardiologist-approved ways to confront the warning signs

"You're one of the lucky ones" is a phrase many newly diagnosed heart patients and survivors of heart attacks have heard. The message is that you've had a warning but are alive and have a fresh chance to set a new course with your diet and lifestyle.

Whether or not you have had one of these warnings, understanding and defining your own risks is the first step in preventing future problems. If you know you have one or more factors that might lead to future heart problems, the best time to start turning things around is now. First recognizing, then lowering your risk factors is the key and there is no reason you can't start today.

It is well within the grasp of almost everyone to craft an approach of better eating and daily walking or other low-impact exercise that will significantly reduce or eliminate coronary risks. For some, medications will be necessary, but in all cases you are still strongly encouraged to maximize the effects of diet and lifestyle to minimize the prescriptions and dosages needed.

MANAGING YOUR CHOLESTEROL LEVELS

Lowering LDL Cholesterol: Low-density lipoproteins (LDL cholesterol) are known villains and are near the top of the list of things most cardiologists want to see brought into line. Excess LDL circulating in the bloodstream tends to deposit itself slowly on artery walls, over time contributing to plaque buildup and narrowing of the vessels to the heart and brain.

The lifestyle approach to lowering LDL cholesterol consists of a combination of diet quality and diet quantity. While exercise has many preventive effects, it does not in itself lower LDL cholesterol unless you lose a fairly substantial amount of weight.

Dietary factors that lower LDL include avoiding trans fats entirely and minimizing saturated fats.

Trans fats are formed during the partial hydrogenation of vegetable oils, a process that converts vegetable oils into semi-solids that have a longer shelf life and, it was previously argued, enhance the palatability of processed baked goods and sweets. Once filling the margarine, cookie and cracker sections of the supermarket, trans fats have been targeted as a clear threat to human health, and they are disappearing from many commercial foods.

Nevertheless, they are still commonly found in such products as deep-fried fast foods, bakery products, packaged snacks, some margarines and crackers. No amount of added trans fats is good for you. They should be avoided entirely. Even if a product states "zero trans fats," check out the ingredients and if a hydrogenated oil is listed, do not use that product. There are trans fats present, but the amount per serving was

"To change one's life:

1. Start immediately,

2. Do it flamboyantly,

3. No exceptions."

WILLIAM JAMES
(1842-1910)

rounded down to zero, and serving sizes are often unrealistically small. Label reading will help you quickly learn which products to choose and which to avoid. Trans fats raise LDL (bad) cholesterol and lower HDL (good) cholesterol.

Saturated fats are found in animal and dairy fats and intake should be carefully limited. Saturated fats are also found in certain vegetable oils, such as palm oil and coconut oil. Overall, saturated fats should make up less than 5 percent of your total calorie intake.

A good rule of thumb is to take your body weight in pounds and divide by 10 to find your daily upper limit of saturated fat. Thus, if you weigh 150 pounds you are allowed 15 grams of saturated fat. At a given meal, a single item should rarely have more than 2 to 3 grams of saturated fat per serving. A 3-ounce piece of chicken breast has less than a gram of saturated fat, while a similar-size hamburger made with regular ground beef has about 6 grams. A glass of whole milk has about 4 grams, a glass of skim not even half a gram. Choices make a difference.

Exceptions: Certain food items, such as fish and nuts, are known to be heart-healthy, thus their saturated fat can be ignored.

The essential plan we use with great success with our patients is two-pronged and not at all complicated:

1) Lower the intake of certain foods, and
2) Replace them with better choices.

Some foods have clearly demonstrated abilities to improve your cholesterol profile.

Dietary items that are known to be LDL cholesterol-lowering include:

- Soluble fiber found in oatmeal, beans and vegetables, such as eggplant and okra
- Nuts, such as almonds and walnuts
- Soy products, such as soymilk, soy burgers, cereals with soy protein and tofu
- Stanol and sterol spreads, such as Take Control and Benecol
- Olive oil and canola oil.

Know Where Trans Fats Lurk

American manufacturers are now required to list trans-fat content in packaged foods. Restaurants and sellers of nonpackaged foods are still free to use hydrogenated fats without warning their customers. Keep a watchful eye on snacks and bakery treats—especially fried pastries and anything with a frosting or creamy filling. In restaurants, be wary of anything deep-fried.

Anyone wanting to avoid serious heart-related risks should aim to eat foods labeled "zero trans fats" and with no partially hydrogenated or hydrogenated fats in their ingredient lists. Amounts vary greatly from brand to brand, so it pays to shop around.

Some of the formerly worst offenders have reformulated their products to reduce or eliminate trans fats—potato chips and fish sticks, for instance.

Trans-Fats Transgressors

Various Manufacturers	High	Low (g)
Biscuit, buttermilk	8	0
Cinnamon roll, mall-style	6	0
Apple pie, fast-food serving	5	3
French fries, fast-food, medium	5	1
Microwave popcorn butter-flavored, 3.5-oz. bag (4 cups)	5	0
Chicken-breast strips fast-food (5)	4.5	2
Pound cake, 2-oz. slice	4.5	0
Chicken nuggets, fast-food (10)	4	0
Doughnut, glazed, 1 regular	4	NA
Cake, frosted, 1 slice	3	2
Fish sandwich, fast-food	2.5	0
Margarine, stick, 1 Tbsp.	2.5	0

Estimates compiled from manufacturers' nutrition information, U.S. Food & Drug Administration, University of Maryland Medical Center, Center for Science in the Public Interest and ConsumerReports.org.

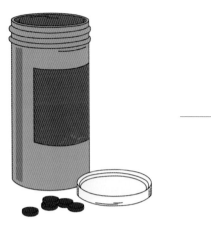

Weight loss, if you are overweight, can also significantly lower LDL cholesterol. Because exercise is a key part of a behavioral weight-loss program, it has an indirect effect on lowering LDL levels.

Lowering Triglycerides: Triglycerides are a chemical form of fat found in food and circulating in our blood plasma. High levels put some people at risk of coronary artery disease. For people with very high triglyceride levels, the diet we recommend is quite different from the diet that lowers LDL cholesterol. There are three basic characteristics of a triglyceride-lowering diet:

1. Limit intake of refined carbohydrates, such as sugar, white bread, pastries, white pasta, white potatoes, white-flour pretzels, etc. These foods fuel the body's ability to manufacture triglycerides.
2. Maintain a healthy weight. If you are overweight, losing just

---

Medications to Optimize Your Lipid Profile

Philosophically, it's attractive to think you can optimize blood lipid levels using diet and exercise, but a great many people need a pharmaceutical assist. If you've done your utmost to practice healthy lifestyle habits, you should not consider the use of medications a "failure."

In reality, for people with known coronary artery problems, lipid-lowering medications are almost universally required. Current recommendations show that for individuals with coronary heart disease, an LDL of 70 mg/dL is optimal and minimizes second coronary events. For those at high risk of coronary heart disease, such as people with diabetes or with peripheral vascular disease, an LDL of less than 100 mg/dL is desired.

MYTH: Your blood cholesterol levels are tied to your intake of cholesterol in foods.

FACT: Your blood cholesterol levels and your levels of (bad) LDL cholesterol are much more closely tied to your intake of saturated fats and trans fats than they are to the actual intake of cholesterol. For this reason, this book will not focus on intake of cholesterol in the diet.

---

5 to 10 pounds can lead to a marked lowering of your triglycerides.
3. Avoid alcohol, or have it rarely. A single drink can keep your triglycerides elevated for 24 hours—if you start with an elevated level.

Exercise has a direct effect on lowering triglyceride levels and a regular program of aerobic exercise can lower triglycerides by 20 percent. Limiting total intake of calories is more important than a strict fat limitation. In fact, since high carbohydrate intake, especially simple sugars, will raise triglyceride levels, a moderate to high intake of healthy oils, such as olive or canola, is encouraged, roughly up to 30 or 35 percent of total calories. Weight gain above normal significantly elevates triglycerides in many people.

Raising HDL Cholesterol: Here is the cholesterol you want. It performs a protective function to keep the negative effects of LDL cholesterol at bay.

LDL-Lowering Medications

Chemical Name (Trade Name)	Dose Range	LDL-Lowering Effects
Fluvastatin	20-80 mg	20-33%
Pravastatin*	10-80 mg	22-37%
Lovastatin*	10-80 mg	24-42%
Simvastatin*	10-80 mg	28-48%
Atorvastatin (Lipitor)	10-80 mg	38-56%
Rosuvastatin (Crestor)	5-40 mg	45-55%

Side Effects
1. Poverty (if your drug plan does not cover them)
2. Muscle cramps (rare)
3. Liver test abnormalities (rare)
4. Kidney problems (very, very rare)

*available as generic

Current theories are that it carries LDL back to the liver, where it can be removed from the bloodstream. Some researchers speculate that HDL can even extract LDL cholesterol from plaque deposits. In short, the more HDL you have, the better.

Everyday practices that raise HDL cholesterol without medical intervention include:

- Exercise
- Stopping smoking
- Weight loss
- Use of olive oil, canola oil and other healthy oils (*see chart, page* 47)
- Following a diet low in refined carbohydrates and sweets (sugar, products made with white flour and white starches).

Overall, these lifestyle factors can combine to raise HDL cholesterol by a very impressive 20 to 30 percent.

WHEN DIET IS NOT ENOUGH

LDL-Lowering Medications: The most effective class of medications for LDL lowering are known as the "statins" or HMG-CoA reductase inhibitors. They lower LDL cholesterol anywhere from 25 to 55 percent, depending on the patient, the specific agent and the specific dose. They have been shown to minimize the occurrence of coronary events and to reduce mortality rates in people at high risk. We've all heard the jokes about statins ("Pass the cheeseburgers, I took my statin"), but their primary effect, demonstrated by many studies, is to prevent heart attacks and prolong life.

Side effects of these agents are fairly rare and well described. About 1 to 2 percent of people taking statins will get a blood test abnormality that signifies liver inflammation, in which case the drug is stopped. This effect is reversible. Anywhere from 1 to 5 percent of people can get mild muscle cramps. If this effect is severe or associated with a blood test finding that shows muscle inflammation, the statin is stopped. This, too, is reversible. However, if this finding is not noticed and the muscle inflammation is allowed to continue, particularly if the individual gets dehydrated, kidney damage can ensue. This effect occurs in less than one in a thousand people who are taking these

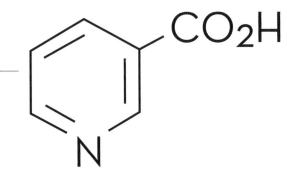

Niacin: The Best Deal in Preventive Cardiology

Niacin is by far the most effective agent to raise HDL. It is cheap, effective and available over the counter.

However, some words of advice are in order regarding niacin (vitamin B_3), particularly the generic form. It, along with aspirin, is *the best deal available in preventive cardiology,* but it can have many side effects and should only be taken with the guidance of your physician. If you buy a quality generic form in a jar of 1,000 pills, for 5 to 10 cents a day you can raise your HDL cholesterol from 20-50 percent, you can lower your triglycerides and you can lower your LDL cholesterol by about 10 percent.

Niacin can have many side effects and it doesn't substitute for a statin in cases of high risk or stubbornly high cholesterol. It should be started at a very low dose, only gradually building up the dose if needed. It should be taken after meals or at bedtime. Common side effects include flushing (which generally disappears with continued use) and possible stomach irritation, and it can activate gout. Individuals with liver disease or who drink alcohol daily should probably not take niacin. (The combination of niacin and alcohol can trigger excessively low blood pressure.)

A pharmaceutical brand of niacin called Niaspan is also available. It causes less flushing but is much more expensive. I sometimes start a patient on Niaspan and then switch to the generic type when we have attained a desirable daily dose.

medications. Risk is increased slightly when a statin is taken in combination with gemfibrozil (Lopid), another cholesterol medication. The risk of side effects is overshadowed by the fact that statins do prevent heart attacks and reduce overall mortality rates. The mechanism of action of these drugs is well understood and involves partially blocking the production of cholesterol in the liver.

Several generic agents are now available at lower cost whereas the two most potent agents, Atorvastatin (Lipitor) and Rosuvastatin (Crestor) are still only available as the brand name.

"The time to repair the roof is when the sun is shining."

JOHN F. KENNEDY (1917-1963)

Other drugs that provide LDL lowering to a lesser degree include ezetamibe (Zetia), colesevelam (WelChol), niacin and the rarely used cholestyramine and colestipol.

Ezetamibe lowers cholesterol by blocking its absorption in the GI tract. Even if the cholesterol in the diet is low, LDL lowering will be substantial. In testing, it had no more side effects than a fake sugar pill (placebo) and it dropped LDL cholesterol by about 15 percent. It is fairly expensive, however. WelChol requires six pills per day in divided doses and, like cholestyramine and colestipol, it works by binding with bile in the gut that contains cholesterol, which is then eliminated. It lowers LDL cholesterol about 10 to 15 percent.

Triglyceride-Lowering Medications

GENERIC NAME (TRADE NAME)	LIPID EFFECTS	SIDE EFFECTS
Gemfibrozil (Lopid)	Lowers triglycerides markedly. Raises HDL cholesterol moderately.	1. Stomach upset
Fenofibrate (Tricor)	Lowers triglycerides markedly. Raises HDL cholesterol moderately. Tricor, but not Lopid, can also decrease LDL levels moderately (15%).	1. Muscle cramps (rare) 2. Fatigue
Niacin/Nicotinic Acid	Lowers triglycerides moderately, raises HDL markedly (20-50%), lowers LDL modestly (15%).	1. Flushing 2. Rashes 3. Stomach upset, ulcers 4. Gout

Triglyceride-lowering medications include gemfibrozil (Lopid), fenofibrate (Tricor) and niacin (*see box, above*).

HERBAL SUPPLEMENTS

Regarding natural or herbal treatments for cholesterol, in individuals who cannot tolerate statins, I have had good success with an agent called (Chinese) **red rice yeast**. This agent contains a low dose of a natural substance similar to lovastatin. Using a dose of one to two daily capsules of 600 mg each, I have collected data in over 25 patients and red rice yeast has been associated with about a 20 to 25 percent drop in LDL cholesterol. The downside is that this agent has not had to stand up to the rigorous clinical trials required by the FDA of standard pharmaceuticals, and the frequency and severity of side effects have not been tallied. Nonetheless, in a setting where the drugs of choice cannot be tolerated, red rice yeast can clearly provide some LDL lowering; check with your physician if you think you might be a candidate. (Among my own patients, Solar Ray red rice yeast has proved effective when other brands were not.)

Other agents that enjoyed early promise have not panned out. **Garlic** in all sorts of forms has been recommended, but when its effects were analyzed scientifically, there was really no measurable effect on LDL cholesterol. It probably can't hurt, but don't count on it to help. **Policosanol**, a derivative of Cuban sugarcane, has been widely recommended by natural medicine physicians, but recent studies performed outside of Cuba showed no significant lipid-lowering effects.

Fish oil, krill oil and omega-3 oil capsules enjoy wide popularity. While their lipid-lowering effects are

"Dad always thought laughter was the best medicine, which I guess is why several of us died of tuberculosis."

JACK HANDY,
SATURDAY NIGHT LIVE

subtle and they mildly to moderately lower triglycerides, these oils may have other beneficial cardiac effects, such as prevention of severe irregular heartbeats, thinning of the blood and improvement of blood vessel function. It is not yet clear if taking omega-3 capsules is more effective than eating fish two or more times weekly in terms of overall cardiac prevention. (*See pages 46-47.*)

BLOOD PRESSURE CONTROL

The most powerful nonpharmacologic methods to control your blood pressure are:

- Weight loss, if you are overweight
- Control of sodium intake to less than 2,300 mg daily
- Regular aerobic physical activity.

Knowing your average blood pressure through a 24-hour period, if you have high blood pressure, is very helpful to your physician. If you can, buy an easy-to-use home blood pressure monitor (available in most pharmacies) to take your own measures to supplement the readings done in your doctor's office. If the systolic averages over 140 or the diastolic averages over 90, you may need to take a medication for blood pressure control.

As always, it makes good sense to maximize non-pharmacologic control before considering medica-tions. An eating plan most commonly recommended for blood pressure is an approach developed by the National Institutes of Health called the DASH eating plan. (DASH stands for Dietary Approaches to Stop Hypertension.) Details about DASH can be obtained from the website: *nhlbi.nih.gov/health/public/heart/hbp/dash/new_dash.pdf.*

The DASH diet is entirely compatible with the dietary approaches recommended in this book. Overall it contains roughly 27 percent of calories from fat, 6 percent or less of calories from saturated fats (we recommend 5 percent), 30 grams of fiber daily, and less than 2,300 mg of sodium per day, with a lower-sodium approach of less than 1,500 per day. The average American man takes in 4,200 mg of sodium per day, the average American woman takes in about 3,300 mg. Many cultures worldwide consume even more sodium, and their rates of heart disease and stroke are even higher than ours.

Overall, highly recommended foods in the DASH diet include whole grains, vegetables, fruits and fat-free or low-fat dairy items. It encourages the use of nuts and seeds, healthy fats and oils, lean meats and poultry, and fish, while recommending little to no sugar and few sweets.

WEIGHT MANAGEMENT

The medical benefits of weight loss are substantial. Even a relatively modest weight loss of 5 to 10 percent of body weight will result in better blood pressure control, a decreased risk of diabetes or insulin resistance, improved lipid levels with lower triglycerides and higher (good) HDL levels, less inflammation and a diminished tendency for your blood to clot.

All of this makes you less likely to develop coronary atherosclerosis. If you have heart disease, weight loss will substantially lower your risk of future problems.

Your weight is determined by the balance between the calories you eat and the calories you burn. There is no way around this basic principle. If you are overweight you are out of balance. Either you are eating too much or burning too little. Being out of balance by just 25 calories a day can result in three pounds gained per year. Over 10 years, that, of course, is 30 pounds.

The amount of calories your body burns is determined by three factors: your basal metabolic rate (50-70 percent of total), the energy you use to digest food (about 10 percent of total) and the energy you expend doing physical activity (20-40 percent of total). The variables you have some control over are calories eaten and calories burned with exercise.

In reality, the factor that you have the most control over is the number of calories you burn per day with exercise. My earnest advice is to make daily exercise a priority in your life. Its value in preventing obesity and in purposefully losing weight is grossly undervalued. (*See Chapter 4.*)

WEIGHT CONTROL BY THE NUMBERS

- A pound of fat has a caloric value of 3,500 calories. That is, if you create a net loss of 3,500 calories burned, or a net gain of 3,500 calories taken in, you will lose or gain approximately one pound of fat, respectively.
- A mile walked will burn 100 calories if you are average weight. If you are 20 percent overweight, you burn 120 calories by walking a mile. It doesn't sound like much, but read on.
- If you walk a mile a day for a year, and if you are 20 percent overweight, you will burn

43,800 calories (120 x 365) and lose 12 pounds of fat, assuming you keep your caloric intake (eating) steady.

- To calculate your daily calorie requirement (the amount you need to eat to *maintain* your current weight), multiply your body weight by 12 (assuming an average amount of physical activity). Thus, if you weigh 200 pounds, your daily caloric requirement to maintain your weight without change would be 2,400 calories. If you weigh 150 pounds, it would be 1,800 calories.
- If you want to lose a pound a week, you should set your daily calorie count at 500 calories less than your maintenance. (That adds up to 3,500 calories per week—the amount in one pound.) So if you weigh 200, it would be 1,900 calories. If you weigh 150 pounds, it would be 1,300 calories.
- In reality, the very best approach to weight control is to both limit calorie intake and increase calories burned with exercise.

BARRIERS TO SUCCESSFUL WEIGHT CONTROL

Losing weight can be made to sound easy, but it is no simple thing for many people. Here are some of the key obstacles:

- Having excess availability of calorie-dense food at home, at work and at most stops in between
- Not recognizing today's excessive portion sizes
- Letting physical activity be largely engineered out of your life
- Having no firm commitment to a long-term exercise program
- Lacking social support to adopt a better weight-management lifestyle
- Leading a life that is too stressful to maintain healthy habits.

Weight Loss Trumps Medications

A 63-year-old man (JR) was referred to me for treatment of hyperlipidemia—high cholesterol. Just three months prior to this visit he weighed 223 pounds at 5 feet 7 inches tall. That comes to a Body Mass Index of 35—officially obese. His triglycerides had been 400 (the target is 150), his LDL cholesterol was 160 (the target is 100). He was taking two pills a day for his cholesterol problem (lovastatin and gemfibrozil) and was also taking two pills for his type 2 diabetes—plus two pills daily for his high blood pressure. In all, JR was taking six pills a day to control risk factors related to his obesity at a cost of more than $200 a month.

By the time he arrived at my office, he had lost 22 pounds in Weight Watchers, which he had initially attended with his son-in-law (who was told he needed to attend by his physician). JR told me that he had felt it was important that he accompany his son-in-law as, without support, the son-in-law would soon drop out. Indeed, his son-in-law opted out after just three weeks, but JR stayed. His persistence was already paying off with more than a shrinking waistline: JR's triglycerides now were in the normal range at 145 and his LDL cholesterol was under good control as well at 101 (the goal in an individual with type 2 diabetes is 100). I encouraged his continued efforts at weight loss and decreased his gemfibrozil dose.

At his next visit, he had lost another 18 pounds, weighing in at 183. I further decreased his gemfibrozil dose and scheduled another visit in three months. In the intervening time (he spent a winter month in Florida), he let his pills run out (all six) and didn't refill them. At his latest visit with me, he weighed 152 pounds (a 71-pound weight loss), was off all pills, his triglycerides were normal at 145, his LDL cholesterol was at 94, his blood pressure was 128/80 and his blood glucose was essentially normal at 101. He said: "When I set my mind to something, I can usually do it." I congratulated him, told him he no longer needed to see me, to recheck all his measures no less than every six months with his primary care M.D. and to "sound the alarm" and get back with Weight Watchers if his weight ever creeps up to 155 or more. I also told him to take one aspirin a day for the rest of his life.

True story.

If you are overweight you are out of balance. Either you are eating too much or burning too little.

Losing weight, first of all, demands a positive attitude, and here are the components of a successful weight-loss program:

1. Determine your daily maintenance calories using the equation of 12 times your weight in pounds.

2. Subtract 500 calories per day to determine your daily calorie goal, planning for a healthy, steady one-pound weight loss per week.

3. Keep dietary records with portion sizes and calorie counts of all items. This gets easier as you get in the habit. An inexpensive pocket calorie counter, such as that offered on *eatingwell.com*, will be needed.

4. Keeping daily records forces you to make food choices. It also teaches you about the physical, temporal and emotional situations where you are most likely to eat excessively.

5. Practice "stimulus control," which means that if you shouldn't eat it, don't keep it in the house. If you were trying to quit smoking, you wouldn't have cigarettes on the kitchen table any more than you should have chocolate chip cookies in the cupboard if they are your downfall.

6. Practice portion control. Many of us eat good-quality food, just too much of it. Learn what a serving size is. For example, a piece of chicken or beef should be the size of a deck of cards, not the size of a baseball glove.

7. Plan for difficult situations. If you know you will be at a party with poor food choices, have a snack or a half a meal before you go so you won't be famished and overeat at the party.

8. Avoid drinking calories. Drinks, such as fruit juice, soda, beer, etc., won't fill you up, but contain hundreds of calories that you should reserve for foods that are both satisfying and nutritious.

9. Be politely assertive if friends or co-workers are offering you food that doesn't fit into your daily plan.

10. By all means exercise. The single best exercise is walking: walk daily and walk far.

The EatingWell Diet

The University-Tested Connection: Weight Loss, Heart Health and Delicious Eating

Physicians tend to look askance at most popular weight-loss programs sold to the public. One that makes sense to me, as a cardiologist, and one being followed by a growing number of my patients who want to manage their weight, is *The EatingWell Diet*, written by my University of Vermont colleague Dr. Jean Harvey-Berino. (For more information, visit *eatingwell.com/diet*.)

With firm footing in behavior-modification science, this approach has been developed by the university's VTrim™ Weight-Loss Program. I think of it as "changing your eating behaviors" rather than "dieting." Like this book, the program also benefits from our joint collaborations with EATINGWELL, whose wealth of delicious, nutritionist-reviewed recipes keeps the pleasures of eating while meeting our medical criteria for healthfulness and for reducing the risks of coronary heart disease.

Weight Loss Without Dieting

In a study we published in the *American Heart Journal* in 2003, we found that 15 cardiac patients were able to lose an average of 4.6 kilograms, or 11 pounds, over 4 months by exercise alone.

These were not seasoned athletes. They were middle-aged and older cardiac patients who were significantly overweight. The intervention was for them to walk almost daily at a moderate pace and to gradually increase the duration up to 45 to 60 minutes a day. We counted food calories and there was no decrease in food intake. Without any intentional diet change whatsoever, they achieved significant weight loss.

An advantage of this approach is that it gives you a nearly foolproof tool to keep the weight off for years and years. Remain committed to a long-term walking program, keep an eye out that you don't increase caloric intake and long-term weight-loss maintenance is assured. If you are able to count calories and subtract calories from your daily maintenance calories (see page 35), you will lose yet more weight.

11. Don't beat yourself up if you have a bad day or a relapse. Don't just collapse and give up. Reassert yourself and balance out your calorie counts over the week.

Don't forget: When you successfully do lose five or more pounds, you'll need to recalculate your maintenance calories and again subtract 500 calories for your new daily goal. Lay out a plan for a year, not for a week or a month.

KEYS TO KEEPING WEIGHT OFF

It turns out that people who lose weight and keep it off for at least a year have several things in common.

- They are physically active most days of the week.
- They frequently measure body weight.
- They keep tabs on food intake.

For a greatly expanded approach to weight control, see *The EatingWell Diet* by Jean Harvey-Berino et al. (The Countryman Press, 2007).

NAVIGATING THE MAZE OF MODERN DIETS

A number of weight-loss diets have been shown to be fairly effective in the short term for moderate weight loss. Sadly, in most cases the hard-won benefits wear off with time. Common sense dictates that for the eating plan to be effective in the long term, it needs to become fully integrated into your lifestyle. There is no magic in any of these diets. To lose weight via a diet, you have to cut your calorie intake.

Rarely do "diets" adequately take into account that, for long-term success, both sides of the weight-control equation need to be addressed: intake must decrease and exercise-related energy expenditure needs to increase. To exercise (or *not* to exercise) is not really an optional decision if long-term weight reduction is your goal. *Say "no" to exercise and you will very likely regain the weight.*

According to Consumer Reports, the vast majority of more than 8,000 successful dieters surveyed listed "my own diet and exercise regimen" as the one that worked. Less than a third consulted a diet book and only 19 percent used a commercial weight-loss program.

WEIGHT-LOSS APPROACHES AND DIETS

The LEARN diet developed by Kelly Brownell, Ph.D., is not actually a diet, as no single food is restricted or recommended, but rather a weight-loss method that helps you make intelligent decisions to meet your daily calorie goal. It acknowledges that as a central focus, eating is a behavior and if you going to modify that behavior, you will need behavior modification techniques. (LEARN stands for Lifestyle, Exercise, Attitudes, Relationships and Nutrition.) Behavioral techniques include: Self-Monitoring, Stimulus Control, Assertiveness Training, Problem Solving, Social Support, Goal Setting and Relapse Prevention. For more information on this weight-loss technique see *The LEARN Program for Weight Management 2000* (American Health Publishing Company, 2004).

One very successful weight-loss program with roots in the LEARN program is the VTrim Diet (*see* "The EatingWell Diet," *page 37*).

The **Weight Watchers** plan does not exclude any food group and does not recommend that you take in any macronutrient—fat, protein or carbohydrates—to an extreme. A daily point system allows the individual to make dietary choices that add up to a daily point total. In essence, this is not greatly different than the LEARN system, which is more direct about its daily caloric allowance. The Weight Watchers system encourages consumption of low-fat, high-fiber meals. Weekly group meetings and weigh-ins provide behavioral support. Weight Watchers groups are widely available in North America and provide the easiest way for individuals who do not want to "go it alone" to find social support. An analysis by Consumer Reports found that Weight Watchers had better long-term adherence rates than other popular diets (Atkins, Zone, Ornish).

LOW-CARBOHYDRATE DIETS

The **Atkins Diet**, developed in the 1970s, was the first of several popular low-carbohydrate plans theoriz-

"Lose 10 lbs. in 2 Weeks!"

EXAMPLE: A 165-pound person normally takes in 2,000 calories per day to maintain his/her weight. In two weeks that would come to a total of 28,000 calories. To lose 10 pounds of fat in two weeks, you would need a *deficit* of 35,000 calories; impossible (unless it came from extreme exercise). To lose five pounds of fat in two weeks you would need a deficit of 17,500 calories. That would allow you to eat 750 calories a day (28,000 − 17,500 divided by 14 = 750 calories a day), which is a very, very severe calorie restriction. Remember, one large bagel is 400 calories. Not much left after the cream cheese. When you see a "diet" making claims like these, move on.

(Impossible!)

ing that overconsumption of carbohydrates is at the root of obesity. The thinking goes that most overweight people are insulin resistant (true), therefore avoidance of foods that cause the greatest rise in blood glucose, and consequent blood-insulin spikes with eating, should be avoided. This is not unreasonable, though difficult to prove.

The Atkins Diet essentially removes all refined carbohydrates and sweets from the diet (soda, cookies, fruit juice, potatoes, etc.) and replaces them with fats (60 percent of dietary calories, one-third of which are saturated fats) and protein (30 percent). By severely restricting carbohydrates, this diet can get you into a metabolic state called "ketosis," which reputedly burns fat, but can make you feel poorly and may diminish your exercise capacity.

The "Induction Phase" of the Atkins Diet is extremely high in animal fats and proteins and extremely

low in carbohydrates. It generally results in rapid weight loss, but most of this weight loss is water. Remember that to lose a pound of fat you need to have a caloric deficit of 3,500 calories. Short of surgery or liposuction, there is no possible physiologic way to lose 10 pounds of fat in two weeks, as you would need a calorie deficit of 35,000 calories, which is simply impossible to accomplish with diet alone.

Down the line, however, the Atkins Diet remains low-calorie and real weight loss occurs. It is probably due to its severe limitation on food choice as much as anything else. However, after a while, people often get bored with unlimited beef and bacon and heavy cream desserts. Carbohydrates, fruits and interesting foods beckon. Well-designed studies published recently in the *Journal of the American Medical Association* showed that at one year, the Atkins Diet yielded an average of 4.6 pounds of weight loss. A quote from Michael Dansinger, M.D., director of obesity research at Tufts University, is informative: "Saying there's one best diet for everyone is a little like saying there's one best type of music for everyone." Therefore, I acknowledge that the Atkins Diet might be right for some, though a long-term diet it is not.

Concerns about the long-term Atkins Diet include the high levels of saturated fat recommended (20 percent of total calories, four times what we recommend), the very low amounts of fiber and fresh fruits, and that it can be dangerous for individuals with kidney disease. Personally, I would dispense with the Induction Phase and instead get on with the long-term diet. For the Atkins Diet to be successful, you need to commit to low carbohydrates for a lifetime, something that is not realistic for most people.

Other low-carbohydrate diets include the **South Beach Diet** and the **Zone Diet**. These diets both recommend an avoidance of processed carbohydrates and an abundance of proteins. The South Beach Diet has a two-week initial phase, which promises that you can "lose up to 13 pounds." As noted above, unless much of this is water, this is impossible. Each of these

10 Simple Weight-Loss Coaching Tips

1. Chew slow.
2. Walk fast.
3. Avoid drinking calories.
4. Keep fewer snacks in the house.
5. Plan out your calories for the day.
6. Drink 8 ounces of water before your meal.
7. Eat filling, high-fiber foods (see *page 50*).
8. Eat bulky, filling, low-calorie foods (see *page 64*).
9. Eat out less.
10. Don't eat in the car or while watching TV.

> **MYTH:** Low-carbohydrate diets can target fat and make you selectively burn off body fat.
>
> **FACT:** Yes, this is a myth.

diets has some good points, such as avoidance of processed carbohydrates, but also has some arbitrary statements and recommendations that are simply not supported by science. The Zone "mini-block" program of distributing portions of fat, protein and carbohydrates is confusing and directly feeds into the sales of Zone products. For both of these diets, the diet book is required as a guidebook, particularly with the Zone diet, and I just don't see how these can be translated into a long-term way of life. Exercise is mentioned but is secondary.

HEART-HEALTHY EATING PLANS

Interest in the so-called "**Mediterranean Diet**" as a preventive heart diet began in the 1960s and '70s when results of the landmark Seven Countries study documented that the residents of Crete and Italy had far lower rates of coronary heart disease than residents of the United States and Finland. Significant differences in diets between these countries pointed to the high use of saturated fats in the U.S. and Finland versus high use of olive oil in Crete and Italy.

The Lyon Diet Heart Study published in 1999 found that patients with CHD who followed a Mediterranean-style diet had 50 percent fewer heart attacks and deaths than individuals who followed a richer, non-Mediterranean French diet.

There is no single, typical "Mediterranean" diet. At least 16 countries border the Mediterranean Sea. Diets vary between these countries and also between regions within a country. Many differences in culture, ethnic background, religion, economy and agricultural production result in different diets. But the common Mediterranean dietary pattern has these characteristics:

- High in fruits, vegetables, bread and non-refined cereals, potatoes, onions, beans, nuts and seeds
- Includes olive oil as an important source of monounsaturated fat
- Dairy products (including butter), fish and poultry consumed in low to moderate amounts, with little red meat, except on special occasions
- Eggs eaten zero to four times weekly
- Wine consumed in low to moderate amounts.

The Mediterranean-style diet used in the Lyon Diet Heart Study was quite comparable to the common pattern but different in a significant way. It was high in alpha-linolenic acid (a type of polyunsaturated

Macronutrient Content of Popular Weight-Loss Diets

Diet	Fat %	Saturated Fat %	Carbohydrate %	Protein %
Weight Watchers	24	7	56	20
Zone	27	7	42	30
South Beach (long-term)	39	9	38	22
Atkins (long-term)	60	20	11	29

(Adapted from Consumer Reports, June 2005)

omega-3 fatty acid found in canola, soybean and flaxseed oils).

It included:

- More bread, more root vegetables (potatoes, carrots, onions, turnips) and green vegetables
- Less beef, lamb and pork (replaced with poultry), more fish
- No day without fruit
- Butter and cream were replaced with margarine high in alpha-linolenic acid.

The diet averaged 30 percent of calories from fat, 8 percent from saturated fat, 13 percent from monounsaturated fat and 5 percent from polyunsaturated fat. Of course, describing a diet in terms of its "macronutrients" is like describing Michelangelo as a man with a paintbrush.

The permutations of this diet are as broad as the Mediterranean, with wonderful taste variations emanating from Italy, Greece, Spain, France, Syria, Israel and Morocco. Furthermore, the principles of this diet can easily be applied to the American diet, which, indeed, is as broad as the range of immigrants who have landed here. (*See page 51.*)

THE PORTFOLIO DIET

The **Portfolio Eating Plan** is a somewhat impractical but instructive diet put together by a Toronto physician-nutritionist, David Jenkins, M.D. Basically, this diet is an intelligently designed combination of cholesterol-lowering foods that demonstrates the extreme cholesterol lowering that can be obtained through diet in individuals with baseline high cholesterols. In fact, these researchers found that the Portfolio diet lowered cholesterol levels as effectively (29 percent) as a regimen of the statin drug lovastatin (30 percent).

Primary aspects of this diet include:

- A high intake of soy proteins (soy burgers, soymilk, tofu, etc.)
- A high intake of soluble fiber (oatmeal, beans, eggplant, okra, psyllium)
- 1 ounce of almonds daily (about 20 almonds)
- Use of plant sterols (Benecol or Take Control spreads).

The point of the Portfolio diet is not to get you to blindly follow this relatively difficult regimen in its entirety, but rather to incorporate components of it into your diet that you find easy enough to do. It is not an entire diet plan, but rather demonstrates the value of certain food groups in lowering cholesterol levels with food.

For more information about the Portfolio eating plan: *portfolioeatingplan.com.*

In the next chapter we will present the EATINGWELL approach to knowing, cooking and eating better foods. It is not a diet, but a menu of facts, techniques and intelligent choices that can help you lower your cardiac risks, maintain a healthy weight and still enjoy delicious, interesting meals.

ON BEING AN ALMOST-VEGETARIAN

If cardiac health were the only consideration in choosing a daily dietary routine, my guess is that a great many people would become "almost-vegetarians."

If we could put our society on a diet of fruits, vegetables, beans, whole grains, seeds, nuts, olives (and oils from seeds, nuts and olives), with fish twice a week, plus a dash of regular exercise, coronary heart disease would be history (assuming we could keep away the tobacco companies). In fact, we can look at large groups of people who eat quasi-vegetarian diets and glean some very enlightening lessons. Societies that eat variations of this diet in places like rural Mexico and rural Africa have low measures of total cholesterol, low measures of (bad) LDL cholesterol, surprisingly low levels of HDL (good) cholesterol and almost negligible rates of coronary heart disease. Animal products are luxuries, not staples, in these societies.

But what most of us eat is not dictated by health alone. Those of us raised on meat, poultry and dairy products are socially steeped in a culture that equates meat and fowl with gustatory fulfillment. Our social celebrations and holiday festivities tend to place animal products at the center of the table. Many patients I see were accustomed to eating meat at every meal of the day.

The powers of heritage, parenting and environment are strong, but I've found that it is very possible to strive for a daily diet that is "almost vegetarian" while still satisfying our cravings for meat. If meat is viewed as a side dish or condiment—sliced or shredded and never served in greater volume than a deck of cards—the primary and most-filling ingredients in most dishes can remain the "good stuff" that we know makes up a heart-healthy diet: vegetables, fruits, beans, whole grains, seeds and nuts. With creative recipes and the right seasonings and spices, small portions of meat or fowl can go a long way and not leave the eater feeling deprived.

Many international dishes do this effectively, and they range from Asian stir-fries and rustic, Italian-style pizza to dishes as American as chicken potpie. The recipe collection in Part II of this book (see page 69) can fit nicely with a goal of becoming more vegetable-oriented in our daily meals.

While some think meat should be the focal point of every supper, an initial step I've seen many people take is to substitute one or two vegetarian meals per week into that slot. My patients who have chosen to shift toward the vegetarian side of the food spectrum have consistently had positive results in lowering their cardiac risks. Their consumption of saturated fat typically decreases, while their intake of fresh vegetables and whole grains rises. Following their example and also boosting fiber, antioxidants and good oils means you can lose excess weight, improve your cholesterol profile and bring other risk factors into line. It is definitely within the abilities of most people to wean themselves from the meat fix.

In the following chapter we delve into the approach that works for the majority of our patients (and those who would prefer not to become our patients). Without using the "V word" or eschewing meat entirely, we obviously follow a vegetarian-influenced theme of skewing back toward a diet that is more plant-based and less dependent on large servings of animal products.

CHAPTER 3

THE EATINGWELL HEALTHY HEART PLAN

A science-based approach that celebrates good food and personal tastes

The EATINGWELL Healthy Heart Plan is based on my work with thousands of cardiac rehabilitation patients over many years, along with my affiliation as an advisor to EATINGWELL since its founding in 1990. A guiding principle we use is that it is simply not realistic to expect that you are going to abandon YOUR DIET.

What you really like to eat is based upon your cultural background, your mother (of course), your politics and your personally negotiated compromise between what, in your view, is healthy and balanced versus what, to you, tastes good and is fun and convenient.

That said, people can evolve, people can learn to substitute good ingredients for bad, people can definitely improve their diets, but rarely can we expect them to undergo a total, permanent eating revolution.

Learning heart-healthy dietary principles will allow you to make over your current diet to fit within the EATINGWELL Healthy Heart Plan while maintaining your culinary, ethnic or family focus. No matter what background you bring to the table, the EATINGWELL Healthy Heart Plan can help you customize foods and dishes that work for you and for your household.

The concepts are straightforward. The Healthy Heart approach *encourages* you to:

> "No disease that can be treated by diet should be treated with any other means."
>
> MAIMONIDES
> (1135-1204)

EAT MORE

- Complex carbohydrates and whole grains
- Soluble and insoluble fiber
- Monounsaturated fats
- Fresh vegetables (including leafy greens and roots), beans and legumes
- Fish (at least twice weekly) and other sources of omega-3 fatty acids (flaxseed, canola and soybean oils)
- Nuts (without added salt)
- Soy proteins (soy burgers, soymilk, tofu, textured soy protein)
- Fruits, but not fruit juice
- Occasional alcohol, up to one drink daily for women, two for men.

EAT LESS

- Trans fats; avoid foods that contain hydrogenated oils or margarines (the tiny amount of trans fats in low-fat dairy and meat is unavoidable)
- Saturated fats, both animal and dairy
- Refined grains and starches (e.g., white flour, white rice, white bread, white pastries, white potatoes, pretzels, white pasta)
- Sugars
- Rich, fatty desserts
- High-sodium (salty) foods
- Processed foods.

SCIENCE, NOT MARKETING

Unlike so many of the popular "diets" of the day, this plan is based on the very best science available to

FATS

Fats make up a class of nutrients of both plant and animal origin. The old days of thinking that the less fat you eat, the healthier your heart, are over. It is not that simple.

It is essential to have some fat in your diet. Fat makes up part of the structure of all cells in your body, it helps you absorb certain essential vitamins (A, D, E and K) and it is a great source of energy for physical activity, particularly activities that require endurance. The problem is that many of us Americans take in too much fat and, in particular, the wrong kinds of fat.

Too much overall fat in the diet predisposes us to obesity and all of its complications (high blood lipids, high blood pressure, diabetes and a tendency toward blood clotting).

The wrong kinds of fat, in particular trans fats and saturated fats, predispose us toward artery-clogging levels of "bad" (LDL) cholesterol.

On the other hand, fat should not be demonized. Several types of fats including monounsaturated fats (olive oil, canola oil, nut oils), polyunsaturated fats (corn, safflower, sunflower) and omega-3 oils (from fish and flaxseed) are notably good for you, as they help maintain high levels of favorable HDL cholesterol.

us. There are no gimmicks, just smart nutrition, along with a great respect for healthy ingredients and foods that people will like.

Healthy heart nutrition starts with a basic understanding of the main food groups within the human diet. For good health, we need carbohydrates and fiber, protein, fats, vitamins, minerals and trace elements. We get these from many food groups: grains, legumes, vegetables, fruits, meats, eggs, fish and seafood, and various types of fat. Because fat is so central to discussions of heart health and diet, we will start here.

Taken in excess, however, all fats and oils can lead to obesity, as fats contain more than double the calories of carbohydrates or protein, gram for gram.

There are four main types of fat:
1. Saturated fats
2. Monounsaturated fats
3. Polyunsaturated fats (includes trans fats)
4. Fish oils and omega-3 fatty acids

Saturated fats include animal fats, dairy fats, palm oil, coconut oil, cocoa butter. These fats are unhealthy. Excessive intake of saturated fats increases your bad cholesterol (LDL cholesterol) and is a well-known precursor to arterial blockages. Saturated fats should be limited to less than 5 percent of your total calories. To figure that out, divide your weight in pounds by 12 to come up with your daily allowance in grams. If you weigh 180 pounds, for example, your daily saturated-fat limit would be 15 grams (180 ÷ 12), or roughly 5 grams per meal.

It helps to know the approximate saturated fat content of mainstay foods in your diet (*see chart, page 46*).

Monounsaturated fats are found primarily in olive and canola oils and to a lesser degree in peanuts, walnuts and avocados. Monounsaturated fats tend to lower blood cholesterol levels without lowering the good cholesterol (HDL cholesterol). Populations that primarily use monounsaturated oils (Greece, Italy, France) tend to have lower rates of coronary heart disease than would be predicted by the rest of their diet.

Polyunsaturated fats are generally vegetable oils and are liquid at room temperature. They include common oils, such as corn oil, safflower oil and cottonseed oil. They tend to lower blood cholesterol

Saturated-Fat Content of Common Foods

	Portion Size	Saturated Fat (grams)
Meats (cooked)		
Ground Beef (80% lean)	3 oz	5.8
Ground Beef (95% lean)	3 oz	2.5
Steak (sirloin)	3 oz	1.9
Ground Pork	3 oz	6.6
Pork Chop (broiled)	3 oz	2.5
Pork Loin Roast	3 oz	2.5
Bacon	2 strips	1.7
Lamb Chop (broiled)	3 oz	3.0
Leg of Lamb	3 oz	2.4
Poultry (cooked)		
Chicken (dark, skinless)	3 oz	2.7
Chicken (white, skinless)	3 oz	0.9
Turkey (dark, skinless)	3 oz	2.0
Turkey (white, skinless)	3 oz	0.2
Eggs & Dairy Products		
Eggs	1 large	1.6
Whole Milk (3.3%)	8 oz	4.2
Reduced-Fat Milk (2%)	8 oz	2.9
Low-Fat Milk (1%)	8 oz	1.4
Fat-Free Milk (skim)	8 oz	0.3
Cottage Cheese (4% fat)	1 cup (8 oz)	6.0
Reduced-Fat Cottage Cheese (2%)	1 cup	2.8
Cheddar Cheese	1 oz	6.0
Butter	1 Tbsp.	7.2

A 3-ounce portion of cooked meat is roughly the size of a deck of cards. Most people eat much more. Note that the fat content of meat cuts is variable based upon the source of the meat, the animal's diet, trimming of fat and other variables. Adapted from the USDA.

Trans fats are a type of processed polyunsaturated fat found in margarines, many packaged foods, such as doughnuts, popcorn, chips, crackers, and deep-fried items, such as French fries. They add to the shelf-life of processed foods, preventing rancidity so that they can last for months or years rather than weeks. Trans fats are solid at room temperature. They raise LDL (bad) cholesterol levels as much as saturated fats but have the doubly dangerous effect of substantially lowering levels of HDL (good) cholesterol.

Recent research by Walter Willett, M.D., at the Harvard School of Public Health has shown that trans fats are substantially more harmful than saturated fats. Trans fats are now listed on food labels but no amount is considered healthy, or allowable. They often hide on the ingredient list as a "hydrogenated" or "partially hydrogenated" oil, such as hydrogenated soybean oil or hydrogenated canola oil. The process of hydrogenation changes a healthy, liquid oil into an unhealthy solid fat. In an interview with EATINGWELL Magazine in 2003, Dr. Willett blamed trans fats for millions of unnecessary premature deaths from coronary artery disease in the United States.

Fish oils contain a type of polyunsaturated fat called omega-3, which lowers the levels of triglycerides in your blood that may contribute to clogged arteries; it also inhibits blood clotting, like aspirin, slightly lowers blood pressure and can prevent irregular heart rhythms. Omega-3 fatty acids are also found in flaxseed oil, canola oil and soybean oil. (*Also see "The Omega Balance," page 49.*) Studies have shown that consuming two or more servings of fish per week is associated with a 30 percent lower risk of developing coronary heart disease over the long term. Benefits of omega-3s in patients with established CHD have been even more impressive and many cardiologists are now recommending omega-3 capsules for individuals who do not eat fish or the right types of fish. The Lyon Heart Study (*see page 41*) was also a diet high in omega-3s (from nonfish sources—canola oil and vegetables) and also demonstrated a decreased

levels and LDL cholesterol levels but also lower the levels of "good" cholesterol (HDL cholesterol).

Percentages of Fat in Cooking Oils & Fats

	Saturated	Poly-unsaturated	Mono-unsaturated
Canola Oil	7%	30%	59%
Safflower Oil	7	14	79
Sunflower Oil	11	64	18
Corn Oil	13	59	24
Olive Oil (extra-virgin)	14	9	77
Soybean Oil	14	58	23
Peanut Oil	18	33	49
Cottonseed Oil	26	52	18
Chicken Fat	30	21	45
Lard	39	11	45
Palm Oil	49	9	37
Beef Tallow	50	4	42
Cocoa Butter	60	3	33
Butter	63	4	26
Palm Kernel Oil	82	2	11
Coconut Oil	87	2	6

particularly those with cardiovascular disease, the benefits of fish and fish oil from a cardiovascular point of view far outweigh, by many orders of magnitude, the small increased risk of cancer or neurological side effects from mercury in most fish. Yet it still seems reasonable for all to avoid the fish species known to be exceptionally high in mercury.

CARBOHYDRATES AND FIBER

Carbohydrates have received a lot of bad publicity with the popularity of various low-carbohydrate weight-reduction diets, yet they are clearly an important component of a healthy diet. Carbohydrates can be divided into complex carbohydrates, such as whole grains (whole wheat, oats, rye), which are desirable, versus highly refined carbohydrates, such as processed grains (white flour, corn flour) and sugar, which we want to eat sparingly.

Whole grains contain substantially more fiber and essential fatty acids, which your body cannot make, compared with processed grains. Processed grains and their manufactured products (white bread, sweet corn-based cereals, pastries, bagels, pretzels) have a

risk of second heart attacks.

The recommended average daily intake of omega-3s is between 650 and 1,000 mg/day from fish or other dietary sources. Eating oily fish, such as salmon or albacore tuna, twice weekly will usually cover the lower-dose recommendation. If fish oil is being taken for triglyceride lowering, higher doses are often recommended (2,000-4,000 mg or 2-4 g/day) and supplements are required.

Many concerns have been expressed about mercury contamination of fish. Mercury is a highly toxic element that concentrates in the oil of large fish. For people at particular risk from mercury, such as pregnant women, nursing mothers and children, fish high in mercury should be avoided. These include shark, king mackerel, swordfish and tilefish. For adult men,

Omega-3 Content in Fish

(cooked)	per 3-ounce serving
Salmon	1,890 mg
Herring	1,870 mg
Tuna (bluefin steak)	1,280 mg
Mackerel	1,120 mg
Tuna (canned white)	790 mg
Halibut	470 mg
Flounder	440 mg
Tuna (canned light)	230 mg
Catfish	220 mg
Haddock	200 mg
Cod	140 mg

high glycemic index which means that they are rapidly converted to glucose in the blood, raising your blood-glucose levels. This is not a good thing and may predispose individuals to type 2 diabetes. The quintessential simple carbohydrate with a high glycemic index is sugar itself. Other high-glycemic foods include peeled white potatoes, doughnuts and low-fiber, high-sugar breakfast cereals. Fiber, such as is found in whole grains, vegetables and fruits, slows absorption of carbohydrates, and the blood sugar is raised to a lesser degree.

Because many carbohydrates contain dietary fiber, one of the most important benefits of eating carbohydrates is the highly desirable fiber they deliver in a palatable way. Commonly called roughage, fiber is an indigestible complex carbohydrate found in plants and has no calories because the body cannot absorb it. Fiber-containing carbohydrates come in two forms—water-insoluble and water-soluble—based on their physical characteristics and effects on the body. Each form functions differently and provides different health benefits.

Insoluble fiber is found in whole wheat, seeds and nuts and many vegetables. It has no effect on cholesterol levels but absorbs water, thereby providing bulk to the stool, and is associated with a lowered risk of colon cancer.

Soluble fiber is found in oatmeal, beans, fruits, selected vegetables, such as eggplant and okra, and is also available as fiber products, such as psyllium (e.g., Metamucil), which has been added to some breakfast cereals. Soluble fiber is associated with a slight reduction in cholesterol levels and LDL levels. A recent review found that a diet rich in whole-grain oats, such as in oatmeal, reduced LDL cholesterol by

"Middle age is when you choose your cereal for the fiber, not the toy."

ANONYMOUS

an average of 7 mg/dL.

A high-fiber diet has been linked with a lower risk of heart disease in a large number of studies that have followed many people for many years. In a Harvard study of more than 84,000 female health professionals, researchers found that a high fiber intake reduced the risk of coronary heart disease by 40 percent, compared to a low fiber intake. Fiber has also been linked with a reduced risk of diabetes and diverticular disease of the colon and may be protective against colon cancer. Moreover, fibers called cellulose and hemicelluloses take up space in the GI tract without yielding calories, promoting the feeling of fullness, which is helpful to those watching their weight.

Recognizing the many health benefits associated with carbohydrates—and especially with diets rich in fruits, vegetables, whole grains and low-fat dairy foods, the Institute of Medicine in 2002 recommended that Americans get the majority of their calories each day from carbohydrates. Specifically, they recommend that:

- Adults should get 45 percent to 65 percent of their calories from carbohydrates.
- The minimum amount of carbohydrate that children and adults need for proper brain function is 130 grams a day.
- For adults 50 years and younger, the recommended total intake for dietary fiber is 38 grams for men and 25 grams for women. For those over 50, it is 30 grams and 21 grams respectively. Most Americans do not come close to these levels.

One of the easiest ways to increase fiber content in your diet is by eating high-fiber cereals at breakfast time. If fiber intake is increased too rapidly it can lead to bloating and flatulence. Do it gradually. Other easy ways to add fiber to the diet are by eating high-fiber breads, using whole wheat and other grains for baking, and by increasing vegetable intake, including various types of beans. (*See chart, page 50.*)

The Omega Balance

Without question, each of us needs omega-6 and omega-3 fatty acids in our diet. But the balance between the two has recently become the center of a hot debate.

These two key polyunsaturated fats are called "essential fatty acids" because our bodies can't manufacture them; they must come from the foods we eat. Each has its own actions in the body, often opposing each other: omega-6s, for example, are converted in the body to substances that assist in responding to inflammation and bleeding; omega-3s, by contrast, convert to substances that slow blood clotting and decrease inflammatory responses. Together, they work as a check-and-balance system of sorts, and some researchers argue that our modern Western diets have thrown that balance out of whack.

Throughout most of human history, since our Paleolithic ancestors first hunted game, speared fish and gathered wild greens, humans have eaten a diet that kept the omega-6 to omega-3 balance fairly equal— "close to a 2 to 1 ratio," notes Artemis Simopoulos, co-author of *The Omega Diet*. This pattern continues in the traditional diet of Crete, where heart disease and cancer rates are among the lowest in the world.

But in the United States, omega-6 fatty acids now dominate the ratio because people are eating more processed foods, such as chips and packaged cookies, which are made with high-omega-6 oils like soybean or cottonseed. Our meats, poultry and dairy products have also become more omega-6 heavy as we feed our animals grains instead of grasses. Today, the omega-6 to omega-3 ratio hovers around 17 to 1, says Simopoulos, explaining that this imbalance is a key contributor to the modern plague of heart disease. "Major dietary studies have shown that when people are fed diets that lower this ratio, their death rates from heart disease fall significantly."

Not everyone agrees that increased omega-6s threaten our health, however. Frank Hu, of the Harvard Nurses' Health Study, argues that omega-6s also have beneficial effects on heart-disease risk. "Because omega-6 has very strong LDL-lowering effects, it actually lowers the LDL to HDL ratio, which is the most powerful predictor of heart disease." Reducing omega-6 levels, then, would take away some of those benefits.

Although he is skeptical, Hu suggests the following for anyone who wants to lower their omega-6 to omega-3 ratio: focus on getting more omega-3s, rather than cutting omega-6s, by eating more fish, freshly ground flaxseeds and walnuts, and by using oils that provide omega-3s, like canola and walnut.

Simopoulos counters, "If you have too many omega-6s, you can't use omega-3s as efficiently. To get the full benefit of omega-3s, you must lower the omega-6 to omega-3 ratio." She recommends following a dietary pattern similar to that of the traditional diet of Crete: vegetable- and fruit-laden, low in saturated fats, generous in omega-3s and stingy with omega-6s.

—JOYCE HENDLEY
EatingWell Magazine, Summer 2004

PROTEIN

Humans must consume adequate amounts of protein for good health, including the essential amino acids that our bodies cannot synthesize from other nutrients. Proteins digest more slowly than carbohydrates and are thus more helpful in providing satiety and energy between meals.

Most members of modern society get enough protein in their diets from animal proteins, such as red meats, poultry and fish. Low-fat and nonfat dairy products are also good sources of protein. Major plant sources of protein include beans, soybeans and nuts. Individuals with kidney disease should avoid high-protein diets, such as the Atkins Diet.

Substitution of soy proteins for animal proteins leads to a moderate decrease of LDL cholesterol. Items high in soy proteins include soy burgers, tofu, soy milk, soy-spiked breakfast cereals and textured soy proteins, which are useful to extend ground beef in recipes like meatloaf and meatballs.

High-Fiber Foods

	Serving Size	Total Fiber (grams)
Lima Beans	1 cup cooked	14.0
Kidney Beans	1 cup cooked	13.1
Chickpeas	1 cup cooked	12.5
White Beans	1 cup cooked	11.3
Sweet Potatoes	1 cup mashed	8.2
Barley	1 cup cooked	6.0
Apples	1 large	5.1
Broccoli	1 cup cooked	4.7
Carrots	1 cup cooked	4.7
Brussels Sprouts	1 cup cooked	4.1
Prunes	½ cup	4.0
Oats	1 cup cooked	4.0
Strawberries	1 cup (about 8)	2.9
Eggplant	1 cup cooked	2.5
Metamucil	1 tablespoon	2.4

VITAMINS, MINERALS & SUPPLEMENTS

With the exception of omega-3 oil and capsules, the American Heart Association frowns on people taking vitamin and mineral supplements. "We recommend that healthy people get adequate nutrients by eating a variety of foods in moderation, rather than by taking supplements," is their official position.

Most cardiologists tend to agree. Among the huge array of health supplements available, there are just a handful with scientific testing that I respect. I consider niacin (vitamin B_3) definitely beneficial, when indicated (to raise HDL cholesterol) and when given under a doctor's care with appropriate followup. As discussed in Chapter 2, fish oil and other omega-3 supplements are potentially beneficial, as are red rice yeast (*page 33*) and green tea (*page 68*). I also routinely recommend an aspirin a day (the coated or enteric form to protect your stomach) as insurance. A tablespoon or two of Metamucil is another safe supplement that can help boost your intake of soluble fiber.

Otherwise, I tell my patients to save their money on most over-the-counter supplements that make unsubstantiated heart-health claims. Eat a varied diet with plenty of vegetables, fruits, whole grains and nuts. A daily multivitamin/mineral supplement makes sense for most people, but there is scant to no evidence that high doses of vitamin and mineral supplements do anything to protect your heart and circulatory system. High doses of vitamin E (above 2,000 mg daily) even appear to have negative health consequences.

By consuming your micronutrients in whole foods, by cooking more meals at home, by filling your daily menu with fresh and minimally processed vegetables and fruits, you should have no need to spend your time and money in the vitamin and supplement aisle.

"Life itself is the proper binge."

JULIA CHILD (1912-2004)

The Mediterranean Diet: Taking the Long View

Following a Mediterranean diet could mean not only a healthier life but also a longer one. In fact, that's precisely what researchers from the Netherlands, France, Spain and Italy recently found. In 2004, they reported that among a large cohort of volunteers who are being studied, those who followed a Mediterranean diet were 23 percent less likely to die over the 10-year study period than those who ate more Western-style diets. Volunteers who combined a Mediterranean diet with physically active lives (and who didn't smoke) cut their risk of dying during the study period by two-thirds.

These remarkable numbers shouldn't really come as a surprise, says Artemis Simopoulos, M.D., who has exhaustively researched the diet of Crete. "The traditional Cretan diet was an ancient one. People on the island made use of what was available to them for many centuries—wild plants foraged from the mountainsides, plentiful fish, olives and olive oil, figs, lemons and other fresh fruit. Their diet closely resembled the Paleolithic diet—what humans ate through most of our evolution. It's the diet our bodies adapted themselves to. No wonder it's so healthy."

12 Ways to Eat Like a Mediterranean

1 Replace butter with olive or canola oil whenever possible.

2 Snack on nuts, seeds or fruit instead of processed foods.

3 Include a generous leafy green salad with most dinners.

4 Help yourself to whole-grain bread, pasta, rice and other grains.

5 Fix at least a couple of vegetarian meals every week.

6 Add a dish or two that contain legumes (beans and lentils) to your weekly menu.

7 Have fish (not breaded and deep-fried) at least twice a week.

8 If you eat meat, favor poultry.

9 Eat red meat only occasionally, and in small servings.

10 If you drink, have no more than a glass or two with a meal.

11 Enjoy fruit for dessert.

12 Set aside enough time to savor every bite.

—PETER JARET
EatingWell Magazine, June/July 2005

SALT

Salt, also known as sodium chloride, is essential to human life, and our palates are genetically predisposed to crave saltiness. Too much, however, very clearly elevates the risk of developing high blood pressure that can, in turn, lead to heart attack and stroke.

Salt intake is usually measured in milligrams of sodium taken in per day. Technically, all people on a healthy-heart diet do not need to severely limit sodium intake although there are clearly no benefits whatsoever of a high-salt diet. Individuals who do need to limit sodium intake include those with high blood pressure (systolic over 140 or diastolic over 90) or borderline high blood pressure (between 120-140 systolic and 80-90 diastolic). Individuals with chronic heart failure, particularly if there is associated edema (swelling) of the legs, should also limit sodium intake.

"To eat is a necessity, but to eat intelligently is an art."

LA ROCHEFOUCAULD
(1613-1680)

A moderate salt restriction is where you take in less than 2,300 mg of sodium per day, while a more severe restriction is less than 1,600 mg sodium per day. This can be difficult to accomplish because sodium is so widely used in food processing. Single servings of most processed soups and entrees can deliver a full third to half a day's sodium allowance. A severe salt limitation cannot really be accomplished unless you avoid processed foods almost entirely.

Individuals who have neither a blood pressure problem nor an edema problem do not need to strictly limit salt intake. The average American man takes in 4,200 mg of sodium per day and the average American woman takes in about 3,300 mg and both of these are quite high. Populations that take in lower levels of salt have less heart disease and stroke, but it is not clear if the damage is done just in individuals with high blood pressure and chronic heart failure or generally across a population. For people without a clinical reason to limit salt, a daily sodium intake of between 2,300 and 3,000 mg is reasonable.

When we cook at home, we can much more easily stay within sodium limits, using low-sodium and zero-sodium ingredients and not oversalting as we cook. Allowing family members to sprinkle on more salt at the table is much better than having a heavy hand with salt at the stove.

As the recipes beginning on page 73 so temptingly illustrate, eating in a manner that is good for your health and heart does not mean forgoing delicious food—even the old family favorites can be transformed with the techniques perfected over two decades in the EATINGWELL Test Kitchen. Rather than deprivation, changing to a healthy-heart diet can bring new food experiences and new joys of eating without guilt.

At Midlife, a Woman Confronts Her Risk Factors

ZR is a 53-year-old woman with no history of heart disease whose 51-year-old younger brother recently died suddenly while bicycling. At his autopsy, he was found to have diffuse coronary heart disease (CHD). ZR was profoundly affected by this and decided to review her own level of risk. She works full time as a lawyer, has three teenage daughters and is happily married.

She scheduled a visit with her internist to evaluate her chances of developing heart disease. The message from her doctor was not reassuring.

They discussed the facts: she is postmenopausal and she had gained 10 pounds over the last five or so years, despite the fact that she was physically active as a younger woman, jogging or biking regularly. Her doctor was somewhat concerned that her cholesterol profile showed high triglycerides (250), low HDL "good cholesterol" (40), moderately elevated LDL "bad" cholesterol at 145, and higher-than-desired total cholesterol of 235. Her blood sugar was in the "intermediate" or "pre-diabetic" range, also known as insulin resistance syndrome, at 118. As both her mother and her brother had adult-onset (type 2) diabetes, this was of particular concern both to her doctor and to ZR herself.

Her doctor arranged an exercise stress test, and ZR was greatly relieved to have normal results. She accepted her physician's suggestion that she see a dietitian. After reviewing her eating habits, she was told that she is already eating a fairly healthy diet, but should reduce her intake of sugar and starchy carbohydrates, such as white breads, pretzels and potatoes, in an effort to decrease her triglycerides. She was also reminded to decrease her intake of hydrogenated oils, animal and dairy fats. "I knew all of this," she says; "I guess it didn't seem to apply to me before."

Most important, to decrease the likelihood of developing diabetes, she was advised to lose 10 to 15 pounds over the next six months and to restart a regular walking program, supplemented by biking and tennis when she can find the time. She was given a calorie target 500 calories per day lower than her maintenance calories—a not-so-drastic program that will allow her to lose one pound per week. ZR's calorie allowance for daily maintenance is calculated at 150 (her weight in pounds) x 12 = 1,800 calories per day, thus her new daily calorie count should be about 1,300 calories per day. She was advised to write down all that she eats in an effort to count calories and to better understand her eating behaviors.

At her three-month follow-up visit with her internist, she had already lost eight pounds by cutting down on refined carbohydrates and walking two miles daily and/or cycling or playing tennis. Her triglycerides have improved to 199, HDL has increased to 45, LDL cholesterol has dropped to 128 and her total cholesterol is 213. The blood sugar is now measured at 108, and she is committed to long-term exercise and continuing to work with her dietitian at least until she gets to her weight goal of 135 pounds. "You shouldn't have to lose a brother to start paying attention to your own health," says ZR. "I'm sorry that's what it took, but I feel more in control of my own health than I have in years. I keep thinking of one day enjoying grandchildren as my reward."

CHAPTER 4

MOVEMENT AS MEDICINE

Exercise can lower your risk of heart disease—and energize your life

I am often asked how many times per week a person needs to exercise. My response, always: "You only need to exercise on days that you eat."

Some get wide-eyed or scoff at this simple rule, but it's hard to forget. (And easy enough to follow if you make the choice to try.) I have as busy a schedule as most professional people I know, and I try to live by this rule. I work hard to cultivate it with my patients, because the results are predictably so beneficial.

Eating and exercise are inextricably linked. You eat to have fuel for your body to function and move. When you move, your body increases its metabolism and use of the energy from the foods you have eaten. You can't really do one without affecting the other.

Overeating seems to get top billing as a cause of obesity, but failure to move deserves equal blame.

"So you wanna dance, Frank, or do you wanna sit here and have a heart attack?"

SCARFACE (1983)

Since weight gain is an imbalance between the calories you take in and the calories you burn, "under-activity" is every bit as important in the development of obesity as is overeating.

Furthermore, if you exercise, you can eat more without putting on weight. Perhaps most important,

people who perform aerobic exercise regularly throughout their adulthood live on average two years longer than sedentary individuals. And no, they do not spend the entire two years exercising and they also consume fewer prescription drugs and enjoy years of higher-quality life.

The two primary types of exercise are aerobic exercise and resistance, or strength, exercise. A third type, flexibility and balance exercise, such as stretching, yoga or Tai Chi, uses less energy but also is of clear benefit, particularly as you age.

Aerobic exercise includes walking, jogging, cycling, swimming and rowing. Aerobic exercise burns far more calories than resistance exercise and therefore is of more direct relevance to weight control. For example, if you are average weight, walking a mile (at any speed) expends 100 calories of energy. If you are 20 percent overweight, it requires 120 calories. One of the few benefits of being overweight is that you burn more calories moving your body over a given distance.

Resistance exercise also is very useful in long-term weight control. If you work on building your strength, you can increase your muscle mass. Since muscle is metabolically active, having a higher muscle mass results in a higher metabolic rate, which will burn extra calories each day, even while you are not exercising. Resistance training also plays a role during dietary-induced weight loss by minimizing loss of muscle mass during the dieting period.

As an example of the obesity-preventing effects of

Benefits of Long-Term Aerobic Exercise

Most of the disease-preventing benefits of exercise are related to long-term aerobic exercise. These include:

- Increased longevity
- Decreased rates of heart disease
- Cholesterol effects including higher (good) HDL cholesterol and lower triglyceride levels
- Lower blood pressure
- Lower rates of obesity and diabetes
- Lower rates of cancer including colon, breast and prostate
- Lower recurrence rates after diagnosis and treatment of breast cancer
- Lower rates of osteoporosis
- Lower rates of mental depression
- Lower rates of disability as you age

Sounds like a pill we would all take if we could.

of Amish men are overweight. Whereas 30 percent of American adults are obese, just 4 percent of Amish people are obese, and these are mostly women. The value of exercise in preventing obesity is starkly demonstrated.

As far as starting an exercise program, a number of questions arise for anyone who has been mostly sedentary: Should you see your doctor first? How much exercise should you do? What type? What intensity? How often?

Simply stated, if you are planning to start on a walking program and plan to advance your exercise program very gradually, you need not "clear" this with your physician, although you might mention it at your next routine visit.

> **MYTH:** Walking or slow jogging is inferior to using exercise machines.
>
> **FACT:** Walking or jogging burns more calories than an equivalent intensity and duration of exercise on a piece of equipment that supports your weight, such as a bicycle or a rowing machine.

If you are planning to undertake a more intense program, such as jogging, you should consider first discussing this with your physician... IF:

- You are a man over 45 and have at least two cardiac risk factors (family history of heart disease, high blood pressure, high cholesterol, smoking, diabetes, obesity, sedentary lifestyle)
- You are a postmenopausal woman with two or more risk factors
- You have known heart disease
- You are taking medications for high blood pressure or high cholesterol
- You have had recent unexplained chest discomfort or shortness of breath.

Individuals with known heart disease can most safely begin their exercise program in a cardiac rehabilitation program.

exercise, take the case of the Amish. As you probably know, Amish individuals work primarily as farmers. They do not drive cars, they do not have computers or electrical appliances, and they live much as people lived in America in the 1800s. They eat a diet that is not particularly heart healthy, with a lot of meat, potatoes, gravy, eggs and notoriously rich pies and cakes. Whereas the average American adult takes 6,000 steps per day (5,000 for women, 7,000 for men), the average Amish man takes more than 18,000 steps on all days but Sunday. Whereas 67 percent of American adults are overweight, only 25 percent

"Walking is the best possible exercise.
Habituate yourself to walk very far."
THOMAS JEFFERSON (1743-1826)

Perhaps the one key element for success in using movement to lower your risks is to make a commitment and a long-term plan. Early on, the goal is to develop an exercise *habit*. It should become as regular as eating or breathing, and every bit as important.

Set small, attainable goals. Early on, a goal might be to exercise every day at an appointed time and place for just five or ten minutes. You are establishing a pattern. Schedule your exercise. Make it an unbreakable habit. Let your family or co-workers know that at a specific time (in the morning before work, lunchtime at work, on the way home) you do not schedule appointments or meetings as you are already committed. Life has its way of throwing you curve balls, so be flexible, but also be firm about your commitment. Start off planning to succeed. I think it is well worth investing in a good pair of walking shoes or an exercise suit, and vowing to wear them out.

THE EXERCISE PRESCRIPTION

The characteristics of your exercise program are called an exercise prescription. An exercise prescription includes: Modality, Frequency, Intensity and Duration.

Modality is nothing more than the mode or type of exercise, such as walking, cycling, rowing, swimming. Go with what you like and what is most convenient for your lifestyle. Walking, jogging and running are most accessible, and most of us can start from our doorstep at home or work and be off and moving.

Walking versus running is hotly debated in some circles. If you walk at 4 mph for an hour and you are

> "Exercise? I get it on the golf course. When I see my friends collapse, I run for the paramedics."
> RED SKELTON (1913-1997)

Feet, Do Your Thing: Walking vs. Faster Pursuits

For equivalent duration and intensity (e.g., equivalent heart rate), walking or jogging will burn more calories than any exercise that is weight-supported, such as cycling or rowing, because you literally weigh less during those activities.

To burn calories, you move a weight (your body) over a distance. The speed doesn't matter. Walk a mile or run a mile, it is roughly 100 calories (perhaps a calorie or two more with running as you lift your legs a bit higher). Mainly you do it faster. An hour of running burns more than an hour of walking because you have gone farther. However, for the same distance the caloric expenditure is about the same.

Another way to look at it is if you walk or jog a mile you will burn more calories than if you bike a mile. Not only does the bicycle seat support you, but in real-life cycling you coast. It gets a bit tricky if you are literally rowing in water or swimming in water because the viscosity of water adds another variable. Remember we are trying to take intensity out of the equation, just minutes per day and distance.

average weight, you will have gone four miles and burned 400 calories. If you run for 30 minutes at a 10 minute-per-mile pace (6 mph) you will have run three miles and burned 300 calories. If you run for 30 minutes at 7:30 minute-per-mile pace (8 mph) you will have gone 4 miles and burned 400 calories.

Walking tends to be easier on the joints and heart and is certainly the exercise form of choice for most people, especially those who want to form a habit that will sustain them for many years to come.

However, if going to the gym or health club works for you, by all means make it your habit. Cross-training, that is varying your exercise somewhat from day to day, is a good idea and minimizes the likelihood of injury or boredom.

Frequency relates to the number of times per week that you plan to exercise. This could range from three times per week to every day. Less than three times per week and you make only very slow progress.

Intensity relates to the percentage of the maximal exercise capacity at which you work. If you know your maximal heart rate, you should generally exercise at 70 to 85 percent of that rate. If you do not know your maximal heart rate, an easy way to gauge your intensity is with the "talk test." If you can carry on a conversation with your partner while exercising, you are almost certainly not above 85 percent of your maximal heart rate.

The *duration* of each exercise session depends in part on the intensity of exercise. Once you are beyond the very early stages of developing the habit, your exercise duration should be at least 20 minutes per session if you are exercising intensely (more is better), whereas it should be 30 minutes or more if you are exercising at a moderate intensity (for example, moderate-pace walking, gardening or cycling). If your goal is to assist with weight loss, the exercise pre-

scription should be at a relatively low intensity, but exercise should be almost daily and should gradually extend for longer periods of time. In one study that we performed with overweight cardiac patients, walking five to seven days per week for durations of eventually up to 45 to 60 minutes per session resulted in 11 pounds of weight loss over four months without making any dietary changes whatsoever. If you also cut calorie intake, the weight loss will be greater.

KEEPING TRACK

An important tool in staying motivated is to keep a log or daily records of your exercise program. This can be as simple as circling the dates on a calendar or as complex as listing daily workouts, distances, durations and calorie counts. Watching your progress is motivating as you will see a clear improvement in your exercise program, also termed the "training effect" after just two to four weeks of exercise.

An optimal way to manage your exercise program is to incorporate as much exercise as possible into your daily routines. This is termed "lifestyle" exercise. This might include walking back and forth to work or to public transportation; taking the stairs at work rather than the elevator; parking far out in the parking lot and walking from there to your office or the supermarket. At the extreme, I have met an obesity researcher from the Mayo Clinic who has rigged up his desk to a treadmill that he keeps at one mile per hour all day long. That is a gentleman who will never become obese and who will never *need* to exercise other than working at his desk.

Unfortunately, for most of us, exercise has been engineered out of our lives. We hop in the car, open and close the garage door with a remote control, drive to work and park near the front door and take the elevator to the fifth floor. Then we spend much of the day in front of a computer or on the phone or attending meetings until it's time to go sit down for lunch. While you can add a bit of lifestyle activity wherever possible, a true exercise session ranging from a long walk to more elaborate health-club exercise becomes a necessity.

Step counters are simple types of pedometers that count your steps throughout the day and are very useful gadgets to help you maintain and advance your exercise program. They are quite inexpensive at $10 to $20 for a basic model and can be purchased at sporting goods stores. To start off, wear the step counter for two to three weekdays and two weekend days and calculate your baseline 24-hour reading. An average daily count for a sedentary individual is about 6,000 steps per day depending on your work and where you live.

Get your daily step count up to 10,000 and you will have a much easier time of losing or managing your weight and will gain feelings of well-being and overall fitness.

"It's easier to go down a hill than up it but the view is much better at the top."

HENRY WARD BEECHER

(1813-1887)

Staying Motivated to Exercise

- Make a strong personal commitment to exercise. Know that you are doing something for yourself or for your family. Make it a high priority.
- Develop an exercise "habit" before seriously increasing intensity or duration of exercise sessions.
- Schedule your exercise during "protected" time.
- Think long-term. There is no need to rush. The habit will become ingrained over time, and your fitness will slowly blossom.
- Set attainable goals. Better to establish targets that seem easy and hit them than to start missing and get discouraged.
- Keep records. Start a personal logbook. It will become an invaluable tool for tracking your progress and staying motivated. Keep a tally of your miles covered, if you wish, and set a target: walking across your county, then your state. Biking across the country, rowing to Hawaii. Some people keep maps and pinpoint their progress.
- Exercise with a partner, or a dog, at least some days per week.

How One Man Got Back in Shape for Life

RF had been a college athlete and, while he had gotten a bit out of shape in middle age, he was surprised when he started getting short of breath and tired after just a short session of snow blowing. He mentioned this to his doctor, who recommended a stress test. He hadn't gone very far on the treadmill when it was stopped because an abnormality was seen and an angiogram was recommended. Just a few days later, severe blockages of his coronary arteries were found and several stents had to be placed. At 60, RF's life had changed.

Looking back, he admits he should have known that he was at high risk for heart disease as he had put on a good deal of weight and his blood pressure was high and difficult to control. He admits he ignored himself, being so busy with work as a university athletic director and being as available as possible for his family. With his diagnosis, he says he had to admit that he had been in denial about his health and physical condition.

"I realized I didn't have a choice," RF says, as he recalls moving beyond the initial shock. He was clearly looking forward to growing old with his wife and seeing his children enjoy adulthood. He dreamed of little things like playing tennis with his daughter and golf with his son. The first order of business was that he knew he needed to eat differently. He and his wife share the cooking, so they committed themselves to working together on heart-healthy shopping, food preparation and eating. He found that he could best control calories and his appetite by limiting his intake of sugar and simple carbohydrates.

Daily exercise became part of his routine. He felt pretty strongly that he needed the support not only of his wife, who has been unwavering, but of his friends and his co-workers as well. He knew that if they knew what he was doing, they would "provide the support that teammates provide." He joined a cardiac rehabilitation program to provide structure for his exercise regimen and plans to continue "until it is 100 percent part of my life." He admits candidly that, while he is internally motivated, "doing this all alone would have been hard."

It has been six months since RF lay on the hard X-ray table in the cardiac catheterization laboratory having stents placed in his coronary arteries. He has lost 45 pounds, he is exercising daily, his energy is back, and he is enjoying his family, his work and his friends as only a person can who has viewed the possibility of being without them. His blood pressure and cholesterol have become much, much easier to control after weight loss, with less need for medication.

CHAPTER 5

LIFELONG STRATEGIES

Proven techniques for making sustainable changes in your diet

Going on a diet for a couple of weeks or even a few months is the easy part. Making your new eating habits permanent is the real challenge and it requires that you lay the foundations properly from the start. Fortunately, it is not a matter of sheer willpower, but more a matter of learning and following a few strategies that we know can work. Start right and this will get easier and easier, not increasingly hard as with most popular diets.

The EATINGWELL Healthy Heart Plan has no induction phase, no crash dieting for radical improvement in two weeks, no sudden encouragement to start a free-for-all binge on grapefruit, white rice, cabbage soup, chocolate, popcorn or whatever the next fad might be. All of these unlimited-single-food diets work on the principle of making all your food choices for you and then getting you good and bored with eating.

"Just 'cause you got the monkey off your back doesn't mean the circus has left town."

GEORGE CARLIN, COMEDIAN

A very different approach is to have you engage with the subject of food and good nutrition. It is important, we believe, that you make the choices and know how to navigate the temptations and clearly unhealthy eating options that are so readily available—and so heavily promoted—in modern life.

CUPBOARD CONCEPTS: A FRIENDLY PANTRY

One of the best first steps in your transition to a healthier diet is to confront your own pantry. Like a vigorous spring cleaning, it is an energizing exercise and one that will make life easier in the weeks and months ahead.

First, you will likely need to get rid of some high-fat, high-sugar, high-sodium ingredients and processed foods. The fancy term for this is "stimulus control." People derive strong feelings of taking control by throwing out (or passing along) jars of gooey Alfredo sauce, boxes of trans-fatty cookies and all those pints of super-premium ice cream in the freezer. "Out of sight, out of mind" is a bit of a cliché, but in working with thousands of heart patients, I've seen it work. Be reassured that you will never regret removing as many temptations as possible from your cupboards, refrigerator, freezer and the little caches of snacks that may be tucked away in your car or desk drawer. I cannot overemphasize the importance of this step. Do not proceed until you have done a thorough cleanout of your refrigerator and pantry shelves.

Next comes the most interesting part: filling all the empty space with things that are tasty, wholesome and essential ingredients for a better way of eating. It is essential to stock up on the appropriate ingredients (*see page 62*) and then keep these on hand in your pantry at all times.

Some people complain that changing to a healthy diet emphasizing fruits, vegetables, whole grains and low-fat dairy products will be too expensive. The reality is that a heart-healthy diet is only minimally more expensive—if you consider yourself a smart shopper, you can definitely find ways to make this work for your own budget. While certain items, such as fish and fresh vegetables, can cost more, you will be spending much less on meats, cheeses and highly processed, expensive snack foods, takeout meals and quick dinner mixes.

MAKING SENSE OF LABELS

Among nutrition-conscious consumers, label reading has become something of a shopping survival skill. Label scrutiny is easy once you've made a habit of it, and it quickly allows you to see beyond the cagey marketing, packaging and clever brand names that are used to sell less-than-desirable foods to the unwary.

Starting from the top of the label, it is first crucial to clarify the serving size. These are often unrealistically small. If the serving size on the label is, for example, 1 cup of cereal, and you normally eat a big bowlful (2 or more cups), you need to multiply all nutritional contents accordingly. Moving down the label, next will be the number of servings per package, to give you a better feel for the serving size. (Snack-food packagers are especially crafty: what seems to be a single portion is often two or more "servings"— with double or triple the calories and fat you might assume from the per-serving information.)

Next is the number of calories per serving, and the calories from fat. The total number of calories is very important if you are attempting to control your weight. The calories from fat is less important. Much more important is the type of fat.

Further down you will find the total fat per serving and the grams of saturated, trans, polyunsaturated and monounsaturated fats. Amounts are rounded to the nearest whole number, so 0.4 gram would be listed as 0 grams, 0.8 gram would be listed as 1 gram and 1.4 grams would also be listed as 1 gram. When the serving size is unrealistic, such as 1 cup of cereal where you might eat 3 cups, 0.4 gram of trans fat will be listed as 0 where you are actually getting a significant 1.2 grams (3 x 0.4) of trans fat in your portion.

You want to limit your saturated fat to 5 percent or less of your total calories (divide your body weight by 12 to get the total daily limit of saturated fat in grams). As for trans fats, you want to limit intake entirely. Polyunsaturated and monounsaturated fats are healthy, so no limitation is needed other than if you are limiting calories.

Further down is cholesterol content. This number is largely irrelevant as your blood cholesterol levels depend more on saturated-fat and trans-fat intake than on cholesterol intake. Ignore this one.

Next comes the sodium and potassium content per serving. Remember that a moderate limitation of sodium is less than 2,300 mg sodium per day, whereas a more severe limitation is less than 1,600 mg per day. Obviously, if you have a bowl of canned soup at more

> MYTH: A healthy diet, with fresh fruits and vegetables and fish, is very expensive to sustain.
>
> FACT: It should not cost much more. You will be saving by spending less on meats, cheeses, quick prepared dinners and highly processed, expensive snack foods.

> "If anything is worth doing, do it with all your heart."
>
> BUDDHA

Nutrition Facts

Serving Size 4 Crackers (14g)
Servings Per Container About 32

Amount Per Serving

Calories 70   Calories from Fat 25

	% Daily Value*
Total Fat 3g	**5%**
Saturated Fat 1g	**5%**
Trans Fat 0g	
Polyunsaturated Fat 1g	
Monounsaturated Fat 1g	
Cholesterol 0mg	**0%**
Sodium 150mg	**6%**
Total Carbohydrate 9g	**3%**
Dietary Fiber less than 1g	**1%**
Sugars 1g	
Protein 1g	

Vitamin A	0%	•	Vitamin C	0%
Calcium	0%	•	Iron	2%

* Percent Daily Values are based on a 2,000 calorie diet. Your daily values may be higher or lower depending on your calorie needs:

	Calories	2,000	2,500
Total Fat	Less than	65g	80g
Sat. Fat	Less than	20g	25g
Cholesterol	Less than	300mg	300mg
Sodium	Less than	2,400mg	2,400mg
Total Carbohydrate		300g	375g
Dietary Fiber		25g	30g

Ingredients: Enriched flour (wheat flour, niacin, reduced iron, thiamin mononitrate [vitamin B₁], riboflavin [vitamin B₂], folic acid), partially hydrogenated soybean and/or cottonseed oil with TBHQ for freshness, sugar, contains two percent or less of salt, leavening (baking soda, sodium acid pyrophosphate, monocalcium phosphate), high fructose corn syrup, corn syrup, sodium sulfite, soy lecithin.

CONTAINS WHEAT AND SOY INGREDIENTS.

THE HEART-HEALTHY PANTRY

Oils, Vinegars & Condiments

Extra-virgin olive oil for cooking and salad dressings

Canola oil for cooking and baking

Flavorful nut and seed oils (toasted sesame oil, walnut oil) for salad dressings and stir-fry seasonings

Vinegars: balsamic, red-wine, white-wine, rice, cider

Asian condiments and flavorings: reduced-sodium soy sauce, fish sauce, hoisin sauce, mirin, oyster sauce, chile-garlic sauce, curry paste

Kalamata olives, green olives

Dijon mustard

Capers

Ketchup

Barbecue sauce

Worcestershire sauce

Mayonnaise, reduced-fat (for a recipe to make your own, see page 228)

Flavorings

Kosher salt, coarse sea salt, fine salt

Black peppercorns

Onions

Fresh garlic

Fresh ginger

Anchovies or anchovy paste for flavoring pasta sauces and salad dressings

Dried herbs: bay leaves, dill, crumbled dried sage, thyme, oregano, tarragon, Italian seasoning blend

Spices: allspice, caraway, chili powder, cinnamon sticks, ground cinnamon, coriander, cumin, curry powder, ground ginger, dry mustard, nutmeg, paprika, cayenne pepper, crushed red pepper, poultry seasoning, turmeric

Lemons, limes, oranges (the zest is as valuable as the juice)

Granulated sugar

Brown sugar

Honey

Pure maple syrup

Unsweetened cocoa powder, natural and/or Dutch-processed

Bittersweet chocolate

Dry Goods

Canned tomatoes, tomato paste

Reduced-sodium chicken broth, beef broth and/or vegetable broth (or go to *eatingwell.com* for homemade broth recipes)

Clam juice

"Lite" coconut milk for Asian curries and soups

Canned beans: cannellini beans, great northern beans, chickpeas, black beans, red kidney beans, pinto beans

Canned lentils

Chunk light tuna, salmon and sardines

Buttermilk powder

Whole-wheat flour and whole-wheat pastry flour (store opened packages in the refrigerator or freezer)

All-purpose flour

Assorted whole-wheat pastas

Brown rice and instant brown rice

Pearl barley, quick-cooking barley

Rolled oats

Whole-wheat couscous

Bulgur

Dried lentils

Yellow cornmeal

Plain dry breadcrumbs

Wild rice

Nuts, Seeds & Fruits
(Store opened packages of nuts and seeds in the refrigerator or freezer.)

Assorted nuts: walnuts, pecans, almonds, hazelnuts, peanuts, pine nuts

Sesame seeds

Natural peanut butter

Tahini (sesame paste)

Assorted dried fruits: apricots, prunes, cherries, cranberries, dates, figs, raisins

Refrigerator Items

Low-fat or nonfat milk

Soymilk

Low-fat or nonfat plain yogurt and/or vanilla yogurt

Reduced-fat or nonfat sour cream

Good-quality Parmesan cheese

Sharp Cheddar cheese

Eggs (large) or egg substitute, such as Egg Beaters

Orange juice

Dry white wine (or nonalcoholic wine)

Water-packed tofu

Freezer Basics

Fruit-juice concentrates (orange, apple, pineapple)

Frozen vegetables: edamame (soybeans), peas, spinach, broccoli, bell pepper and onion mix, corn, chopped onions, small whole onions, uncooked hash browns

Frozen berries

Italian turkey sausage (to flavor fast pasta sauces)

Low-fat vanilla ice cream or frozen yogurt (for impromptu desserts)

NO ROOM IN THE PANTRY

Saying goodbye to these is the hard part, for some. These foods are the heavy hitters in raising levels of LDL (bad) cholesterol. You will *rarely* need them, therefore they need not be in your cupboard. If you recently stopped smoking, would you keep a carton of cigarettes in your closet or ashtrays on your table?

Butter	Heavy cream
Stick margarine	Whipped cream
Whole milk	Ice cream
Half-and-half	Bacon

than 800 mg of sodium, it is going to be difficult to finish the day without going over your limit. The EATINGWELL target for most main courses is less than 700 mg of sodium, which is enough to satisfy most palates and keep you within your daily limits. A high dietary intake of potassium can help lower blood pressure; a good source of potassium has 15 percent of the Daily Value (525 mg). On the other hand, people with kidney disease or individuals on certain medications need to limit potassium intake.

Carbohydrate content is the next listing on the label and, unfortunately, current rules do not require labels to distinguish whole grains from processed grains. The label does give information on dietary fiber but does not distinguish between soluble and insoluble fiber. As a rule of thumb, men should take in more than 38 grams of total fiber per day and women should take in more than 25 grams of total fiber. Cereals and crackers that appear to be wholesome and dense with whole grains often come up with surprisingly scant amounts of fiber per serving. Compare the labels of different brands and you are sure to discover surprising differences.

Sugar is next; less is better. None is best in many foods that are too often made less healthy with the addition of sugars (such as canned tomatoes). Still, even unsweetened tomatoes have natural sugar, which shows up on the label. The label does not distinguish between natural and added sugars, so check the ingredients list to spot added sugars—a frequent culprit is high-fructose corn syrup.

And finally, protein is listed as total protein. Chances are, your protein intake is adequate, and I usually don't suggest tallying it.

At the bottom of the label, vitamins are listed generally as percent of total daily recommendation.

Ingredients: Here is the core of the label. Ingredients are listed in order of weight. You should carefully check ingredients for contents like *partially hydrogenated* and *hydrogenated* oils, as these signify the presence of trans fats. If these are near the top of the

ingredients list, check to see how realistic the serving size is, as you don't want to be a victim of an unrealistically small serving size with trans fats "rounded" down to zero. Fortunately, it's getting easier and easier just to find brands that have no hydrogenated fats among the ingredients. Also look for added sugars (see above) and whole grains—the label must say "whole," not just "wheat flour."

At the extreme right of the label you'll see each nu-

"Live not as though there were a thousand years ahead of you. Fate is at your elbow; make yourself good while life and power are still yours."

MARCUS AURELIUS (121-180), THE EMPEROR-PHILOSOPHER

trient's percentage of your total daily intake based upon the guess that you take in 2,000 calories a day. Since this amount of calories would be appropriate only for an individual weighing 166 pounds, I find this section quite useless if you don't happen to weigh 166 pounds. I suggest that you focus on the actual grams or milligrams of the nutrients in question, and not percentages of a nutrient in your total diet. While label rules have gradually improved, they still could be made simpler to understand *and* more informative.

Surprising things turn up in the ingredients list. "Pure Juice" cranberry juice, for example, may not be as it sounds. Cheaper brands use inexpensive concentrated *grape juice* to sweeten and dilute the pricier cranberry juice. Many products posing as "maple syrup" are nothing more than high-fructose corn syrup with traces of flavoring. When buying packaged foods, read the fine print and make a habit of buying products that live up to their name and that use ingredients you would want to put in your body.

Safe Substitutions

Old recipes can have fresh new lives, often without losing their essential flavors and appeal. Learning options for safe substitutions is a key concept. A limited list of common heart-healthy substitutions is given here, with many more to be found in the recipe section. These substitutes don't always work exactly on a one-to-one ratio, so be patient and willing to experiment.

Original	Substitute
Heavy Cream	Nonfat Half-and-Half, Nonfat Sour Cream, Nonfat Evaporated Milk, Nonfat Yogurt
Whole Milk	Nonfat (Skim) Milk (add powdered milk to thicken if you wish)
Ice Cream	Nonfat Frozen Yogurt, Low-Fat Ice Cream, Sherbet, Sorbet
Butter or Margarine for baking and cooking	Canola Oil, Nut Oils
Salt for popcorn	Brewer's Yeast, Powdered Cheddar Cheese
Whole Egg	Two Egg Whites, Egg Beaters
Soy Sauce	Reduced-Sodium Soy Sauce
Cream Cheese	Reduced-Fat Cream Cheese
Sour Cream	Reduced-Fat or Nonfat Sour Cream, Yogurt Cheese (yogurt drained through cheesecloth)

MINDFUL SNACKING

Snacking and grazing are part of life. If you plan ahead for healthy snacking, you will always have a choice of heart-healthy items available when the urge hits. In moderation and with wise choices, snacking need not be a guilt-ridden escape from sensible eating.

- **Fresh fruit** (Keep the fruit bowl filled and inviting; let it change with the seasons and buy produce when it's fresh and ripe.)
- **Fresh vegetables** (Cut vegetables, such as carrots, celery, bell peppers, into bite-size pieces and serve with a yogurt-based dip.)
- **Popcorn** (air-popped, seasoned with brewer's yeast or garlic powder)
- **Whole-wheat pretzels** (scrape off the salt)
- **Baked corn chips** with salsa
- **Fruit-juice popsicles**
- **Nonfat yogurt** with fresh fruit and wheat germ
- **Smoothies** (yogurt blended with bananas and fruit juice)
- **Nuts**, with no added oil (best are walnuts, pecans, almonds, then peanuts)
- **Low-fat granola** (Be careful, many commercial brands are very high in hydrogenated oils and sugars.)
- **Fat-free crackers** with reduced-fat or nonfat cottage cheese
- **Rice cakes**
- **Whole-grain cereal** with nonfat milk

EATING OUT

For reasons that escape logic, many people feel that food eaten at a restaurant doesn't "count" as part of their healthy diet. The thinking seems to be that your body will not "notice" the rich restaurant food. This, of course, is nonsense.

On the other hand, you have far more control over nutritional content and serving size when you do eat at home. It is very challenging to adhere to a good diet, from the point of view of both weight management and heart health, when you routinely consume restaurant meals and greasy, heavy take-out food.

Still, most of us find going to a restaurant fun and socially rewarding, and this experience need not be removed from your agenda. A few suggestions can steer you around the pitfalls of eating out:

- If you frequent a restaurant often, politely but clearly let them know how you would like your food prepared (no butter, no cream, etc.). Don't hesitate: they virtually always want your continued business. Most restaurateurs are remarkably service-oriented. That is, they want to please and they understand that happy eaters will return.
- In most situations, ask for sauces and dressings on the side and use minimally. Substitute a wedge of lemon or flavored vinegar for a creamy sauce.
- Be careful at the salad bar. Many of the items and dressings are extremely high in fat. Stick to the vinaigrette if you can.
- Avoid soups made with cream, eggs or cheese.
- In Asian restaurants, wok-fried vegetables are generally acceptable as peanut oil is typically used. Ask what kind of oil they fry in. Avoid batter-dipped selections. Be careful of high salt and/or MSG (monosodium glutamate).
- Ask for fish grilled, baked or sautéed in olive oil.
- Avoid deep-fried anything unless you know the oil is trans-fat free.
- Ask for vegetables without butter or cream sauce.
- If no healthy items appear to be available at a restaurant, ask for them. Popular demand will often shape their next menu.
- Serving sizes can be inordinately large. You need not finish everything on your plate. Bring food home for the dog or for lunch the next day.

- Do not go to the restaurant or a party hungry, particularly if you suspect that the fare will all be heavy and unhealthy. Have a heart-healthy snack before leaving home and partake of the party food in moderation.
- Bring snacks when traveling on planes. Airline food and airports often offer very little in the way of healthy selections, unless you plan ahead.

WHERE DO THESE FIT IN?

Alcohol: Numerous dietary studies have shown quite clearly that individuals who take in moderate amounts of alcohol (1 to 2 drinks daily) actually have less heart disease than people who abstain. The mechanism of this effect probably relates to its favorable effect on (good) HDL cholesterol, which it raises. Wine, in particular, has anti-platelet effects similar to those of aspirin. (Platelets are cell remnants that can clump together as part of a clot.) Wine "thins" the blood and it also contains flavonoids, which are antioxidant and may protect against LDL cholesterol being taken up by the walls of your arteries. Interestingly, grape juice, without alcohol, also has these same effects. If you are taking aspirin, it is not clear if grape juice or wine has a supplemental effect. The downside of alcohol is that it can raise blood triglycerides, particularly if you start with high levels, and that it contains somewhat "empty calories" if you are working to control your weight.

A drink is defined as 12 ounces of beer, 5 ounces of wine or 1.5 ounces of liquor or 80-proof spirits. Higher amounts of alcohol—more than two drinks a day for men and one more than drink a day for (smaller) women—are associated with increased rates of cancer, liver disease, high blood pressure, ulcers and a shortened life span. I rarely recommend that anyone take up drinking if they don't currently drink, but if an individual currently has a drink or two per day, I do not discourage their continuing to imbibe. You should be honest with your physician about how often and how much you drink, to evaluate alcohol's health effects for you. Most important, alcohol use will in no way protect you if other risk factors (smoking, obesity, high cholesterol, high blood pressure) are left untreated.

Chocolate: If only chocolate were good for the heart. Life would be magical! The scientific verdicts about the supposed health benefits of chocolate are still in flux. Studies, mostly funded by the chocolate industry, suggest that cocoa butter, the primary ingredient in dark chocolate, is rich in flavonoids (like red wine), which can have antioxidant and blood thinning effects. Overall, dark chocolate has a neutral effect on blood lipids. Unfortunately, most of the chocolate that we like to eat is in the form of milk chocolate, where sugar is usually the first ingredient and the "milk" component consists of unhealthy milk fat and/or other unhealthy oils. Fortunately, it is quite easy to incorporate chocolate into your baking in a healthy manner by combining cocoa powder with a healthy oil and other ingredients to make delicious cakes, cookies and bars (*see Dark Fudgy Brownies, page 239*). One Harvard study suggested that, like alcohol, chocolate in small doses (three times per month) may indeed have health benefits compared to higher doses or no chocolate at all. In summary, chocolate cannot yet be labeled a health food, but it can easily be incorporated into heart-healthy baking and an occasional snack of good dark chocolate brings no harm.

Nuts: An increased intake of nuts has been shown in numerous studies to be associated with a decreased risk for the development of coronary heart disease. These include studies in women, men, Iowans, Seventh-Day Adventists, nurses and physicians. Individuals who eat nuts two to four days or more per week have less heart disease than those who eat less. Nuts included in these studies and therefore associated with these benefits include walnuts, pecans, almonds, hazelnuts, pine nuts, pistachios and peanuts (actually a legume). They are all characterized by a relatively high content of monounsaturated fats, a relatively high content of polyunsaturated fats including omega-3s and a low content of saturated fats.

Nuts, however, are high in calories: roughly 200 calories per ounce, which is about 15 or so nuts, depending on the nut. Thus, they can make a healthy but high-calorie snack. If you are adding nuts to your diet, subtract something else. Peanut and almond butters are healthy spreads, but be sure there are no added unhealthy oils, such as trans/hydrogenated oils, or added sugar. Watch the salt content as well.

In addition to nuts, seeds like flaxseed, pumpkin seeds and sunflower seeds also have potential heart benefits due to their high content of omega-3 fatty acids. Avoid the presalted varieties. Ground flaxseed and flaxseed flour also add fiber to baked items, such as breads or muffins.

Coffee: A freshly brewed cup of coffee tastes so good that it has been assumed over the years that it must be bad for you. Certainly it contains caffeine, which has been tied to blood pressure elevations and irregular heartbeats. However, most studies of large populations have shown no increase in overall rates of coronary heart disease or high blood pressure related to coffee. To the contrary, some health benefits have emerged. It appears that coffee drinkers have lower rates of type 2 diabetes and Parkinson's disease. On the other hand, some individuals are sensitive to coffee, which can cause migraine headaches and stomach ulcers. If you are a regular drinker of caffeinated coffee and you stop abruptly, the caffeine-withdrawal headaches can last from part of a day to up to a week or more.

When coffee is prepared the American way, which is to drip-brew it through a paper filter, it has no adverse effects on blood cholesterol levels. When it is prepared the European way, which is to boil ground coffee in water or to filter it through a metal plunger filter, 4 cups or more a day can slightly raise cholesterol levels on the order of 4 mg/dL. Caffeine is not

"Getting the Elephant Off My Chest"

BV had no warning symptoms before the afternoon he was driving home and felt a pressure that was "like an elephant sitting on my chest." He first thought it might be indigestion, but it persisted for almost an hour so he spoke with his wife and decided to go to the emergency room. He was having a heart attack and he was taken immediately to the cardiac catheterization laboratory where a clot was removed from one of his coronary arteries and a coronary stent was placed to keep the blood flowing freely.

Looking back, BV did not think that he had been at high risk for a heart attack. While there was a lot of obesity in his family and he was carrying almost 300 pounds on his 6-foot-1-inch frame, he had no family history of heart problems and his cholesterol levels and blood pressures had been good. He had never smoked. He was active though he didn't exercise.

After he returned home, his cardiologist put it to him directly: "How long do you want to survive?" BV quickly summed up in his mind that his life was good and replied, "I want more!" While he was not afraid to make changes, he very much wanted to do it in a controlled way.

As advised, he entered a cardiac rehabilitation program and quickly focused on the importance of losing weight and taking on a long-term exercise program. He says he "became a believer" and "logged every bite" to attain his goal of no more than 1,600 calories per day. He found that an easy initial way to control calories was to cut out entirely the soft drinks that had become a staple of his day.

His wife, LV, was his greatest supporter and found a health-oriented cookbook to learn the ins and outs of better eating, cooking and label reading. She quickly found that the trans and saturated fats they had been consuming also needed to be brought into line. One key she learned was to always have fresh fruit or a filling salad with beans or other protein ready in the fridge so that—if the urge hits—he (or she) can eat something healthy and satisfying rather than "falling off the wagon." She wanted to avoid blandness and drudgery in their everyday eating and says she enjoys keeping things varied and interesting.

BV has enjoyed and accepted the positive encouragement and support he has received from friends and neighbors. He knew he could set his mind to it and is proud of losing 85 pounds, of getting fit and of keeping the weight off for almost three years. He says, candidly, that this has been a challenge, particularly when traveling. A key to the maintenance of his weight loss has been the planned availability of a healthy snack when he gets hungry, and physical activity. He logs two to three hours per week of exercise at the cardiac rehab center and gets out every single day for at least a half-hour walk. In addition, he always parks at the farthest spot in the parking lot and keeps busy on his job, which includes property management and development.

LV quietly but confidently states that, while she enthusiastically supported her husband's efforts, he had to decide for himself to control what he eats. She has enjoyed a bit of weight loss herself, and has found that their life now follows a new routine that is no harder than the old one. They say they have too many plans to enjoy life not to change a few of the habits that led them to the emergency room.

the culprit but rather the cholesterol-raising effect of oils found in coffee. Surprisingly, decaffeinated coffee has this effect to a greater degree than caffeinated coffee, as stronger beans are used to stand up to the decaffeination process. Thus, consumption of four cups of caffeinated coffee or less per day prepared by dripping through a paper filter has no bad effects on cholesterol levels. Enjoy!

Tea: I always hesitate when they say that "5,000 years of Chinese medicine can't be wrong." In my mind, I wonder, "What did they know about medicine in China—or anywhere else for that matter—5,000 years ago?" In the case of tea, they may have been right. Tea is the second-most widely consumed beverage in the world, after water. Tea can be categorized into three types, depending on the level of fermentation: green (unfermented), oolong (partially fermented) and black (fermented) tea. Of these, green tea contains the highest concentration of antioxidants that may be protective with regards to cardiovascular health. While some studies show that both black and green tea consumption lower cholesterol levels, this has not been a consistent finding. Tea, particularly green tea, has also been shown in some studies to increase arterial blood flow.

While this topic has been incompletely studied, one study from Japan published in the *Journal of the American Medical Association* in 2007 showed that green tea consumption was associated with lower overall mortality, partly due to a lower rate of cardiovascular disease. So, regular drinking of green or black tea may be cardioprotective, but is not nearly as beneficial as controlling your blood pressure,

managing your diabetes, not smoking, maintaining a healthy weight and exercise.

Most herbal teas are a blend of leaves, flowers and roots from plants, so they are not true "tea." It is simply not clear if herbal teas have health benefits and there are scores of herbal teas to consider. I see no reason to think they are harmful, however.

YOUR CHOICES (AND MINE)

Heart disease is a much-feared diagnosis, yet so many of the patients I see had either accepted it as an inevitable part of life or something that happens as a stroke of bad luck.

The most important message I can leave you with is something my colleagues and patients have heard me emphasize many times: "A healthy heart is a choice you make." In my own case, I could have sunk into an acceptance of a family history of early cardiac events. Had I just accepted my fate, I might very well not be here today to write this book.

In the vast majority of people, premature coronary artery disease is highly preventable. Even for patients who have early warning signs and many risk factors, and even for those who have already had a cardiac event, the odds of living a long and fulfilling life can be dramatically shifted in your favor by following the advice presented in this book. There is simply no reason to feel powerless against something that can be avoided or even reversed by paying attention to diet, maintaining a healthy weight, eliminating risk factors and exercising at least moderately every day that you eat.

As the many delicious recipes that follow will clearly attest, following a healthy-heart way of life can be a time of enjoying some of the best foods you have ever eaten. Look at them as part of the reward for choosing to have a healthy heart and vibrant life.

"A healthy heart is a choice you make."

PHILIP ADES, CARDIOLOGIST

INTRODUCTION TO HEART-HEALTHY COOKING

Simple changes and makeover techniques for eating well every day

EATINGWELL for a healthy heart means enjoying food that tastes great and is good for you. It means eating the foods you know and love, and trying new healthy foods from around the globe. All it takes are a few simple changes.

We know that you don't want to feel deprived when you're eating dinner. A recipe must taste wonderful to make it a hit. But we also know that we need to keep a recipe simple, easy and accessible for it to become a part of your monthly (or weekly) rotation. So you'll find that most of the recipes in this book can be made even on a busy weeknight, in 45 minutes or less. Many have fewer than 10 ingredients—nearly all of which you can easily find at your supermarket. When we call for more exotic items, we tell you either where to find them or what to substitute.

We believe that eating a balanced diet every day is essential, which means we don't follow the fads—low-carb, no-carb, low-fat, high-protein diets are not what we're about. Our approach to healthy cooking is actually quite simple. We use whole foods instead of processed foods as much as possible to eliminate unwanted additives like trans fats and excess sodium. We load up on fruits and vegetables and opt for healthy oils like olive and canola, which are high in unsaturated fats. We choose lean meats, low-fat dairy products and whole grains that still have their key nutrients and fiber intact.

In this collection of recipes, you will find some of our favorite healthy-cooking techniques, perfected over the years. These techniques are the combined work of many talented recipe developers, writers from around the country and the world, and our staff here in the EATINGWELL Test Kitchen. Sometimes we have come up with healthy solutions for a recipe only after testing and tasting it numerous times. When we were trying to bump up the nutrients on a pizza, we discovered that replacing some of the tomato sauce with pumpkin puree boosted the beta carotene and fiber and still tasted delicious. After taking a look at the list of ingredients (not to mention the trans fat) in many store-bought crispy taco shells, we set out to make a delicious oven-baked version. (We found that an oven rack stood in as a perfect "hanger" to drape corn tortillas over.)

We've also included makeovers of classics like meatloaf and lasagna, as well as inherently healthy dishes like grilled salmon. If you're already a healthy-cooking pro, there are plenty of exciting recipes like Gorgonzola & Prune Stuffed Chicken to add to your repertoire. If this is the beginning of your transition to a heart-healthy lifestyle, then the makeover recipes are an easy place for you to start—they are foods that you may already know and love, just made healthier.

Once you try these makeover recipes at home you will be on your way to learning healthy-cooking techniques that you can incorporate into your cooking every day. The changes are easy to make and the nutritional improvements are simply jaw-dropping. Take our lasagna, for instance: we replace some of the meat with mushrooms, onions and carrots. Flavorful, lean turkey sausage is our choice for meat because it has a big flavor impact with minimal fat and calories. We also swap whole-wheat pasta for regular pasta and low- or nonfat cheeses for their high-fat counterparts. Our final recipe nets out with two-thirds the calories of regular lasagna, one-quarter of the fat and one-fifth of the saturated fat. Meanwhile we've bumped up the fiber from 4 grams to 9 and reduced the sodium by almost 900 milligrams. Throughout the book, we tell you exactly how we change our makeover recipes to be more healthful—and at least as delicious—so you can start applying these tricks to your favorite recipes that could use a little makeover. You'll find a section of makeover recipes beginning on page 73 to get you started, and the rest throughout the recipe chapters.

There is something for everyone from a taste perspective in this collection, from pepperoni pizza to Stir-Fried Noodles with Green Tea. Try them and we're sure you'll find that it's simple *and delicious* to make heart-healthy eating a way of life *every day*.

10 SIMPLE CHANGES TO GET YOU ON YOUR WAY TO EATINGWELL EVERY DAY:

1. CHOOSE WHOLE GRAINS OVER PROCESSED GRAINS. Processed grains are stripped of many key nutrients that whole grains have. Try whole-wheat flour instead of all-purpose flour, whole-wheat pasta instead of regular, whole-grain bread instead of white and brown rice instead of white.

2. SUBSTITUTE HEART-HEALTHY OILS FOR BUTTER. Pick oils like olive, canola or walnut oil. These are high in heart-healthy unsaturated fats, as opposed to butter, which is loaded with saturated fat. But keep in mind that even though unsaturated fat is better for your heart, these oils are still high in calories and need to be used in moderation to maintain a healthy weight.

3. MAKE SURE YOU HAVE A SET OF NONSTICK PANS. These allow you to sauté meats and vegetables in just a teaspoon or two of oil without having the food stick to the pan. You don't need ½ cup of oil (or butter) to cook two chicken breasts!

4. CHOOSE LOW-FAT OR NONFAT DAIRY PRODUCTS INSTEAD OF THE HIGH-FAT VERSIONS. Part-skim mozzarella, nonfat milk, nonfat ricotta cheese and nonfat sour cream are great dairy products that you can include in a heart-healthy diet and skip all the saturated fat in their full-fat counterparts.

5. ADD VEGETABLES. In order to keep a serving of food generous but still healthy, use less of the higher-calorie ingredients like meat or pasta and add in more vegetables. See the makeovers of Hamburger Helper (*page 204*) or lasagna (*page 74*) for ideas on how to sneak in more vegetables.

6. GO FOR SHARP, STRONG CHEESES. When you use cheeses with a big flavor, a little goes a long way. So look for the sharpest Cheddar you can find or the best real Parmesan you can afford.

7. CHOOSE LEANER MEATS. That means picking skinless chicken or ground meats with a lower percentage of fat. Also look for cuts with "loin" or "tenderloin" in the name, which tend to be lean. Trim visible fat off meat before you cook it.

8. OPT FOR LOWER-SODIUM PRODUCTS. Many convenient packaged goods have added sodium. Luckily, there are often lower-sodium versions of canned tomatoes, broths, soy sauce and beans available. Look for products labeled "low-sodium," "reduced-sodium" or "no-salt added." Also compare the nutrition labels of different brands to find the ones with the least sodium. If you have time, using fresh or homemade ingredients is an even better way to control the sodium.

9. SKIP THE DEEP FRYER. With just a bit of breading or batter and a little oil or cooking spray, you can get a crispy, delicious coating on fish (*page 80*), chicken (*page 76*) or even zucchini (*page 233*) without a Fry-Daddy in sight!

10. USE FRESH HERBS. Grow them if you have the right weather, space and time or pick them up at the market. Rather than relying on lots of butter or salt, you can use herbs to give dishes nuance and flavor without extra calories or fat. —*Jessie Price, Food Editor*

RECIPE GUIDELINES & NUTRIENT ANALYSES

NUTRITION ICONS:

Our nutritionists have highlighted recipes likely to be of interest to those following various dietary plans. Recipes that meet specific guidelines are marked with these icons:

Healthy ✕ Weight

To qualify for this icon, an entree has reduced calories, fats and saturated fats, as follows:

CALORIES ≤ 350, TOTAL FAT ≤ 20g, SAT FAT ≤ 5g

For soups, salads and side dishes, the upper limits are:

CALORIES ≤ 250, TOTAL FAT ≤ 10g, SAT FAT ≤ 5g

For muffins, breads and desserts, the upper limits are:

CALORIES ≤ 230, TOTAL FAT ≤ 10g, SAT FAT ≤ 5g

Lower ⬇ Carbs

This icon means a recipe has 22 grams or less of carbohydrate per serving.

High ⬆ Fiber

This icon means a recipe provides 5 grams or more of fiber per serving.

HEART-HEALTHY CRITERIA:

Entrees have 3 grams or less of saturated fat, except for fish entrees, which have 5 grams or less of saturated fat. All other recipes have 2 grams or less of saturated fat. All recipes in this book meet this criteria.

NUTRITION BONUSES:

Nutrition bonuses are indicated for recipes that provide 15% or more of the Daily Value (DV) of specific nutrients. The daily values are the average daily recommended nutrient intakes for most adults that you see listed on food labels. In addition to the nutrients listed on food labels (vitamins A and C, calcium, iron and fiber), we have included bonus information for other nutrients, such as folate, magnesium, potassium, selenium and zinc, when a recipe is particularly high in one or more of these. We have chosen to highlight these nutrients because of their importance to good health and the fact that many Americans may have inadequate intakes of them.

ANALYSIS NOTES:

Each recipe is analyzed for calories, total fat, saturated (SAT) and monounsaturated (MONO) fat, cholesterol, carbohydrate, protein, fiber, sodium and potassium. (Numbers less than 0.5 are rounded down to 0; 0.5 to 0.9 are rounded up to 1.) We use Food Processor SQL software (ESHA Research) for analyses.

When a recipe states a measure of salt "or to taste," we analyze the measured quantity. (Readers on sodium-restricted diets can reduce or eliminate the salt.) Recipes are tested with iodized table salt unless otherwise indicated. Kosher or sea salt is called for when the recipe will benefit from the unique texture or flavor. We assume that rinsing with water reduces the sodium in canned foods by 35%.

When alternative ingredients are listed, we analyze the first one suggested. Optional ingredients and garnishes are not analyzed. We do not include trimmings or marinade that is not absorbed in analyses. Portion sizes are consistent with healthy-eating guidelines.

DEFINING "ACTIVE TIME" AND "TOTAL":

Testers in the EATINGWELL Test Kitchen keep track of the time needed for each recipe.

Active Time includes prep time (the time it takes to chop, dice, puree, mix, combine, etc. before cooking begins), but it also includes the time spent tending something on the stovetop, in the oven or on the grill—and getting it to the table. If you can't walk away from it, we consider it active time.

Total includes both active and inactive time and indicates the entire amount of time required for each recipe, start to finish.

Recipes ready to eat in 45 minutes or less are marked with this icon.

To Make Ahead gives storage instructions to help you plan.

If special **Equipment** is needed to prepare a recipe, we tell you that too.

MENUS

A SAMPLING OF HEART-HEALTHY DINNERS

Item or Recipe	Per Serving	
	Calories	Sat. Fat (g)
Tomato, Tuna & Tarragon Salad (p.111)	255	2
Whole-wheat pita pocket	170	0
Warm Chocolate Pudding (p.240)	164	1
TOTAL	**589**	**3**
Tortellini & Zucchini Soup (p.117)	203	2
Corn & Broccoli Calzones (p.131)	334	2
Strawberry-Mango Margarita Compote (p.243)	134	0
TOTAL	**671**	**4**
Yucatan Lemon Soup (p.122)	149	1
The EatingWell Taco (p.207)	261	1
Tomato Salsa (p.229)	21	0
Lemon Poppy-Seed Cake (p.238)	215	1
TOTAL	**646**	**3**
Baby Spinach Salad with Raspberry Vinaigrette (p.227)	70	0
Hamburger Buddy (p.205)	297	3
Oven-Fried Zucchini Sticks (p.233)	108	0
Chocolate & Nut-Butter Bites (p.243)	79	2
TOTAL	**554**	**5**
Spring Pea & Scallion Soup (p.127)	141	1
Paprika-Spiced Butter Beans & Polenta (p.136)	210	2
Pear Crumble (p.242)	257	1
TOTAL	**608**	**4**
Fresh Corn & Red Pepper Bisque (p.116)	201	2
Grilled Chicken Salad with Fresh Strawberry Dressing (p.104)	321	2
Cherries with Ricotta & Toasted Almonds (p.243)	133	0
TOTAL	**655**	**4**
Pureed Zucchini Soup (p.126)	87	2
Five-Spice Chicken & Orange Salad (p.106)	278	2
Whole-wheat pita pocket	170	0
"Cocoa-Nut" Bananas (p.243)	80	0
TOTAL	**615**	**4**

Item or Recipe	Per Serving	
	Calories	Sat. Fat (g)
Watercress & Pickled Ginger Salad (p.228)	76	0
Honey-Soy Broiled Salmon (p.186)	234	3
Green Bean & Cherry Tomato Sauté (p.231)	71	0
Brown rice (p.229)	110	0
Broiled Mango (p.243)	69	0
TOTAL	**560**	**3**
EatingWell's Oven-Fried Chicken (p.76)	226	2
Garden Pasta Salad (p.103)	205	2
Savoy Cabbage Slaw (p.228)	69	1
Dark Fudgy Brownies (p.239)	86	1
TOTAL	**586**	**6**
Blue Ribbon Meatloaf (p.82)	259	2
Oven-Fried Potatoes (p.232)	103	1
Roasted Broccoli with Lemon (p.230)	54	1
Nutty Baked Apples (p.243)	165	0
TOTAL	**581**	**4**
Snap Pea Salad with Radish & Lime (p.228)	110	1
Fillet of Sole with Spinach & Tomatoes (p.195)	138	0
Brown rice (p.229)	110	0
Strawberry-Raspberry Sundaes (p.243)	130	0
TOTAL	**488**	**1**
Baby Spinach Salad with Raspberry Vinaigrette (p.227)	70	0
Chicken à la King (p.78)	271	1
Whole-wheat pasta (1 cup)	174	0
Apple, medium	72	0
TOTAL	**587**	**1**
Romaine & Fresh Herb Salad (p.227)	46	0
Classic Lasagna (p.74)	357	3
Italian bread	100	0
Olive oil for dipping (2 teaspoons)	90	0
Fresh berries (1 cup)	60	0
TOTAL	**653**	**3**
Pork Medallions with Prune-Ginger Sauce (p.222)	262	2
Oven-Fried Potatoes (p.232)	103	1
Brussels Sprouts with Walnut-Lemon Vinaigrette (p.230)	108	1
Strawberry-Raspberry Sundaes (p.243)	130	0
TOTAL	**603**	**4**

RECIPE MAKEOVERS

IN THIS CHAPTER:

Classic Lasagna 74

EatingWell's Oven-Fried Chicken 76

Chicken à la King 78

Crispy Fish Sandwich with Pineapple Slaw 80

Blue Ribbon Meatloaf 82

ELSEWHERE IN THE BOOK:

EatingWell Waffles 90

Garden Pasta Salad 102

Old-Fashioned Chicken & Dumplings 154

EatingWell's Pepperoni Pizza 170

Hamburger Buddy 204

The EatingWell Taco 206

EatingWell's Chicken-Fried Steak 208

PER SERVING:

357 calories;

8 g fat (3 g sat, 2 g mono);

32 mg cholesterol; 46 g carbohydrate;

22 g protein; 9 g fiber; 698 mg sodium;

396 mg potassium.

NUTRITION BONUS: Fiber (36% DAILY VALUE), Calcium (30% DV).

High ⬆ Fiber

ACTIVE TIME: 1 HOUR

TOTAL: 2 HOURS

TO MAKE AHEAD: Prepare through Step 5. Store in an airtight container in the refrigerator for up to 2 days or freeze for up to 3 months. Thaw before baking.

CLASSIC LASAGNA

Here's an old-fashioned meat-and-cheese lasagna made lighter. Whole-wheat lasagna noodles taste great in this recipe, plus they help boost the fiber to 9 grams, which is more than a third of the recommended daily intake and especially good news for a healthy heart. (Photograph: page 73.)

MEAT SAUCE

- ½ tablespoon extra-virgin olive oil
- 4 ounces hot *or* sweet Italian turkey sausage, casings removed
- 2 onions, finely chopped
- 1 carrot, finely chopped
- 12 ounces mushrooms, wiped clean and chopped
- 2 cloves garlic, minced
- ⅛ teaspoon salt
   Freshly ground pepper to taste
- ¼ cup dry red wine
- 2 28-ounce cans plum tomatoes, drained and chopped
- ½ cup sun-dried tomatoes (*not* packed in oil), slivered
- 1 teaspoon dried oregano
- 1 teaspoon dried basil
- 1 teaspoon dried thyme
- ¼ teaspoon crushed red pepper, or to taste

PASTA & CHEESE FILLING

- 12 whole-wheat lasagna noodles (12 ounces)
- 2 cups nonfat ricotta cheese
- ⅛ teaspoon salt
   Freshly ground pepper to taste
   Ground nutmeg to taste
- 1 cup shredded part-skim mozzarella
- ½ cup freshly grated Parmesan cheese
- 2 tablespoons chopped fresh parsley

1. TO PREPARE MEAT SAUCE: Heat oil in a large heavy pot or Dutch oven over medium-high heat. Add sausage and cook, breaking up clumps, until browned, 3 to 5 minutes. Reduce heat to medium. Add onions and carrot; cook, stirring, until softened, 2 to 3 minutes. Add mushrooms and garlic; season with salt and pepper. Cook, stirring frequently, until mushroom liquid evaporates, 4 to 6 minutes.

2. Stir in wine, plum tomatoes, sun-dried tomatoes, oregano, basil, thyme and crushed red pepper. Bring to a simmer; reduce heat to low, cover and simmer, stirring occasionally, for 45 minutes. Uncover and cook, stirring frequently, until the sauce is very thick, 30 to 45 minutes more. Adjust seasoning with salt and pepper.

3. TO PREPARE FILLING & ASSEMBLE LASAGNA: Bring a large pot of lightly salted water to a boil. Preheat oven to 350°F. Coat a 9-by-13-inch baking dish with cooking spray.

4. Cook noodles until just tender, about 10 minutes or according to package directions. Drain, then cool by plunging noodles into a large bowl of ice-cold water. Lay the noodles out on kitchen towels.

5. Season ricotta with salt, pepper and nutmeg. Spread about 1½ cups meat sauce in the prepared pan. Layer 3 noodles on top. Spread another 1 cup sauce over the noodles. Dot about ⅔ cup ricotta over the sauce, then sprinkle with ¼ cup mozzarella and 2 tablespoons Parmesan. Continue layering the noodles, sauce and cheeses, finishing with the sauce, mozzarella and Parmesan. Sprinkle with parsley; cover with foil.

6. Bake the lasagna until the sauce is bubbling, 35 to 40 minutes. Uncover and bake until golden, 5 to 10 minutes more. Let cool for 10 minutes before cutting.

MAKES 8 SERVINGS.

	EatingWell's Classic Lasagna	Regular Meat Lasagna
Calories	357	671
Fat	8 g	34 g
Saturated Fat	3 g	17 g
Sodium	698 mg	1,594 mg
Fiber	9 g	4 g

To cut the fat and saturated fat in the meat sauce we use turkey sausage rather than ground beef or pork. Because sausage is so flavorful, we can use less of it than plain ground beef or pork and still get a big impact on flavor.

A generous amount of vegetables like onions, carrot, mushrooms and tomatoes stand in for some of the high-calorie meat and dairy products. That helps keep the serving size generous while reducing fat and calories.

We opt for nonfat ricotta and part-skim mozzarella rather than their full-fat counterparts to cut the fat content by nearly 27 grams and the saturated fat by 15 grams.

	EatingWell's Oven-Fried Chicken	Traditional Fried Chicken
Calories	226	431
Fat	7 g	26 g
Saturated Fat	2 g	7 g
Sodium	353 mg	441 mg
Fiber	1 g	0 g

We remove and discard the chicken skin, which is high in saturated fat. To maintain a crispy "fried chicken-like" coating, we dredge the chicken in whole-wheat flour, paprika and sesame seeds. This gives it a great full flavor with less fat.

Instead of frying, we spray the coated chicken with cooking spray and bake it in the oven on a wire rack. The result is a delicious, crispy outer crust that is significantly lower in total fat, saturated fat and calories.

EATINGWELL'S OVEN-FRIED CHICKEN

Marinating the chicken legs in buttermilk keeps them juicy, and the light coating of flour, sesame seeds and spices, misted with olive oil, forms a flavorful, crunchy crust during baking. It's even good cold so it's a good option for a picnic.

½	cup buttermilk (see *Tip*)
1	tablespoon Dijon mustard
2	cloves garlic, minced
1	teaspoon hot sauce, such as Tabasco
2½-3	pounds chicken legs, skin removed, trimmed and cut into thighs and drumsticks
½	cup whole-wheat flour
2	tablespoons sesame seeds
1½	teaspoons paprika
1	teaspoon dried thyme
1	teaspoon baking powder
⅛	teaspoon salt
	Freshly ground pepper to taste
	Olive oil cooking spray

1. Whisk buttermilk, mustard, garlic and hot sauce in a shallow glass dish until well blended. Add chicken and turn to coat. Cover and marinate in the refrigerator for at least 30 minutes or for up to 8 hours.

2. Preheat oven to 425°F. Line a baking sheet with foil. Set a wire rack on the baking sheet and coat it with cooking spray.

3. Whisk flour, sesame seeds, paprika, thyme, baking powder, salt and pepper in a small bowl. Place the flour mixture in a paper bag or large sealable plastic bag. Shaking off excess marinade, place one or two pieces of chicken at a time in the bag and shake to coat. Shake off excess flour and place the chicken on the prepared rack. (Discard any leftover flour mixture and marinade.) Spray the chicken pieces with cooking spray.

4. Bake the chicken until golden brown and no longer pink in the center, 40 to 50 minutes.

MAKES 4 SERVINGS.

PER SERVING:

226 calories;

7 g fat (2 g sat, 2 g mono);

130 mg cholesterol; 5 g carbohydrate;

34 g protein; 1 g fiber; 353 mg sodium;

423 mg potassium.

NUTRITION BONUS: Potassium (21% DAILY VALUE).

Healthy ✕ Weight

Lower ⬇ Carbs

ACTIVE TIME: 20 MINUTES

TOTAL: 1 HOUR 35 MINUTES (including marinating time)

TO MAKE AHEAD: Marinate the chicken for up to 8 hours.

TIP:

No **buttermilk**? You can use buttermilk powder prepared according to package directions. Or make "sour milk": the ratio is 1 tablespoon lemon juice or vinegar to 1 cup milk.

	EatingWell's Chicken à la King	Traditional Chicken à la King
Calories	271	718
Fat	8 g	59 g
Saturated Fat	1 g	30 g
Sodium	401 mg	682 mg
Fiber	1 g	3 g

Instead of heavy whipping cream we use low-fat (1%) milk to cut down on fat and saturated fat. Then to thicken the sauce we add flour, which gives it a rich, creamy mouthfeel with significantly less fat.

We replace some of the meat with extra mushrooms and green pepper to bump up the flavor and keep the calories reasonable.

Fresh mushrooms stand in for canned mushrooms to reduce sodium.

CHICKEN A LA KING

There's no need to feel guilty over this classic creamy combination of chicken, peppers and mushrooms. Our version uses low-fat milk and flour for thickening to make it plenty rich without all the saturated fat. Serve over whole-wheat egg noodles.

- 1½ **pounds boneless, skinless chicken breast, trimmed and cut into 1-inch cubes**
- ½ **cup all-purpose flour**
- 2 **tablespoons canola oil, divided**
- 10 **ounces white mushrooms, quartered**
- 1 **large green bell pepper, diced**
- ¾ **teaspoon salt**
- ½ **teaspoon freshly ground pepper**
- 1 **cup dry sherry (see *Note*)**
- 1 **cup reduced-sodium chicken broth**
- 1 **cup low-fat milk**
- 1 **4-ounce jar sliced pimientos, rinsed**
- ½ **cup sliced scallions**

1. Toss chicken and flour in a medium bowl until coated. Heat 1 tablespoon oil in a large skillet over medium-high heat. Reserving the remaining flour, add the chicken to the pan and cook, stirring occasionally, until lightly browned, 2 to 4 minutes. Transfer the chicken to a plate.
2. Reduce heat to medium and add the remaining 1 tablespoon oil to the pan. Add mushrooms, bell pepper, salt and pepper, and cook, stirring often, until the mushrooms are softened and starting to brown, 3 to 5 minutes. Pour in sherry; bring to a boil and cook, stirring to scrape up any browned bits, 3 minutes.
3. Whisk broth and milk into the reserved flour until smooth. Stir the mixture into the pan. Bring to a simmer, stirring often. Stir in pimientos and the chicken and return to a simmer. Reduce heat to maintain a gentle simmer and cook until the vegetables are tender and the chicken is cooked through, 5 to 7 minutes. Stir in scallions and serve immediately.

MAKES 6 SERVINGS, ABOUT 1 CUP EACH.

PER SERVING:

271 calories;

8 g fat (1 g sat, 4 g mono);

66 mg cholesterol; 15 g carbohydrate;

28 g protein; 1 g fiber; 401 mg sodium;

529 mg potassium.

NUTRITION BONUS: Vitamin C (70% DAILY VALUE), Selenium (40% DV), Potassium & Vitamin A (15% DV).

Healthy ⚖ Weight

Lower ⬇ Carbs

ACTIVE TIME: 35 MINUTES

TOTAL: 35 MINUTES

INGREDIENT NOTE:

Sherry is a type of fortified wine originally from southern Spain. Don't use the "cooking sherry" sold in many supermarkets—it can be surprisingly high in sodium. Instead, purchase **dry sherry** that's sold with other fortified wines in your wine or liquor store.

	EatingWell's Crispy Fish Sandwich with Pineapple Slaw	Traditional Fried Fish Sandwich
Calories	425	533
Fat	9 g	30 g
Saturated Fat	1 g	4 g
Sodium	684 mg	1,055 mg
Fiber	7 g	1 g

Instead of deep-fat frying, we cook the fish on the stovetop using a nonstick skillet. The result is a crispy golden outer crust, without the added fat from frying.

We boost the fiber in this recipe by using whole-wheat bread instead of plain hamburger buns.

Reduced-fat mayonnaise and yogurt dress the creamy coleslaw in the sandwich. Our reduced-fat coleslaw takes the place of usual coleslaw or tartar sauce, which are typically made with full-fat mayonnaise.

Pineapple in the coleslaw adds great flavor along with extra vitamin C and fiber.

CRISPY FISH SANDWICH WITH PINEAPPLE SLAW

A fish sandwich doesn't have to be deep-fried and doesn't have to be off your list of "healthy" foods. Try our version with a tangy, zesty pineapple slaw. It's worth taking the extra minute to chop pineapple slices instead of using crushed pineapple—the crushed is too small and disappears into the slaw. Try this with Oven-Fried Potatoes (page 232).

2	tablespoons reduced-fat mayonnaise
2	tablespoons nonfat plain yogurt
2	teaspoons rice vinegar
1/8-1/4	teaspoon crushed red pepper
1	8-ounce can pineapple chunks *or* rings, drained and coarsely chopped
2	cups coleslaw mix (see *Tip*)
1/4	cup cornmeal
1¼	pounds haddock *or* Pacific cod, skinned and cut into 4 portions
1/2	teaspoon Cajun seasoning
1/4	teaspoon salt
4	teaspoons canola oil, divided
8	slices whole-wheat country bread, toasted

1. Whisk mayonnaise, yogurt, vinegar and crushed red pepper to taste in a medium bowl. Add pineapple and coleslaw mix and stir to combine.

2. Place cornmeal in a shallow dish. Sprinkle both sides of fish with Cajun seasoning and salt. Dredge the fish in the cornmeal.

3. Heat 2 teaspoons oil in a large nonstick skillet over medium-high heat. Add half the fish and cook until golden, about 2 minutes per side. Transfer to a plate and repeat with the remaining 2 teaspoons oil and fish, adjusting heat as necessary to prevent burning.

4. Top toasted bread with the fish and pineapple slaw to make sandwiches. Serve immediately.

MAKES 4 SERVINGS.

PER SERVING:

425 calories;

9 g fat (1 g sat, 4 g mono);

105 mg cholesterol; 42 g carbohydrate;

44 g protein; 7 g fiber; 684 mg sodium;

865 mg potassium.

NUTRITION BONUS: Vitamin C (45% DAILY VALUE), Iron (20% DV), Calcium (15% DV).

High ⬆ Fiber

ACTIVE TIME: 25 MINUTES

TOTAL: 25 MINUTES

SHOPPING TIP:

Look for convenient pre-shredded cabbage-and-carrot **"coleslaw mix"** near other prepared vegetables in the produce section of the supermarket.

	EatingWell's Blue Ribbon Meatloaf	Traditional Meatloaf
Calories	259	342
Fat	9 g	15 g
Saturated Fat	2 g	6 g
Sodium	339 mg	1,200 mg
Fiber	2 g	2 g

We replace regular ground beef and pork with a combination of lean ground beef and turkey. The result: the total fat and saturated fat are cut almost in half.

Substituting an egg white for a whole egg cuts down on calories and saturated fat.

To reduce sodium we replace ketchup and plain white bread with dark beer and whole-wheat breadcrumbs.

BLUE RIBBON MEATLOAF

Here's a meatloaf that has plenty of meaty robustness, without all the fat and saturated fat. We use a combination of lean beef and turkey along with beer-simmered sweet onions to pack it with flavor but keep it "slim."

2	**teaspoons canola oil**
1	**medium sweet onion, chopped (2 cups)**
1	**12-ounce bottle dark or amber beer**
1	**teaspoon dried thyme leaves**
1	**teaspoon dry mustard**
3/4	**teaspoon salt**
	Freshly ground pepper to taste
1¼	**pounds 95%-lean ground beef**
1¼	**pounds 93%-lean ground turkey**
1	**cup fresh whole-wheat breadcrumbs (see *Tip*)**
¼	**cup chopped fresh parsley**
1	**large egg, lightly beaten**
1	**egg white, lightly beaten**

1. Preheat oven to 375°F. Coat an 8½-by-4½-inch loaf pan with cooking spray.

2. Heat oil in a large nonstick skillet over medium-high heat. Add onion and cook, stirring often, until translucent and starting to brown, about 5 minutes. Pour in beer and increase heat to high. Bring to a vigorous boil; cook until the liquid is quite syrupy and the mixture reduces to about ¾ cup, 8 to 10 minutes. Transfer to a large bowl. Stir in thyme, dry mustard, salt and pepper. Let cool for 10 minutes.

3. Add beef, turkey, breadcrumbs, parsley, beaten egg and egg white to the onion mixture. With clean hands, mix thoroughly and transfer to the prepared pan.

4. Bake the meatloaf until an instant-read thermometer registers 160°F when inserted into the center, about 1 hour 20 minutes. Let rest for 5 minutes; drain accumulated liquid from the pan and slice.

MAKES 8 SERVINGS, ONE 1-INCH SLICE EACH.

PER SERVING:

259 calories;

9 g fat (2 g sat, 2 g mono);

105 mg cholesterol; 11 g carbohydrate;

31 g protein; 2 g fiber; 339 mg sodium;

51 mg potassium.

NUTRITION BONUS: Zinc (20% DAILY VALUE), Iron (15% DV).

Healthy ⚖ Weight

Lower ⬇ Carbs

ACTIVE TIME: 30 MINUTES

TOTAL: 2 HOURS

TIP:

To make **fresh breadcrumbs**, trim crusts from firm sandwich bread. Tear the bread into pieces and process in a food processor until coarse crumbs form. One slice of bread makes about ⅓ cup crumbs.

Creamy Wheat Berry Hot Cereal

Honey Oat Quick Bread

Banana-Bran Muffins

Scandinavian Muesli

BREAKFAST

Banana-Berry Smoothie 86

Papaya Smoothie 86

Cantaloupe Smoothie 87

Winter Fruit Salad 87

Quick Breakfast Tacos 88

Egg-white omelet technique 89

MAKEOVER: EatingWell Waffles 90

Buttermilk-Oatmeal Pancakes 92

Chunky Blueberry Sauce 93

Scandinavian Muesli 94

Creamy Wheat Berry Hot Cereal 95

Apricot-Wheat Germ Muffins 96

Banana-Bran Muffins 98

Honey Oat Quick Bread 99

> ‘When you wake up in the morning, Pooh,’ said Piglet at last,
> ‘what’s the first thing you say to yourself?’
> ‘What’s for breakfast?’ said Pooh. ‘What do *you* say, Piglet?’
> ‘I say, I wonder what’s going to happen exciting *today*?’ said Piglet.
> Pooh nodded thoughtfully.
> ‘It’s the same thing,’ he said.
>
> A.A. MILNE, WINNIE-THE-POOH

135 calories;

2 g fat ($\bigcirc$ g sat, 0 g mono);

0 mg cholesterol; 27 g carbohydrate;

4 g protein; 3 g fiber; 19 mg sodium;

376 mg potassium.

NUTRITION BONUS: Vitamin C (93% DAILY VALUE).

Healthy)(Weight

ACTIVE TIME: 5 MINUTES

TOTAL: 5 MINUTES

BANANA-BERRY SMOOTHIE

This bright and easy breakfast packs two servings of fruit plus soy protein and fiber.

1¼	**cups orange juice**
1	**ripe medium banana, peeled and sliced**
1	**cup frozen blueberries, blackberries *or* raspberries**
½	**cup silken tofu**
2	**ice cubes, crushed**
1	**tablespoon sugar (optional)**

Combine orange juice, banana, berries, tofu and crushed ice in a blender; cover and blend until smooth and frothy. Sweeten with sugar, if desired. Serve immediately.

MAKES 3 SERVINGS, 1 CUP EACH.

---

176 calories;

1 g fat ($\bigcirc$ g sat, 0 g mono);

2 mg cholesterol; 42 g carbohydrate;

3 g protein; 2 g fiber; 74 mg sodium;

365 mg potassium.

NUTRITION BONUS: Vitamin C (100% DAILY VALUE), Vitamin A (25% DV).

Healthy)(Weight

ACTIVE TIME: 10 MINUTES

TOTAL: 10 MINUTES

PAPAYA SMOOTHIE

This fresh, tropical smoothie starts your day off with plenty of vitamins A, C and folate as well as dietary fiber and potassium.

1	**papaya, peeled, seeded and coarsely chopped (1¼ cups)**
¾	**cup bottled fruit nectar, such as papaya, mango *or* peach**
½	**cup buttermilk (see *Tip, page 244*)**
2½	**tablespoons sugar, preferably superfine**
2	**tablespoons fresh lime juice**
5	**ice cubes**

Combine all ingredients in a blender; cover and blend until very smooth and frothy. Pour into 2 tall glasses and serve.

MAKES 2 SERVINGS, ABOUT 1¼ CUPS EACH.

CANTALOUPE SMOOTHIE

If on a hurried morning you eat nothing but this smoothie, you will still be doing your body a favor with satisfying protein, fruit and a serving of dairy.

- 1 **ripe banana**
- 1/4 **ripe cantaloupe, seeded and coarsely chopped**
- 1/2 **cup nonfat *or* low-fat yogurt**
- 2 **tablespoons nonfat dry milk**
- 1 1/2 **tablespoons frozen orange juice concentrate**
- 2 **teaspoons honey**
- 1/2 **teaspoon vanilla extract**

Place unpeeled banana in the freezer overnight (or for up to 3 months). Remove banana from the freezer and let it sit until the skin begins to soften, about 2 minutes. Remove the skin with a paring knife. (Don't worry if a little fiber remains.) Cut the banana into chunks; combine in a blender or food processor with cantaloupe, yogurt, dry milk, orange juice, honey and vanilla. Cover and blend until smooth.

MAKES 1 SERVING.

PER SERVING:

314 calories;

1 g fat (0 g sat, 0 g mono);

4 mg cholesterol; 72 g carbohydrate;

11 g protein; 4 g fiber; 135 mg sodium;

1,052 mg potassium.

NUTRITION BONUS: Vitamin C (160% DAILY VALUE), Vitamin A (90% DV), Potassium (30% DV), Calcium (28% DV), Folate (23% DV).

Healthy ⅟ Weight

ACTIVE TIME: 10 MINUTES

TOTAL: 10 MINUTES (plus overnight to freeze banana)

WINTER FRUIT SALAD

Fruit salad isn't just for summer; winter fruits combine for a satisfying dish your body craves.

- 4 **seedless oranges, peeled**
- 3 **pink grapefruits, peeled**
- 1 **pineapple, peeled, quartered, cored and sliced**
- 2 **star fruit, sliced**
- 1 **pomegranate, cut in half and seeds removed**

Remove white pith from oranges and grapefruits; quarter the fruit lengthwise and cut into 1/4-inch slices. Place in a large bowl and toss with pineapple, star fruit and pomegranate seeds.

MAKES 8 SERVINGS, ABOUT 3/4 CUP EACH.

PER SERVING:

110 calories;

0 g fat (0 g sat, 0 g mono);

0 mg cholesterol; 28 g carbohydrate;

2 g protein; 4 g fiber; 2 mg sodium;

400 mg potassium.

NUTRITION BONUS: Vitamin C (160% DAILY VALUE), Vitamin A (20% DV), Fiber (16% DV).

Healthy ⅟ Weight

ACTIVE TIME: 25 MINUTES

TOTAL: 25 MINUTES

153 calories;

2 g fat (1 g sat, 0 g mono);

3 mg cholesterol; 15 g carbohydrate;

17 g protein; 0 g fiber; 453 mg sodium;

207 mg potassium.

Healthy)(Weight

Lower ⬇ Carbs

ACTIVE TIME: 15 MINUTES

TOTAL: 15 MINUTES

QUICK BREAKFAST TACOS

A smaller cousin of the breakfast burrito, the breakfast taco made with reduced-fat Cheddar and egg substitute is a satisfying and healthy breakfast option.

- **2 corn tortillas**
- **1 tablespoon salsa**
- **2 tablespoons shredded reduced-fat Cheddar cheese**
- **½ cup liquid egg substitute, such as Egg Beaters**

Top tortillas with salsa and cheese. Heat in the microwave until the cheese is melted, about 30 seconds. Coat a small nonstick skillet with cooking spray and heat over medium heat. Add egg and cook, stirring, until cooked through, about 1½ minutes. Divide the scrambled egg between the tortillas.

MAKES 1 SERVING.

EGG-WHITE OMELET TECHNIQUE

The fastest meal on the planet is a simple folded omelet, also known as a French-style omelet. If you just use egg substitutes or egg whites, an omelet is a satisfying part of a heart-healthy diet. Here are the basics:

- Use ½ cup egg substitute, such as Egg Beaters, or 4 egg whites to make an omelet for one serving, 1 cup or 8 egg whites to make an omelet for two.
- Use a heavy 7- to 10-inch nonstick or well-seasoned skillet with low, sloping sides and a comfortable sturdy handle that won't get hot. A small heat-resistant, flexible spatula is essential.
- Have the filling prepared and warmed, if it was refrigerated, before you start. Don't overstuff: figure ¼ cup filling per serving. The filling can be just about anything (*see "Filling Ideas," below*).

1. Heat 1 teaspoon olive oil in a 7- to 10-inch skillet over medium-high heat until hot. Tilt to coat the pan with oil. Pour the eggs into the pan and immediately stir with a heat-resistant rubber spatula or fork for 5 to 10 seconds. Then push the cooked portions at the edge toward the center, tilting the pan to allow uncooked egg to fill in around the edges. When no more egg runs to the sides, continue to cook until almost set and the bottom is light golden. (The omelet will continue to cook as it is filled and folded.) This whole step takes about 1 minute.

2. Remove the pan from the heat and spoon filling onto the center third of the omelet perpendicular to the handle. Use the spatula to fold the third of the omelet closest to the handle over the filling. Then, grasping the handle from underneath and using the spatula as a guide, tip the omelet onto a warm plate so that it lands folded in thirds, seam-side down.

FILLING IDEAS
- Cooked broccoli, sun-dried tomatoes (reconstituted) and shredded mozzarella
- Steamed spinach and tomatoes
- Mushrooms sautéed with rosemary and thyme
- Sautéed apple slices, minced fresh sage and shredded Gruyère
- Sautéed pear slices, sliced almonds and crumbled Stilton

1. Push cooked egg at the edge into the center.

2. Fold the omelet over the filling.

3. Tip the omelet onto a plate, seam-side down.

	EatingWell Waffles	Traditional Waffles
Calories	241	560
Fat	4 g	27 g
Saturated Fat	0 g	18 g
Sodium	450 mg	938 mg
Fiber	3 g	2 g

We reduce the calories and fat and eliminate the saturated fat by using canola oil in place of butter.

Using egg whites in place of whole eggs cuts down on calories and saturated fat.

By replacing all-purpose flour with whole-wheat flour we add fiber.

We suggest topping the waffles with fresh fruit or yogurt instead of whipped cream or additional butter to keep the fat and saturated fat down.

EATINGWELL WAFFLES

Top with fresh berries or sliced peaches and yogurt: you'll never miss the butter (and the saturated fat) that is normally in waffle recipes.

- 1 **cup whole-wheat flour**
- 1 **cup all-purpose flour**
- 1½ **teaspoons baking powder**
- ½ **teaspoon salt**
- ¼ **teaspoon baking soda**
- 2 **cups nonfat buttermilk (see *Tip*)**
- 1 **large egg, separated**
- 1 **tablespoon canola oil**
- 1 **tablespoon vanilla extract (optional)**
- 2 **large egg whites**
- 2 **tablespoons sugar**

1. Stir whole-wheat flour, all-purpose flour, baking powder, salt and baking soda in a large bowl. Whisk buttermilk, the egg yolk, oil and vanilla (if using) in a separate bowl. Add the wet ingredients to the dry ingredients and stir with a wooden spoon just until moistened.

2. Beat the 3 egg whites in a grease-free mixing bowl with an electric mixer until soft peaks form. Add sugar and continue beating until stiff and glossy. Whisk one-quarter of the beaten egg whites into the batter. Fold in the remaining beaten egg whites with a rubber spatula.

3. Preheat a waffle iron. Brush the surface lightly with oil. Fill the waffle iron two-thirds full of batter. Cook until the waffles are crisp and golden, 5 to 6 minutes. Repeat with the remaining batter, brushing the surface with oil before cooking each batch.

MAKES 6 SERVINGS.

PER SERVING:

241 calories;

4 g fat (0 g sat, 2 g mono);

37 mg cholesterol; 41 g carbohydrate;

11 g protein; 3 g fiber; 450 mg sodium;

285 mg potassium.

NUTRITION BONUS: Selenium (17% DAILY VALUE), Folate (16% DV).

Healthy Weight

ACTIVE TIME: 40 MINUTES

TOTAL: 40 MINUTES

TIP:

No **buttermilk**? You can use buttermilk powder prepared according to package directions. Or make "sour milk": the ratio is 1 tablespoon lemon juice or vinegar to 1 cup milk.

271 calories;

5 g fat (1 g sat, 2 g mono);

39 mg cholesterol; 46 g carbohydrate;

12 g protein; 4 g fiber; 675 mg sodium;

293 mg potassium.

NUTRITION BONUS: Folate (23% DAILY VALUE), Calcium (22% DV).

Healthy ⧓ Weight

ACTIVE TIME: 35 MINUTES

TOTAL: 55 MINUTES

TO MAKE AHEAD: Store the batter in an airtight container in the refrigerator (Step 1) overnight.

TIP:

No **buttermilk**? You can use buttermilk powder prepared according to package directions. Or make "sour milk": the ratio is 1 tablespoon lemon juice or vinegar to 1 cup milk.

BUTTERMILK-OATMEAL PANCAKES

Here is a hearty, high-grain way to start the day. Maple syrup is a perennial favorite topping; Chunky Blueberry Sauce (page 93) or sliced bananas would also complement their oat flavor.

2½	**cups nonfat buttermilk (see *Tip*)**
¾	**cup rolled oats**
1	**cup all-purpose flour**
½	**cup whole-wheat flour**
¼	**cup toasted wheat germ**
¼	**cup packed light brown sugar**
2	**teaspoons baking powder**
1	**teaspoon baking soda**
1	**teaspoon ground cinnamon**
½	**teaspoon salt**
1	**large egg**
2	**large egg whites**
2	**teaspoons canola oil, divided**
	Maple syrup (optional)

1. Combine buttermilk and rolled oats in a small bowl; let rest for 20 to 30 minutes to soften oats. Stir all-purpose flour, whole-wheat flour, wheat germ, brown sugar, baking powder, baking soda, cinnamon and salt in a medium bowl. Whisk egg, egg whites and 1 teaspoon oil in a separate bowl. Add the oat mixture and the flour mixture and stir with a wooden spoon until just combined.

2. Heat a large nonstick skillet over medium heat and brush lightly with a little of the remaining 1 teaspoon oil. Using ¼ cup batter for each pancake, pour batter onto the skillet and cook until the underside is browned and the bubbles on top remain open, 2 to 3 minutes. Turn the pancakes over and cook until the underside is browned, about 1 to 2 minutes. Transfer to a platter and keep warm in a 200°F oven. Repeat with remaining batter, brushing skillet with a little of the remaining oil as needed. Serve hot, topping with maple syrup if desired.

MAKES 6 SERVINGS, 2 PANCAKES EACH.

CHUNKY BLUEBERRY SAUCE

Easy to make and intensely flavored, this is equally at home on a stack of pancakes or a scoop of vanilla frozen yogurt.

- **2   cups fresh or frozen (*not* thawed) blueberries**
- **¼   cup honey**
- **1   teaspoon freshly grated lemon zest**
- **2   tablespoons lemon juice**

Stir blueberries, honey, lemon zest and juice in a medium saucepan. Bring to a boil; reduce heat to maintain a simmer and cook, stirring occasionally, until thickened, about 15 minutes. Let cool for 10 minutes; serve warm.

MAKES ABOUT 1⅓ CUPS.

PER TABLESPOON:

21 calories;

0 g fat (0 g sat, 0 g mono);

0 mg cholesterol; 6 g carbohydrate;

0 g protein; 0 g fiber; 0 mg sodium;

15 mg potassium.

ACTIVE TIME: 35 MINUTES

TOTAL: 35 MINUTES

TO MAKE AHEAD: Store in an airtight container in the refrigerator for up to 1 week or freeze for up to 1 month.

PER SERVING:

196 calories;

5 g fat (1 g sat, 2 g mono);

0 mg cholesterol; 34 g carbohydrate;

6 g protein; 5 g fiber; 6 mg sodium;

209 mg potassium.

NUTRITION BONUS: Fiber (18%
DAILY VALUE).

Healthy)(Weight

High ⬆ Fiber

ACTIVE TIME: 10 MINUTES

TOTAL: 2½ HOURS (including cooling time)

TO MAKE AHEAD: Store the muesli in an airtight container in the refrigerator for up to 2 weeks.

INGREDIENT NOTE:

Rye or **wheat flakes** are simply rye or wheat kernels that have been steamed and rolled, oatmeal-style. Look for them in natural-foods stores.

TIP:

Grind **flaxseeds** in a clean coffee grinder or dry blender just before using.

SCANDINAVIAN MUESLI

Serve this Scandinavian cereal with low-fat yogurt or nonfat milk to start your day off with whole grains and some protein and calcium-rich dairy. You can substitute any combination of chopped dried or fresh fruit for the raisins—apricots, apples, figs, cherries or cranberries would all be delicious. Try walnuts or hazelnuts instead of the almonds if you like. Ground flaxseeds stirred in at the end provide a boost of heart-healthy omega-3s.

- **2   cups old-fashioned** *or* **quick-cooking (***not* **instant) rolled oats**
- **²/₃ cup rye flakes** *or* **wheat flakes (see** *Note***)**
- **¹/₃ cup coarsely chopped almonds (1³/₄ ounces)**
- **2   tablespoons flaked coconut (sweetened** *or* **unsweetened)**
- **¹/₂ cup raisins**
- **2   tablespoons honey**
- **¹/₂ teaspoon vanilla extract**
   Pinch of cinnamon
- **¹/₄ cup flaxseeds, ground (optional; see** *Tip***)**

1. Preheat oven to 350°F. Coat a baking sheet with cooking spray. Spread oats and rye (or wheat) flakes on the baking sheet. Bake for 10 minutes. Stir in almonds and coconut; bake until the oats are fragrant, about 8 minutes. Turn off the oven. Stir raisins into the muesli.
2. Microwave honey for 10 seconds in a glass measuring cup. Stir in vanilla and cinnamon; drizzle over the muesli and stir to coat. Return the muesli to the turned-off warm oven and let cool completely, about 2 hours. Stir in flaxseeds, if using.

MAKES 8 SERVINGS, ABOUT ½ CUP EACH.

CREAMY WHEAT BERRY HOT CEREAL

This warming whole-grain cereal pairs cooked wheat berries with rolled oats, fruit and nuts for a filling, fiber-rich breakfast. Even better, the oats contain soluble fiber, the most important kind in lowering LDL cholesterol. Substitute heart-friendly walnuts for the almonds if you prefer.

1¼	**cups old-fashioned rolled oats**
½	**cup raisins**
2	**cups nonfat milk *or* reduced-fat soymilk**
⅛	**teaspoon salt**
1¼	**cups cooked wheat berries (see *Grain-Cooking Guide*, page 236)**
2	**teaspoons brown sugar**
1	**teaspoon ground cinnamon**
¼	**cup slivered almonds, toasted (see *Tip*, page 244)**

Place oats, raisins, milk (or soymilk) and salt in a large, microwave-safe bowl. (*No microwave? See stovetop variation, right.*) Stir to combine. Microwave on High, uncovered, for 3 minutes. Stir in cooked wheat berries and microwave again until hot, 1 to 2 minutes more. Let stand for 1 minute. Stir in brown sugar and cinnamon. Sprinkle with toasted almonds and serve.

MAKES 4 SERVINGS, ABOUT ¾ CUP EACH.

PER SERVING:

340 calories;

6 g fat (0 g sat, 2 g mono);

3 mg cholesterol; 59 g carbohydrate;

14 g protein; 7 g fiber; 304 mg sodium;

392 mg potassium.

NUTRITION BONUS: Fiber (28% DAILY VALUE), Calcium (21% DV), Iron (15% DV).

Healthy ⚖ Weight

High ⬆ Fiber

ACTIVE TIME: 10 MINUTES

TOTAL: 10 MINUTES

STOVETOP VARIATION:

Bring milk (or soymilk) to a boil in a medium saucepan over medium-high heat. Stir in oats, raisins and salt. Reduce heat to low, cover, and cook for 3 minutes. Stir in cooked wheat berries and cook until heated through, about 1 minute more. Remove from the heat. Stir in brown sugar and cinnamon; let stand for 1 minute. Sprinkle with toasted almonds and serve.

220 calories;

7 g fat (1 g sat, 3 g mono);

36 mg cholesterol; 34 g carbohydrate;

7 g protein; 3 g fiber; 185 mg sodium;

284 mg potassium.

Healthy ⨯ Weight

ACTIVE TIME: 30 MINUTES

TOTAL: 1 HOUR

♥ HEART-HEALTHY TIP

Whole-Wheat Flour:

Because whole grains are rich in dietary fiber, antioxidants and protective compounds like lignans, plant sterols and plant stanols, people who eat more whole grains, including whole wheat, have a lower risk of inflammatory heart disease and less thickening of their carotid artery.

APRICOT-WHEAT GERM MUFFINS

Nutty toasted wheat germ and tangy dried apricots give these muffins a homey, satisfying flavor along with a boost of fiber. Plumping the dried fruit before adding it to the batter keeps the muffins moist.

- ³/₄ **cup dried apricots, chopped**
- ½ **cup orange juice, divided**
- 1 **cup whole-wheat flour**
- ³/₄ **cup all-purpose flour**
- ³/₄ **cup plus 1 tablespoon toasted wheat germ, divided**
- 1½ **teaspoons baking powder**
- ½ **teaspoon baking soda**
- ¼ **teaspoon salt**
- 2 **large eggs**
- ½ **cup packed light brown sugar**
- 1 **cup buttermilk (see *Tip*, page 244)**
- ¼ **cup canola oil**
- 2 **tablespoons freshly grated orange zest**
- 1 **teaspoon vanilla extract**

1. Preheat oven to 400°F. Coat 12 muffin cups with cooking spray.
2. Combine apricots and ¼ cup orange juice in a small bowl. Cover with vented plastic wrap and microwave on High for 1 minute. (*Alternatively, bring to a simmer in a small saucepan. Remove from the heat.*) Set aside to plump.
3. Whisk whole-wheat flour, all-purpose flour, ¾ cup wheat germ, baking powder, baking soda and salt in a large bowl.
4. Whisk eggs and brown sugar in a medium bowl until smooth. Whisk in buttermilk, oil, orange zest, vanilla and remaining ¼ cup orange juice. Add to the dry ingredients and mix with a rubber spatula just until moistened. Add apricots and juice and mix just until blended. Scoop the batter into the prepared muffin cups. Sprinkle with remaining 1 tablespoon wheat germ.
5. Bake the muffins until lightly browned and the tops spring back when touched lightly, 15 to 25 minutes. Let cool in the pan for 5 minutes. Loosen the edges and turn muffins out onto a wire rack to cool slightly before serving.

MAKES 1 DOZEN MUFFINS.

203 calories;

6 g fat (1 g sat, 3 g mono);

36 mg cholesterol; 34 g carbohydrate;

6 g protein; 4 g fiber; 184 mg sodium;

219 mg potassium.

NUTRITION BONUS: Fiber (17% DAILY VALUE).

Healthy ⚥ Weight

PREP TIME: 30 MINUTES

TOTAL: 1 HOUR

INGREDIENT NOTE:

Unprocessed wheat bran, also known as miller's bran, is the outer layer of the wheat kernel, removed during milling. Look for it in the baking section. Do not substitute bran cereal in this recipe.

♥ HEART-HEALTHY TIP

The potassium in **bananas** helps maintain normal heart function and the balance of sodium and water in the body. It is especially important for people taking diuretics for heart disease, which combat sodium and water retention but also strip potassium from the body in the process.

BANANA-BRAN MUFFINS

By the end of the week, any bananas left in the fruit bowl are past their prime—just right for these moist bran muffins. Add a handful of dark chocolate chips to entice children to enjoy a fiber-rich treat.

2	large eggs
2/3	cup packed light brown sugar
1	cup mashed ripe bananas (2 medium)
1	cup buttermilk (see *Tip, page 244*)
1	cup unprocessed wheat bran (see *Note*)
1/4	cup canola oil
1	teaspoon vanilla extract
1	cup whole-wheat flour
3/4	cup all-purpose flour
1 1/2	teaspoons baking powder
1/2	teaspoon baking soda
1/2	teaspoon ground cinnamon
1/4	teaspoon salt
1/3	cup chopped walnuts (optional)

1. Preheat oven to 400°F. Coat 12 muffin cups with cooking spray.
2. Whisk eggs and brown sugar in a medium bowl until smooth. Whisk in bananas, buttermilk, wheat bran, oil and vanilla.
3. Whisk whole-wheat flour, all-purpose flour, baking powder, baking soda, cinnamon and salt in a large bowl. Make a well in the dry ingredients; add the wet ingredients and stir with a rubber spatula until just combined. Scoop the batter into the prepared muffin cups (they'll be quite full). Sprinkle with walnuts, if using.
4. Bake the muffins until the tops are golden brown and spring back when touched lightly, 15 to 25 minutes. Let cool in the pan for 5 minutes. Loosen edges and turn muffins out onto a wire rack to cool slightly before serving.

MAKES 1 DOZEN MUFFINS.

HONEY OAT QUICK BREAD

This bread has a pleasant flavor and divinely moist, tender crumb. It requires minimal mixing and cleanup, calls for ingredients usually stocked in the pantry, and is tasty yet healthful.

2	tablespoons plus 1 cup old-fashioned rolled oats *or* quick-cooking (*not* instant) oats, divided
1⅓	cups whole-wheat flour *or* white whole-wheat flour (see *Note, page 245*)
1	cup all-purpose flour
2¼	teaspoons baking powder
¼	teaspoon baking soda
1¼	teaspoons salt
8	ounces (scant 1 cup) nonfat *or* low-fat plain yogurt
1	large egg
¼	cup canola oil
¼	cup clover honey *or* other mild honey
¾	cup nonfat *or* low-fat milk

1. Position rack in middle of oven; preheat to 375°F. Generously coat a 9-by-5-inch (or similar size) loaf pan with cooking spray. Sprinkle 1 tablespoon oats in the pan. Tip the pan back and forth to coat the sides and bottom with oats.

2. Thoroughly stir together whole-wheat flour, all-purpose flour, baking powder, baking soda and salt in a large bowl. Using a fork, beat the remaining 1 cup oats, yogurt, egg, oil and honey in a medium bowl until well blended. Stir in milk. Gently stir the yogurt mixture into the flour mixture just until thoroughly incorporated but not overmixed (excess mixing can cause toughening). Immediately scrape the batter into the pan, spreading evenly to the edges. Sprinkle the remaining 1 tablespoon oats over the top.

3. Bake the loaf until well browned on top and a toothpick inserted in the center comes out clean, 40 to 50 minutes. (It's normal for the top to crack.) Let stand in the pan on a wire rack for 15 minutes. Run a table knife around and under the loaf to loosen it and turn it out onto the rack. Let cool until barely warm, about 45 minutes.

MAKES 12 SLICES.

PER SLICE:

193 calories;

6 g fat (1 g sat, 3 g mono);

18 mg cholesterol; 31 g carbohydrate;

6 g protein; 3 g fiber; 396 mg sodium;

100 mg potassium.

NUTRITION BONUS: Iron (15% DAILY VALUE).

Healthy ⚖ Weight

ACTIVE TIME: 15 MINUTES

TOTAL: 1¾ HOURS (including cooling time)

TO MAKE AHEAD: Store cooled bread, tightly wrapped, for up to 1 day at room temperature. If desired, warm (wrapped in foil) at 375°F before serving.

Warm Bean & Arugula Salad

Grilled Chicken Salad with Fresh Strawberry Dressing

Five-Spice Chicken & Orange Salad

Tomato, Tuna & Tarragon Salad

MAIN-DISH SALADS

MAKEOVER: Garden Pasta Salad.............**102**

Grilled Chicken Salad with
    Fresh Strawberry Dressing................**104**

    Fresh Strawberry Dressing...............**105**

Five-Spice Chicken &
    Orange Salad.....................................**106**

Lebanese Fattoush Salad with
    Grilled Chicken **108**

Warm Chicken Sausage &
    Potato Salad......................................**109**

Warm Bean & Arugula Salad **110**

Tomato, Tuna &
    Tarragon Salad **111**

Smoked Salmon
    Salad Niçoise **113**

Additional salad recipes:

SIDE SALADS **227**

> "To remember a successful salad is generally to remember a successful dinner; at all events, the perfect dinner necessarily includes the perfect salad."
>
> GEORGE ELLWANGER, PLEASURES OF THE TABLE

	EatingWell's Garden Pasta Salad	Traditional Pasta Salad
Calories	205	573
Fat	9 g	41 g
Saturated Fat	2 g	8 g
Sodium	291 mg	516 mg
Fiber	4 g	3 g

We replace regular white pasta with whole-wheat pasta to add fiber.

Using a combination of reduced-fat mayonnaise, low-fat yogurt and olive oil instead of regular mayonnaise cuts down the calories and saturated-fat content.

We add lots of tomatoes, carrots and peppers and cut back on the pasta. This allows for a generous serving size with significantly fewer calories.

GARDEN PASTA SALAD

Serve on a crisp bed of greens. Toss in canned chunk light tuna, cooked chicken or flavored baked tofu (see Note, page 244) to add protein and make it more substantial.

2	cups whole-wheat rotini (6 ounces)
⅓	cup reduced-fat mayonnaise
⅓	cup low-fat plain yogurt
2	tablespoons extra-virgin olive oil
1	tablespoon red-wine vinegar *or* lemon juice
1	clove garlic, minced
⅛	teaspoon salt
	Freshly ground pepper to taste
1	cup cherry *or* grape tomatoes, halved
1	cup diced yellow *or* red bell pepper (1 small)
1	cup grated carrots (2-4 carrots)
½	cup chopped scallions (4 scallions)
½	cup chopped pitted kalamata olives
⅓	cup slivered fresh basil

1. Bring a large pot of lightly salted water to a boil. Cook pasta, stirring occasionally, until just tender, 8 to 10 minutes, or according to package directions. Drain and refresh under cold running water.
2. Whisk mayonnaise, yogurt, oil, vinegar (or lemon juice), garlic, salt and pepper in a large bowl until smooth. Add the pasta and toss to coat. Add tomatoes, bell pepper, carrots, scallions, olives and basil; toss to coat well.

MAKES 6 SERVINGS, 1 CUP EACH.

PER SERVING:

205 calories;

9 g fat (**2** g sat, 5 g mono);

1 mg cholesterol; 29 g carbohydrate;

6 g protein; 4 g fiber; 291 mg sodium;

269 mg potassium.

NUTRITION BONUS: Vitamin C (97% DAILY VALUE), Vitamin A (70% DV), Fiber (17% DV).

Healthy)(Weight

ACTIVE TIME: 35 MINUTES

TOTAL: 35 MINUTES

TO MAKE AHEAD: Store in an airtight container in the refrigerator for up to 1 day.

♥ HEART-HEALTHY TIP

Olives and olive oil are good sources of monounsaturated fat, which helps prevent oxidation of LDL cholesterol and reduces the risk of plaque buildup.

321 calories;

17 g fat (2 g sat, 11 g mono);

49 mg cholesterol; 17 g carbohydrate;

25 g protein; 5 g fiber; 356 mg sodium;

633 mg potassium.

NUTRITION BONUS: Vitamin C (110% DAILY VALUE), Selenium (24% DV), Magnesium (21% DV), Iron & Vitamin A (20% DV), Potassium (19% DV), Folate (17% DV).

Healthy ♓ Weight

Lower ⬇ Carbs

High ⬆ Fiber

ACTIVE TIME: 35 MINUTES

TOTAL: 35 MINUTES

TO MAKE AHEAD: Blanch the vegetables up to 4 hours before serving; store in the refrigerator under barely moistened paper towels.

TIP:

Sugar snaps have a fibrous seam on the inside curve. To remove it, grasp the stem protruding from one end and pull it down the inside curve as if you were unzipping the pea.

GRILLED CHICKEN SALAD WITH FRESH STRAWBERRY DRESSING

Balsamic vinegar, strawberries and black pepper are a classic Italian trio: spicy and sweet, refined and earthy. Studies show that strawberries, which are loaded with antioxidants, may have positive effects on fighting heart disease and in particular on lowering systolic blood pressure. This dressing is also great on a salad of arugula, goat cheese and pecans.

- ³/₄ **cup Fresh Strawberry Dressing (*page 105*)**
- ¹/₂ **pound thin asparagus, stem ends snapped off, cut into 2-inch pieces (about 2 cups)**
- ¹/₂ **pound sugar snap peas, stemmed (2 cups) (see *Tip*)**
- ¹/₂ **pound snow peas, stemmed (2 cups)**
- 2 **tablespoons fresh lemon juice**
- 1 **tablespoon almond oil (see *Note, page 105*) or canola oil**
- ¹/₄ **teaspoon salt**
- ¹/₄ **teaspoon freshly ground pepper**
- ¹/₂ **cup chopped scallions**
- 12 **ounces boneless, skinless chicken breasts, trimmed**
- 2 **teaspoons canola oil**
- 1 **teaspoon salt-free lemon-pepper seasoning**
- ¹/₄ **cup sliced almonds, toasted**
- 4 **whole strawberries for garnish**

1. Put a large pot of water on to boil for cooking vegetables. Make Fresh Strawberry Dressing. Prepare a grill or preheat broiler.
2. Blanch asparagus, sugar snaps and snow peas in boiling water for 2 minutes. Drain, rinse with cold water to refresh, then blot dry with paper towels. Whisk lemon juice, almond oil (or canola oil), salt and pepper in a medium bowl. Add vegetables and scallions; toss to coat.
3. Rub chicken breasts with 2 teaspoons canola oil and sprinkle with lemon-pepper seasoning. Lightly oil the grill rack by rubbing it with an oil-soaked paper towel (use tongs to hold the paper towel). Place the chicken on the grill, close the cover and cook until lightly browned and no longer pink in the center, about 6 minutes per side. (*Alternatively, broil chicken 4 to 6 inches from the heat source for about 6 minutes per side.*) Let rest for 5 minutes.

4. Cut the chicken crosswise into ¼-inch-thick slices. Divide the vegetable mixture among 4 plates. Arrange the chicken slices over the vegetables. Spoon about 3 tablespoons Fresh Strawberry Dressing over each salad. Sprinkle with almonds and garnish each serving with a strawberry. Serve immediately.

MAKES 4 SERVINGS, ABOUT 2 CUPS EACH.

FRESH STRAWBERRY DRESSING

Pureed strawberries make a distinctive base for a colorful dressing with a creamy consistency, and you still get the nutritional benefits—fiber, vitamin C, heart-healthy phytonutrients—of eating the whole berries.

- 1 **cup strawberries (6 large berries), rinsed, hulled and sliced**
- 1 **tablespoon balsamic vinegar**
- ³/₄ **teaspoon freshly ground pepper**
- ½ **teaspoon sugar**
- ¼ **teaspoon salt**
- 2 **tablespoons almond oil (see *Note*) or canola oil**

Place strawberries, vinegar, pepper, sugar and salt in a blender or food processor; process until pureed, stopping once or twice to scrape down the sides. Add oil and process until smooth.

MAKES ABOUT ³/₄ CUP.

PER TABLESPOON:

26 calories;

2 g fat (0 g sat, 2 g mono);

0 mg cholesterol; 1 g carbohydrate;

0 g protein; 0 g fiber; 49 mg sodium;

20 mg potassium.

ACTIVE TIME: 10 MINUTES

TOTAL: 10 MINUTES

TO MAKE AHEAD: Store in an airtight container in the refrigerator for up to 2 days.

INGREDIENT NOTE:

Almond oil is an unrefined oil pressed from almonds. You can find it in many supermarkets and natural-foods stores. Store it in the refrigerator.

INGREDIENT NOTE:

Often a blend of cinnamon, cloves, fennel seed, star anise and Szechuan peppercorns, **five-spice powder** was originally considered a cure-all miracle blend encompassing the five elements (sour, bitter, sweet, pungent, salty). Look for it in the supermarket spice section.

FIVE-SPICE CHICKEN & ORANGE SALAD

Five-spice powder is a Chinese seasoning shortcut combining multiple flavors in one convenient package. Tossed with orange juice and chicken, it makes a terrific salad with a complex, layered taste that belies the simple recipe.

- 6 teaspoons extra-virgin olive oil, divided
- 1 teaspoon five-spice powder (see *Note*)
- 1 teaspoon kosher salt, divided
- ½ teaspoon freshly ground pepper, plus more to taste
- 1 pound boneless, skinless chicken breasts, trimmed
- 3 oranges
- 12 cups mixed Asian *or* salad greens
- 1 red bell pepper, cut into thin strips
- ½ cup slivered red onion
- 3 tablespoons cider vinegar
- 1 tablespoon Dijon mustard

1. Preheat oven to 450°F. Combine 1 teaspoon oil, five-spice powder, ½ teaspoon salt and ½ teaspoon pepper in a small bowl. Rub the mixture into both sides of the chicken breasts.

2. Heat 1 teaspoon oil in a large ovenproof nonstick skillet over medium-high heat. Add chicken breasts; cook until browned on one side, 3 to 5 minutes. Turn them over and transfer the pan to the oven. Roast until the chicken is just cooked through (an instant-read thermometer inserted into the center should read 165°F), 6 to 8 minutes. Transfer the chicken to a cutting board; let rest for 5 minutes (it will finish cooking as it rests).

3. Meanwhile, peel and segment two of the oranges (*see Tip, page 244*), collecting segments and any juice in a large bowl. (Discard membranes, pith and skin.) Add the greens, bell pepper and onion to the bowl. Zest and juice the remaining orange. Place the zest and juice in a small bowl; whisk in vinegar, mustard, the remaining 4 teaspoons oil, remaining ½ teaspoon salt and freshly ground pepper to taste. Pour the dressing over the salad; toss to combine. Slice the chicken and serve on the salad.

MAKES 4 SERVINGS.

INGREDIENT NOTE:

The tart berries of a particular type of **sumac** add another element to many Middle Eastern dishes. Find them whole or ground in Middle Eastern markets or online at *kalustyans.com* or *lebaneseproducts.com*.

LEBANESE FATTOUSH SALAD WITH GRILLED CHICKEN

Fattoush is a popular salad in Lebanon made with mixed greens and pita bread pieces. Toasting the pita adds crunch and a sprinkle of ground sumac—which grows wild all over Lebanon—adds depth. Let the salad sit for a bit to let the pita soak up the lemony dressing.

SALAD

- 2 6-inch whole-wheat pitas, split
- 3 tablespoons extra-virgin olive oil, divided
- 1¼ teaspoons ground sumac (*see Note*), divided
- ¼ cup lemon juice
- ½ teaspoon salt
- ¼ teaspoon freshly ground pepper
- 1 large head romaine lettuce, coarsely chopped
- 2 large tomatoes, diced
- 2 small salad cucumbers *or* 1 large cucumber, seeded and diced (peeled if desired)
- ½ cup thinly sliced red onion
- ⅓ cup thinly sliced fresh mint

CHICKEN

- 1½ pounds boneless, skinless chicken breasts, trimmed
- 1½ teaspoons extra-virgin olive oil
- ¼ teaspoon salt
  Freshly ground pepper to taste

1. TO PREPARE SALAD: Preheat oven to 350°F. Place pita halves rough-side up on a large baking sheet. Brush with 1 tablespoon oil and sprinkle with 1 teaspoon sumac. Bake until golden and crisp, about 15 minutes. When cool, break into bite-size pieces.

2. Whisk lemon juice, salt, pepper and the remaining 2 tablespoons oil and ¼ teaspoon sumac in a large bowl. Add lettuce, tomatoes, cucumber, onion, mint and the pita pieces; toss to coat. Let stand for 15 minutes.

3. TO PREPARE CHICKEN: Meanwhile, preheat grill to medium-high. Rub the chicken with oil and season with salt and pepper. Grill until no longer pink inside, 3 to 4 minutes per side. (*Alternatively, broil chicken 4 to 6 inches from the heat source for about 6 minutes per side.*) Slice the chicken thinly and serve on top of the salad.

MAKES 6 SERVINGS.

WARM CHICKEN SAUSAGE & POTATO SALAD

This warm bistro-style salad is perfect on a chilly winter's night. There are plenty of flavors and brands of chicken sausage available in major supermarkets these days. Look for brands with the least amount of saturated fat.

- 1 **pound small potatoes, cut in half**
- 1 **5-ounce bag arugula (about 4 cups, gently packed)**
- 12 **ounces precooked chicken sausage, cut crosswise into ¹/₂-inch pieces**
- ¹/₃ **cup cider vinegar**
- 1 **tablespoon maple syrup**
- 1 **tablespoon whole-grain *or* Dijon mustard**
- 1 **tablespoon extra-virgin olive oil**
  Freshly ground pepper to taste

1. Bring 1 inch of water to a boil in a Dutch oven. Place potatoes in a steamer basket and steam, covered, until just cooked through, about 15 minutes. Transfer to a large bowl and add arugula; cover with foil to keep warm.

2. Cook sausage in a medium skillet over medium heat, stirring often, until browned and heated through, about 5 minutes. Add to the potato-arugula mixture.

3. Remove the pan from the heat and whisk in vinegar, maple syrup and mustard, scraping up any browned bits. Gradually whisk in oil. Pour the dressing over the salad and toss until the arugula is wilted. Season with pepper.

MAKES 4 SERVINGS, ABOUT 1³/₄ CUPS EACH.

PER SERVING:

258 calories;

9 g fat (1 g sat, 3 g mono);

60 mg cholesterol; 27 g carbohydrate;

15 g protein; 2 g fiber; 483 mg sodium;

103 mg potassium.

NUTRITION BONUS: Vitamin C (45% DAILY VALUE).

Healthy ⑆ Weight

ACTIVE TIME: 30 MINUTES

TOTAL: 30 MINUTES

> ♥ **HEART-HEALTHY TIP**
>
> The beta carotene and vitamin C in **arugula** are potent antioxidants that defend our bodies from oxidative damage. Scientific evidence suggests a diet high in food sources of antioxidants (rather than supplements) protects our hearts and reduces the risk of cardiovascular disease.

196 calories;

11 g fat (2 g sat, 7 g mono);

4 mg cholesterol; 24 g carbohydrate;

9 g protein; 7 g fiber; 430 mg sodium;

510 mg potassium.

NUTRITION BONUS: Folate (40% DAILY VALUE), Fiber (31% DV), Potassium (17% DV), Calcium (15% DV).

Healthy ⋈ Weight

High ⬆ Fiber

ACTIVE TIME: 35 MINUTES

TOTAL: 35 MINUTES

TO MAKE AHEAD: Store the bean mixture in an airtight container in the refrigerator for up to 2 days.

WARM BEAN & ARUGULA SALAD

Studies have shown that getting more beans into your diet can help reduce cholesterol levels and reduce the risk of developing heart disease. In this salad, saucy, lemony beans stand in for a warm dressing, coating the arugula and wilting it just a bit to mellow its naturally assertive character. Add a piece of warm crusty bread and a glass of crisp white wine to make this an excellent light supper.

1	ounce thinly sliced prosciutto, cut into strips
¼	cup extra-virgin olive oil
1	medium red onion, finely chopped
4	cloves garlic, minced
2	15-ounce cans white beans, rinsed
⅓	cup reduced-sodium chicken broth
¼	cup lemon juice
¼	cup chopped fresh parsley
	Freshly ground pepper to taste
8	cups arugula

1. Cook prosciutto in a large nonstick skillet over medium heat, stirring frequently, until crispy, about 5 minutes. Drain on paper towels.
2. Add oil to the pan and place over medium-low heat. Add onion and garlic; cook, stirring occasionally, until softened, being careful not to brown the garlic, 3 to 5 minutes. Stir in beans and broth; cook until heated through, stirring occasionally, about 4 minutes. Add lemon juice, parsley and pepper; stir to combine. Place arugula in a large bowl. Add the bean mixture and toss to coat. Top with the prosciutto.

MAKES 6 SERVINGS.

TOMATO, TUNA & TARRAGON SALAD

Tomatoes and tuna were meant for each other, and fresh tarragon seals the deal. This is a delightful way to get some tuna, which is high in heart-healthy omega-3s, into your dinner routine. Soaking the onion in cold water tames the heat and sweetens its taste.

- ½ cup diced red onion
- ⅓ cup reduced-fat mayonnaise
- ¼ teaspoon kosher salt
  Freshly ground pepper to taste
- 2 6-ounce cans chunk light tuna in olive oil, drained
- 2 stalks celery, thinly sliced (about 1 cup)
- ¼ cup packed coarsely chopped fresh tarragon leaves
- 8 cups torn lettuce *or* mixed greens
- 1 pound small ripe tomatoes, cut into wedges
- 1 lemon, cut into 8 wedges

1. Place onion in a small bowl and cover with cold water. Refrigerate for 20 minutes. Drain.

2. Whisk mayonnaise, salt and pepper in a medium bowl. Add tuna, celery, tarragon and onion; stir to combine. Serve on top of the lettuce (or mixed greens) with tomato and lemon wedges.

MAKES 4 SERVINGS.

PER SERVING:

255 calories;

10 g fat (**2** g sat, 3 g mono);

15 mg cholesterol; 14 g carbohydrate;

27 g protein; 3 g fiber; 668 mg sodium;

694 mg potassium.

NUTRITION BONUS: Vitamin C (50% DAILY VALUE), Vitamin A (30% DV), Potassium (20% DV).

Healthy ⵊ Weight

Lower ⬇ Carbs

ACTIVE TIME: 30 MINUTES

TOTAL: 30 MINUTES

TO MAKE AHEAD: Store in an airtight container in the refrigerator for up to 1 day.

SMOKED SALMON SALAD NIÇOISE

This twist on a classic salade Niçoise *uses smoked salmon in place of tuna and adds extra vegetables in place of hard-boiled eggs and olives. Lovely served as an untraditional brunch, special weekend lunch or light supper.*

- **8** ounces small red potatoes, scrubbed and halved
- **6** ounces green beans, preferably thin haricots verts, trimmed and halved
- **2** tablespoons reduced-fat mayonnaise
- **1** tablespoon white-wine vinegar
- **1** teaspoon lemon juice
- **1** teaspoon Worcestershire sauce
- **1** teaspoon Dijon mustard
- **½** teaspoon dried dill
- **¼** teaspoon freshly ground pepper
- **6** cups mixed salad greens
- **½** small cucumber, halved, seeded and thinly sliced
- **12** small cherry or grape tomatoes, halved
- **4** ounces smoked salmon, cut into 2-inch pieces

1. Place a large bowl of ice water next to the stove. Bring 1 inch of water to a boil in a large saucepan. Place potatoes in a steamer basket over the boiling water, cover and steam until tender when pierced with a fork, 10 to 15 minutes. Transfer the potatoes with a slotted spoon to the ice water. Add green beans to the steamer, cover and steam until tender-crisp, 4 to 5 minutes. Transfer the green beans with a slotted spoon to the ice water. Transfer the potatoes and beans to a towel-lined baking sheet to drain.

2. Meanwhile, whisk mayonnaise, vinegar, lemon juice, Worcestershire sauce, mustard, dill and pepper in a large bowl. Add the potatoes and green beans, salad greens, cucumber and tomatoes; toss gently to coat.

3. Divide the salad and smoked salmon between 2 plates.

MAKES 2 SERVINGS.

PER SERVING:

291 calories;

7 g fat (**1** g sat, 2 g mono);

17 mg cholesterol; 40 g carbohydrate;

19 g protein; 9 g fiber; 651 mg sodium;

1,092 mg potassium.

NUTRITION BONUS: Vitamin A & Vitamin C (120% DAILY VALUE), Potassium (31% DV), Iron (25% DV), Calcium (15% DV), high omega-3s.

Healthy ⚖ Weight

High ⬆ Fiber

ACTIVE TIME: 30 MINUTES

TOTAL: 30 MINUTES

TO MAKE AHEAD: Store the potatoes and beans (Step 1) in an airtight container in the refrigerator for up to 2 days.

♥ HEART-HEALTHY TIP

A fatty fish, **salmon** is high in both EPA and DHA, two health-promoting omega-3 fatty acids that help to regulate healthy cardio-vascular function. They slow growth of arterial plaque, lower triglyceride levels and reduce the risk of irregular heartbeat.

Manhattan Crab Chowder

Pureed Zucchini Soup

Chicken Mulligatawny

Middle Eastern Chickpea & Rice Stew

SOUPS

MAIN-DISH SOUPS

Fresh Corn & Red Pepper
  Bisque...116

Tortellini & Zucchini Soup.....................117

Wheat Berry-Lentil Soup........................118

Middle Eastern Chickpea &
  Rice Stew.......................................119

Chicken Mulligatawny.............................120

Manhattan Crab Chowder.........................121

Yucatan Lemon Soup..............................122

SIDE-DISH SOUPS

Egg Thread Soup
  with Asparagus..................................124

Japanese Noodle &
  Shiitake Soup...................................125

Pureed Zucchini Soup............................126

Spring Pea & Scallion Soup.....................127

" Do you have a kinder, more adaptable friend in the food world than soup?
Who soothes you when you are ill? Who refuses to leave you when you are
impoverished and stretches its resources to give a hearty sustenance
and cheer? Who warms you in the winter and cools you in the summer?
Yet who also is capable of doing honor to your richest table and impressing
your most demanding guests? Soup does its loyal best, no matter what
undignified conditions are imposed upon it. You don't catch steak hanging
around when you're poor and sick, do you? "

JUDITH MARTIN (MISS MANNERS)

201 calories;

6 g fat (2 g sat, 3 g mono);

11 mg cholesterol; 32 g carbohydrate;

9 g protein; 5 g fiber; 314 mg sodium;

477 mg potassium.

NUTRITION BONUS: Vitamin C (120% DAILY VALUE), Vitamin A (45% DV).

Healthy ⋈ Weight

High ⬆ Fiber

ACTIVE TIME: 25 MINUTES

TOTAL: 40 MINUTES

TO MAKE AHEAD: Store in an airtight container in the refrigerator for up to 2 days.

REMOVING CORN FROM THE COB:

Stand an uncooked ear of **corn** on its stem end in a shallow bowl and slice the kernels off with a sharp, thin-bladed knife. This technique produces whole kernels that are good for adding to salads and salsas. If you want to use the corn kernels for soups, fritters or puddings, you can add another step to the process. After cutting the kernels off, reverse the knife and, using the dull side, press it down the length of the ear to push out the rest of the corn and its milk.

FRESH CORN & RED PEPPER BISQUE

The flavor of this soup depends on the quality of the corn, so be sure to use the freshest and sweetest ears you can find. We use just a bit of reduced-fat sour cream in this soup to give it a creamy body, without the heavy cream usually used in a bisque.

- 2 teaspoons extra-virgin olive oil
- 1 cup chopped sweet onion, such as Vidalia
- 3 cups fresh corn kernels (about 6 ears; see *Tip*)
- 1 large clove garlic, minced
- 4 cups reduced-sodium chicken broth *or* vegetable broth
- ¼ teaspoon salt
  Freshly ground pepper to taste
- ¼ cup reduced-fat sour cream
- 1 tablespoon yellow cornmeal
- 1 small red bell pepper, diced (about 1 cup)
- 1 scallion, white and pale green part, thinly sliced
- 2 tablespoons finely chopped parsley *or* cilantro
  Hot sauce, such as Tabasco sauce, to taste
- 1 lime, cut into wedges

1. Heat oil in a large heavy saucepan over medium heat. Add onion and cook, stirring often, until lightly browned, 6 to 7 minutes. Add corn and garlic; cook, stirring often, until the corn is lightly browned, about 5 minutes. Add broth and simmer until the corn is tender, 12 to 15 minutes. Stir in salt and pepper.

2. Using a slotted spoon, transfer 1½ cups of the corn mixture to a blender or food processor. Add sour cream and ½ cup cooking liquid and process until the mixture is smooth, about 2 minutes. (Use caution when pureeing hot liquids.) Return the puree to the pan.

3. Whisk in cornmeal; bring the soup to a boil over medium-high heat and cook, whisking constantly, until it thickens. Add bell pepper, scallion, parsley (or cilantro) and hot sauce; heat through. Serve with lime wedges.

MAKES 4 SERVINGS, 1½ CUPS EACH.

TORTELLINI & ZUCCHINI SOUP

Everyone knows tortellini make a quick weeknight pasta dinner—but they also add substance that turns this quick, colorful vegetable soup into a meal. One caveat: Read the label carefully; avoid pasta products made with hydrogenated oils or unnecessary preservatives. Enjoy this soup with a slice of multigrain baguette and a spinach salad.

- **2 tablespoons extra-virgin olive oil**
- **2 large carrots, finely chopped**
- **1 large onion, diced**
- **2 tablespoons minced garlic**
- **1 teaspoon chopped fresh rosemary**
- **2 14-ounce cans vegetable broth**
- **2 medium zucchini, diced**
- **9 ounces (about 2 cups) fresh *or* frozen tortellini, preferably spinach-&-cheese**
- **4 plum tomatoes, diced**
- **2 tablespoons red-wine vinegar**

1. Heat oil in a Dutch oven over medium heat. Add carrots and onion; stir, cover and cook, stirring occasionally, until the onion is soft and just beginning to brown, 6 to 7 minutes. Stir in garlic and rosemary and cook, stirring often, until fragrant, about 1 minute.

2. Stir in broth and zucchini; bring to a boil. Reduce heat to a simmer and cook, stirring occasionally, until the zucchini is beginning to soften, about 3 minutes. Add tortellini and tomatoes and simmer until the tortellini are plump and the tomatoes are beginning to break down, 6 to 10 minutes. Stir vinegar into the hot soup just before serving.

MAKES 6 SERVINGS, ABOUT 1½ CUPS EACH.

PER SERVING:

203 calories;

8 g fat (2 g sat, 4 g mono);

10 mg cholesterol; 28 g carbohydrate;

7 g protein; 4 g fiber; 386 mg sodium;

400 mg potassium.

NUTRITION BONUS: Vitamin A (80% DAILY VALUE), Vitamin C (35% DV).

Healthy ⚖ Weight

ACTIVE TIME: 25 MINUTES

TOTAL: 40 MINUTES

♥ HEART-HEALTHY TIP

Very low in calories and with good amounts of folate and vitamin A, **zucchini** also contains potassium. Some people with heart failure are advised to take a diuretic to combat sodium and water retention, and potassium is often lost in this process. Many physicians advise replacing it by eating potassium-rich foods like zucchini or bananas.

343 calories;

9 g fat (1 g sat, 5 g mono);

0 mg cholesterol; 53 g carbohydrate;

15 g protein; 12 g fiber; 818 mg sodium;

633 mg potassium.

NUTRITION BONUS: Vitamin A (170% DAILY VALUE), Folate (61% DV), Iron & Vitamin C (25% DV).

Healthy)(Weight

High ⬆ Fiber

ACTIVE TIME: 45 MINUTES

TOTAL: 45 MINUTES

TO MAKE AHEAD: Store in an airtight container in the freezer for up to 1 month.

♥ HEART-HEALTHY TIP

An excellent source of high-quality, plant-based protein, **lentils** are also a great source of cholesterol-lowering soluble fiber.

WHEAT BERRY-LENTIL SOUP

Perfect for a weeknight supper with a hunk of crusty whole-grain bread, this soup is packed with heart-healthy, fiber-rich wheat berries and lentils. It freezes beautifully; you can keep individual portions in the freezer for healthy weekday lunches.

- 1½ cups French green or brown lentils (see *Note, page 245*), sorted and rinsed
- 4 cups vegetable broth
- 4 cups cold water
- 3 tablespoons extra-virgin olive oil
- 3 large carrots, finely chopped
- 1 medium red onion, diced
- ¾ teaspoon salt
- ¼ teaspoon freshly ground pepper, plus more to taste
- 4 cloves garlic, minced
- 1½ teaspoons ground cumin
- 1½ cups cooked wheat berries (see *Grain-Cooking Guide, page 236*)
- 1 bunch rainbow or red chard, large stems discarded, leaves coarsely chopped
- 3 tablespoons lemon juice

1. Combine lentils, broth and water in a Dutch oven. Bring to a boil over high heat, reduce heat, cover, and simmer gently until the lentils are tender, but not mushy, 25 to 30 minutes (brown lentils take a little longer than green).

2. Meanwhile, heat oil in a large skillet over medium heat. Add carrots, onion, salt and pepper. Cook, stirring occasionally, until the vegetables begin to brown, about 15 minutes. Add garlic and cumin and cook, stirring constantly, for 30 seconds more. Remove from the heat.

3. When the lentils are tender, stir cooked wheat berries and chard into the pot. Cover and simmer until the chard has wilted, about 5 minutes. Stir in the carrot mixture and lemon juice.

MAKES 6 SERVINGS, 1²⁄₃ CUPS EACH.

MIDDLE EASTERN CHICKPEA & RICE STEW

The nutty goodness of slowly browned onions, spices and sweet potato are offset by a burst of fresh cilantro. Serve this hearty dish with whole-wheat pita and a salad of sliced cucumbers tossed with yogurt and a pinch of salt.

1	**tablespoon extra-virgin olive oil**
3	**medium onions, halved and thinly sliced (about 3 cups)**
2	**teaspoons ground cumin**
2	**teaspoons ground coriander**
1	**cup orange juice**
4	**cups reduced-sodium chicken broth or vegetable broth**
2	**15-ounce cans chickpeas, rinsed**
3	**cups peeled and diced sweet potato (about 1 pound)**
²/₃	**cup brown basmati rice**
¹/₄	**teaspoon salt**
¹/₄	**teaspoon freshly ground pepper**
¹/₂	**cup chopped fresh cilantro**

Heat oil in a large saucepan over medium heat; add onions and cook, stirring often, until tender and well browned, 10 to 12 minutes. Add cumin and coriander and stir for about 15 seconds. Add orange juice and broth. Stir in chickpeas, sweet potato, rice and salt. Bring to a boil; reduce heat to a gentle simmer and cover. Cook, stirring occasionally, until the rice is tender and the sweet potatoes are breaking down to thicken the liquid, about 45 minutes. Season with pepper. (The stew will be thick and will thicken further upon standing. Add more broth to thin, if desired, or when reheating.) Serve topped with cilantro.

MAKES 6 SERVINGS, 1¹/₂ CUPS EACH.

PER SERVING:

317 calories;

5 g fat (1 g sat, 2 g mono);

3 mg cholesterol; 58 g carbohydrate;

12 g protein; 9 g fiber; 362 mg sodium;

461 mg potassium.

NUTRITION BONUS: Vitamin A (220% DAILY VALUE), Vitamin C (50% DV), Fiber (37% DV), Iron (15% DV).

Healthy ✕ Weight

High ⬆ Fiber

ACTIVE TIME: 30 MINUTES

TOTAL: 1 HOUR 25 MINUTES

230 calories;

6 g fat (3 g sat, 1 g mono);

38 mg cholesterol; 25 g carbohydrate;

20 g protein; 2 g fiber; 284 mg sodium;

128 mg potassium.

Healthy ⅝ Weight

ACTIVE TIME: 45 MINUTES

TOTAL: 1 HOUR

SHOPPING TIP:

Hot Madras curry powder, located in the spice aisle of most supermarkets, adds a pleasant level of heat. Substitute regular curry powder for a milder soup.

CHICKEN MULLIGATAWNY

Mulligatawny, which literally means "pepper water," is an English interpretation of an Indian dish. It has seemingly limitless versions, but most have curry and a bit of chicken. We've added tart Granny Smith apples, plenty of spice and a touch of coconut milk.

1	tablespoon canola oil
1	large yellow onion, diced
2	stalks celery, diced
3	cloves garlic, minced
2	Granny Smith apples, peeled and diced
1½	teaspoons hot Madras curry powder (see *Tip*)
½	teaspoon ground cumin
½	teaspoon ground coriander
½	teaspoon ground ginger
6	cups reduced-sodium chicken broth
½	cup white basmati rice
12	ounces chicken breast tenders, cut into bite-size pieces
1	cup "lite" coconut milk
1	tablespoon lemon juice
¼	teaspoon salt
¼	teaspoon freshly ground pepper
3	tablespoons sliced almonds, toasted (see *Tip, page 244*), optional

1. Heat oil in a Dutch oven over medium-high heat. Add onion, celery and garlic; cook, stirring often, until softened, about 5 minutes. Add apples, curry powder, cumin, coriander and ginger and cook, stirring often, until the apples begin to soften, about 2 minutes. Add broth and rice; bring to a boil. Reduce heat to a simmer and cook, uncovered, for 12 minutes.

2. Add chicken, return to a simmer and cook until the chicken is cooked through and the rice is tender, 8 to 10 minutes more. Stir in coconut milk and return to a simmer. Remove from the heat; stir in lemon juice, salt and pepper. Garnish with almonds (if using).

MAKES 6 SERVINGS, ABOUT 1½ CUPS EACH.

MANHATTAN CRAB CHOWDER

Manhattan chowder is the red kind, made with disease-fighting lycopene-rich tomatoes. This version substitutes crab for the clams. To make it cook faster, take your time to finely dice the vegetables. We call for convenient canned crushed tomatoes, but you only need 2 cups; store leftover tomatoes in an airtight container for 1 week in the refrigerator or months in the freezer. Then take them out to toss into other soups or sauces—you can't go wrong with adding tomatoes, from a heart-health perspective! All you need is crusty bread or oyster crackers and a tossed salad and you've got dinner.

2	tablespoons extra-virgin olive oil
1	cup finely diced onion
1	cup finely diced cored fennel bulb, plus 2 tablespoons chopped fronds, divided
2	tablespoons minced garlic
2	teaspoons Italian seasoning blend
⅛	teaspoon salt
½	teaspoon freshly ground pepper
1	14-ounce can reduced-sodium chicken broth *or* vegetable broth
1½	cups water
2	cups precooked diced potatoes (see *Tip*)
2	cups canned crushed tomatoes
1	pound pasteurized crabmeat, drained if necessary

1. Heat oil in a large saucepan over medium heat. Add onion, diced fennel, garlic, Italian seasoning, salt and pepper and cook, stirring often, until the vegetables are just starting to brown, 6 to 8 minutes.

2. Add broth, water and potatoes; bring to a boil. Reduce heat to a simmer and cook until the vegetables are tender, 3 to 5 minutes. Stir in tomatoes, crabmeat and fennel fronds. Return to a boil, stirring often; immediately remove from heat.

MAKES 6 SERVINGS, ABOUT 1½ CUPS EACH.

PER SERVING:

210 calories;

5 g fat (1 g sat, 4 g mono);

88 mg cholesterol; 21 g carbohydrate;

19 g protein; 3 g fiber; 648 mg sodium;

515 mg potassium.

NUTRITION BONUS: Iron (35% DAILY VALUE), Vitamin C (30% DV), Calcium (15% DV).

Healthy ⚖ Weight

Lower ⬇ Carbs

ACTIVE TIME: 30 MINUTES

TOTAL: 40 MINUTES

SHOPPING TIP:

Look for **precooked diced potatoes** in the refrigerated section of most supermarket produce departments—near other fresh, prepared vegetables.

149 calories;

2 g fat (1 g sat, 0 g mono);

177 mg cholesterol; 3 g carbohydrate;

27 g protein; 0 g fiber; 600 mg sodium;

234 mg potassium.

NUTRITION BONUS: Selenium (61% DAILY VALUE), Vitamin C (15% DV), good source of omega-3s.

Healthy)(Weight

Lower ↓ Carbs

ACTIVE TIME: 20 MINUTES

TOTAL: 30 MINUTES

TO MAKE AHEAD: Store the spiced broth (Step 1) in an airtight container in the freezer for up to 3 months. Defrost and return the broth to a simmer before continuing with Step 2.

SUBSTITUTION TIP:

Meyer lemon juice concentrate can be purchased online from *perfectpuree.com*. Although nothing can replicate the distinct sweet, tart, floral taste of a **Meyer lemon**, you can use 2 tablespoons regular lemon juice plus 1 tablespoon orange juice to replace the 3 tablespoons juice in this recipe, and regular lemons for the zest.

YUCATAN LEMON SOUP

Although it's traditionally made with limes (and you could certainly make it that way), Meyer lemons add a gentler, subtle twist to this Mexican classic with shrimp, garlic and lots of fresh cilantro. Meyer lemons are usually available only during the winter months; they are rounder and smoother than common lemons. Serve this soup as a light entree with a big salad or as a special starter.

- 4 **cups reduced-sodium chicken broth**
- 1 **medium onion, cut into quarters**
- 2 **jalapeño peppers, seeded and quartered**
- 8 **cloves garlic, crushed and peeled**
- 3 **tablespoons finely grated Meyer lemon zest (see *Tip*)**
- ½ **teaspoon cumin seeds**
- 1 **4-inch cinnamon stick**
- 4 **whole cloves**
- 1 **pound raw shrimp (26-30 per pound), peeled and deveined**
- 3 **tablespoons Meyer lemon juice (see *Tip*)**
- ½ **teaspoon salt**
- ¼ **teaspoon hot sauce, or to taste (optional)**
- ½ **cup chopped fresh cilantro**

1. Bring broth, onion, jalapeños, garlic, zest, cumin seeds, cinnamon stick and cloves to a simmer in a large saucepan or Dutch oven. Cover, reduce heat, and continue to simmer for 20 minutes. Strain the broth (discard solids).

2. Return the broth to the pan and bring to a low simmer. Add shrimp, lemon juice, salt and hot sauce (if using). Cook until the shrimp are pink and firm, about 3 minutes. Stir in cilantro and serve.

MAKES 4 SERVINGS, 1 CUP EACH.

PER SERVING:

108 calories;

3 g fat (1 g sat, 1 g mono);

111 mg cholesterol; 11 g carbohydrate;

10 g protein; 1 g fiber; 254 mg sodium;

138 mg potassium.

NUTRITION BONUS: Calcium (25% DAILY VALUE), Folate (23% DV).

Healthy)(Weight

Lower ⬇ Carbs

ACTIVE TIME: 20 MINUTES

TOTAL: 20 MINUTES

COOKING TIP:

Peeling the stem ends of the **asparagus** will make them even more tender.

EGG THREAD SOUP WITH ASPARAGUS

Stirring eggs into simmering broth is a classic technique for adding nourishment and body to soup. Asparagus gives it a mild, sweet flavor and a bit of texture. Garnish this quick soup with grated Parmesan.

   8   **cups reduced-sodium chicken broth**
  1/2 **cup pastina or other tiny pasta, such as alphabet or stars**
  12   **ounces asparagus, trimmed and cut into 1 1/2-inch diagonal pieces (2 cups)**
   4   **large eggs**
  1/2 **teaspoon fresh lemon juice**
  1/4 **teaspoon salt**

1. Bring broth to a boil in a Dutch oven or soup pot. Stir in pasta. Cook, uncovered, over medium-high heat, stirring occasionally, until pasta is just tender, about 5 minutes. Stir in asparagus; cook for 2 minutes. Reduce heat to medium.
2. Break eggs into a large measuring cup and whisk until well blended. Add to the gently boiling soup in a thin, steady stream, stirring constantly with a fork. (Slow stirring will produce large threads; rapid stirring will break the threads up into small pieces.) Remove from heat and stir in lemon juice and salt.

MAKES 8 SERVINGS, ABOUT 1 CUP EACH.

JAPANESE NOODLE & SHIITAKE SOUP

Daikon is a long, white radish with a mild flavor. It provides a crunchy, cool contrast to the hot soup.

- **8 ounces dried soba (buckwheat) noodles**
- **8 cups reduced-sodium chicken broth**
- **1 tablespoon finely grated fresh ginger**
- **4 ounces fresh shiitake mushrooms, stems removed, slivered (about 1 cup)**
- **2 tablespoons sake *or* mirin (see *Note*)**
- **2 tablespoons reduced-sodium soy sauce *or* tamari**
- **1 tablespoon rice vinegar**
- **2 tablespoons miso (see *Note*)**
- **1 cup packed spinach leaves, washed, dried and coarsely chopped**
- **4 scallions, finely chopped**
- **¼ cup grated daikon radish (see *Note*)**

1. Bring at least 3 quarts water to a boil in a large pot. Slowly add soba. When water returns to a boil, add ½ cup cold water. Repeat steps of returning water to a boil and adding cold water 2 or 3 times, until the noodles are just tender. (It will take 5 to 7 minutes total.) Drain and rinse with cold water, working your fingers through the strands to separate them. Set aside.

2. Combine broth and ginger in the large pot and bring to a boil. Reduce the heat to medium-low, add mushrooms and simmer for 8 minutes. Add sake (or mirin), soy sauce (or tamari) and vinegar.

3. Whisk a ladleful of the broth with miso in a small bowl to dissolve it; return the mixture to the pot, along with spinach. Simmer for 2 minutes more and remove from the heat. Divide the noodles among soup bowls and ladle the soup over the top. Garnish with scallions and daikon.

MAKES 8 SERVINGS, ABOUT 1¼ CUPS EACH.

PER SERVING:

150 calories;

1 g fat (1 g sat, 0 g mono);

5 mg cholesterol; 27 g carbohydrate;

9 g protein; 1 g fiber; 685 mg sodium;

150 mg potassium.

Healthy ⚖ Weight

ACTIVE TIME: 45 MINUTES

TOTAL: 45 MINUTES

INGREDIENT NOTES:

Mirin is a sweet, low-alcohol rice wine essential in Japanese cooking. Look for it in your supermarket with the Asian or gourmet ingredients.

Miso is fermented bean paste made from barley, rice or soybeans. It is available in different colors; in general, the lighter the color, the more mild the flavor. Look for miso alongside the refrigerated tofu in the market. It will keep, in the refrigerator, for more than a year.

Daikon is a long, white radish; it can be found in Asian groceries and most natural-foods stores. Commercially prepared pickled daikon radish can be found in Asian markets.

PUREED ZUCCHINI SOUP

This is one of the few soups that make the cut in summer. Serve it chilled to take the edge off a hot August night. Pick the sharpest Cheddar cheese you can find, to give the biggest flavor impact with the least amount of saturated fat.

3	cups reduced-sodium chicken broth
1½	pounds zucchini (about 3 medium), cut into 1-inch pieces
1	tablespoon chopped fresh tarragon *or* dill *or* 1 teaspoon dried
½	cup shredded reduced-fat Cheddar cheese
¼	teaspoon salt
¼	teaspoon freshly ground pepper

Place broth, zucchini and tarragon (or dill) in a medium saucepan; bring to a boil over high heat. Reduce to a simmer and cook, uncovered, until the zucchini is tender, 7 to 10 minutes. Puree in a blender, in batches if necessary, until smooth. (Use caution when pureeing hot liquids.) Return the soup to the pan and heat over medium-high, slowly stirring in cheese until it is incorporated. Remove from heat and season with salt and pepper. Serve hot or chilled.

MAKES 4 SERVINGS, 1¼ CUPS EACH.

SPRING PEA & SCALLION SOUP

You can use fresh or frozen peas, either of which delivers B vitamins, iron and fiber, in this soup, but if you do take the time to shell fresh peas, you will be rewarded with a special bright, springy flavor.

2	**teaspoons extra-virgin olive oil**
1¹/₂	**cups chopped scallions (about 3 bunches)**
4	**cups reduced-sodium chicken broth**
3	**cups shelled fresh peas (4¹/₂ pounds unshelled) *or* frozen peas**
¹/₈	**teaspoon salt**
	Freshly ground pepper to taste
2	**tablespoons fresh chervil *or* tarragon leaves for garnish (optional)**

1. Heat oil in a large heavy saucepan or Dutch oven over medium-high heat. Add scallions and cook, stirring, until softened, about 2 minutes. Add broth and bring to a boil. Add peas and reduce heat to low. Cover and simmer until peas are tender, 5 to 10 minutes.

2. In batches, transfer soup to a blender and puree. (Use caution when pureeing hot liquids.) Strain through a fine sieve into another saucepan, pressing on the solids. Reheat gently. Season with salt and pepper.

3. Ladle soup into bowls. Garnish with chervil (or tarragon), if desired, and serve.

MAKES 4 SERVINGS.

PER SERVING:

141 calories;

3 g fat (1 g sat, 2 g mono);

5 mg cholesterol; 19 g carbohydrate;

10 g protein; 6 g fiber; 340 mg sodium;

264 mg potassium.

NUTRITION BONUS: Vitamin A (50% DAILY VALUE), Vitamin C (45% DV), Folate (20% DV).

Healthy ⅟ Weight

Lower ⬇ Carbs

High ⬆ Fiber

ACTIVE TIME: 30 MINUTES

TOTAL: 30 MINUTES

♥ HEART-HEALTHY TIP

High in potassium and soluble fiber, which helps lower LDL cholesterol, **peas** are a great low-fat source of plant-based protein.

Mini Chile Relleno Casseroles

Indian-Spiced Eggplant & Cauliflower Stew

Creamy Squash Risotto

Stir-Fried Noodles with Green Tea

VEGETARIAN

Corn & Broccoli Calzones........................131

Zesty Wheat Berry-Black
    Bean Chili 132

Mini Chile Relleno Casseroles.................135

Paprika-Spiced Butter Beans
    & Polenta 136

Creamy Squash Risotto 138

Athenian Pasta Primavera....................139

Egyptian Edamame Stew.....................140

Stir-Fried Noodles with
    Green Tea...................................143

Sweet & Sour Tofu 144

Ginger Fried Rice 145

Saag Tofu 146

Indian-Spiced Eggplant &
    Cauliflower Stew...........................149

Quinoa & Smoked Tofu Salad 150

Lentil & Almond Burgers......................151

"Did you ever stop to taste a carrot? Not just eat it, but taste it?
You can't taste the beauty and energy of the earth in a Twinkie."

ASTRID ALAUDA

CORN & BROCCOLI CALZONES

Here's proof that you need not feel deprived on a heart-healthy diet—you can still enjoy a calzone! Nonfat ricotta and a bit of melted mozzarella go a long way without all the saturated fat normally in a calzone. Plus each calzone has plenty of veggies and even more if you serve them with your favorite marinara sauce for dipping.

1½	**cups chopped broccoli florets**
1½	**cups fresh corn kernels (about 3 ears; see *Tip*, page 244)**
1	**cup shredded part-skim mozzarella**
⅔	**cup nonfat ricotta cheese**
4	**scallions, thinly sliced**
¼	**cup chopped fresh basil**
½	**teaspoon garlic powder**
¼	**teaspoon salt**
¼	**teaspoon freshly ground pepper All-purpose flour for dusting**
20	**ounces prepared whole-wheat pizza dough (see *Tip*), thawed if frozen**
2	**teaspoons canola oil**

1. Position racks in the upper and lower thirds of oven; preheat to 475°F. Coat 2 baking sheets with cooking spray.

2. Combine broccoli, corn, mozzarella, ricotta, scallions, basil, garlic powder, salt and pepper in a large bowl.

3. On a lightly floured surface, divide dough into 6 pieces. Roll each piece into an 8-inch circle. Place a generous ¾ cup filling on one half of each circle, leaving a 1-inch border of dough. Brush the border with water and fold the top half over the filling. Fold the edges over and crimp with a fork to seal. Make several small slits in the top to vent steam; brush each calzone with oil. Transfer the calzones to the prepared baking sheets.

4. Bake the calzones, switching the pans halfway through, until browned on top, about 15 minutes. Let cool slightly before serving.

MAKES 6 CALZONES.

PER CALZONE:

334 calories;

5 g fat (**2** g sat, 2 g mono);

17 mg cholesterol; 50 g carbohydrate;

16 g protein; 4 g fiber; 503 mg sodium;

218 mg potassium.

NUTRITION BONUS: Vitamin C (35% DAILY VALUE), Calcium (25% DV), Vitamin A (20% DV).

Healthy ♓ Weight

ACTIVE TIME: 30 MINUTES

TOTAL: 45 MINUTES

SHOPPING TIP:

Look for balls of **whole-wheat pizza dough** at your supermarket, fresh or frozen and without any hydrogenated oils.

386 calories;

11 g fat (1 g sat, 7 g mono);

0 mg cholesterol; 61 g carbohydrate;

14 g protein; 15 g fiber; 703 mg sodium;

311 mg potassium.

NUTRITION BONUS: Vitamin C (130% DAILY VALUE), Fiber (72% DV), Folate (48% DV), Iron & Vitamin A (25% DV).

High ⬆ Fiber

ACTIVE TIME: 25 MINUTES

TOTAL: 1 HOUR

SHOPPING TIP:

Canned chipotle peppers (smoked jalapeños) in adobo sauce add heat and a smoky flavor. Look for the small cans with other Mexican foods in large supermarkets. Once opened, store in an airtight container for up to 2 weeks in the refrigerator or 6 months in the freezer.

ZESTY WHEAT BERRY-BLACK BEAN CHILI

Feel free to add an additional chipotle pepper to crank up the heat in this one-pot meal. Cooked wheat berries will keep for up to 1 month in your freezer; there's no need to thaw them—stir them directly into the chili.

2	tablespoons extra-virgin olive oil
1	large yellow onion, chopped
1	large yellow bell pepper, chopped
5	cloves garlic, minced
2	teaspoons chili powder
1½	teaspoons ground cumin
1	teaspoon dried oregano
½	teaspoon salt
½	teaspoon freshly ground pepper
2	15-ounce cans black beans, rinsed
2	14-ounce cans no-salt-added diced tomatoes, undrained
1-2	canned chipotle peppers in adobo sauce, minced (see *Tip*)
2	cups vegetable broth
2	teaspoons light brown sugar
2	cups cooked wheat berries (see *Grain-Cooking Guide, page* 236)
	Juice of 1 lime
1	avocado, diced
½	cup chopped fresh cilantro

1. Heat oil in a Dutch oven over medium-high heat. Add onion, bell pepper, garlic, chili powder, cumin, oregano, salt and pepper, and cook, stirring occasionally, until tender, about 5 minutes. Add beans, tomatoes, chipotle to taste, broth and brown sugar. Bring to a boil over high heat, reduce heat, cover, and simmer for 25 minutes.

2. Stir in cooked wheat berries and heat through, about 5 minutes more. (If using frozen wheat berries, cook until thoroughly heated.) Remove from the heat. Stir in lime juice. Garnish each bowl with avocado and cilantro.

MAKES 6 SERVINGS, ABOUT 1½ CUPS EACH.

MINI CHILE RELLENO CASSEROLES

Everyone gets an individual portion with this vegetarian, Tex-Mex mini casserole. A normal-size casserole like this would take close to an hour to bake—these are ready in half the time. Heatproof ramekins are a cook's best friend—we use them all the time to hold ingredients while cooking. You can buy them at most grocery stores.

2	4-ounce cans diced green chiles, drained and patted dry
³/₄	cup frozen corn, thawed and patted dry
4	scallions, thinly sliced
1	cup shredded reduced-fat Cheddar cheese
1¹/₂	cups nonfat milk
6	large egg whites
4	large eggs
¹/₄	teaspoon salt

1. Preheat oven to 400°F. Coat eight 6-ounce or four 10-ounce heatproof ramekins with cooking spray and place on a baking sheet.

2. Equally divide green chiles, corn and scallions among the ramekins. Top each with cheese. Whisk milk, egg whites, eggs and salt in a medium bowl until combined. Divide the egg mixture evenly among the ramekins.

3. Bake the mini casseroles until the tops begin to brown and the eggs are set, about 25 minutes for 6-ounce ramekins and about 35 minutes for 10-ounce ramekins.

MAKES 4 SERVINGS, TWO 6-OUNCE OR ONE 10-OUNCE CASSEROLE EACH.

PER SERVING:

215 calories;

7 g fat (**3** g sat, 3 g mono);

219 mg cholesterol; 14 g carbohydrate;

23 g protein; 3 g fiber; 726 mg sodium;

421 mg potassium.

NUTRITION BONUS: Selenium (46% DAILY VALUE), Calcium (35% DV), Vitamin C (25% DV).

Healthy ⋈ Weight

Lower ⬇ Carbs

ACTIVE TIME: 10 MINUTES

TOTAL: 35-45 MINUTES

EQUIPMENT: Eight 6-ounce or four 10-ounce heatproof ramekins

♥ HEART-HEALTHY TIP

Chile peppers: The capsaicin in chiles (which is the compound that makes them hot) may decrease LDL cholesterol absorption, delaying the buildup of plaque deposits in the arteries.

INGREDIENT NOTE:

Smoked paprika is available in three varieties: sweet, bittersweet and hot. Sweet is the most versatile, but choose hot if you like a bit of heat. Find it in well-stocked supermarkets, specialty-foods stores or online at *tienda.com*.

PAPRIKA-SPICED BUTTER BEANS & POLENTA

This is a satisfying vegetarian meal complete with plenty of heart-healthy spinach, onions, peppers and beans. The bold flavors of smoked paprika and sherry vinegar give it punch and a Spanish flair.

- 4 teaspoons extra-virgin olive oil, divided
- 1 16-ounce tube prepared plain polenta, cut into ½-inch cubes
- 1 clove garlic, minced
- 1 small onion, halved and thinly sliced
- 1 red bell pepper, diced
- ½ teaspoon paprika, preferably smoked, plus more for garnish (see *Note*)
- 1 15-ounce can butter beans, rinsed
- 4 cups packed baby spinach
- ¾ cup vegetable broth
- ½ cup shredded Manchego or Monterey Jack cheese
- 2 teaspoons sherry vinegar

1. Heat 2 teaspoons oil in a large nonstick skillet over medium-high heat. Add polenta and cook in a single layer, stirring occasionally, until beginning to brown, 8 to 10 minutes. Transfer to a plate.

2. Reduce the heat to medium, add the remaining 2 teaspoons oil and garlic to the pan, and cook, stirring, until fragrant, 30 seconds. Add onion and bell pepper; cook, stirring, until just tender, 3 to 5 minutes. Sprinkle with paprika; cook, stirring, for 30 seconds. Stir in beans, spinach and broth; cook, stirring, until the beans are heated through and the spinach is wilted, 2 to 3 minutes. Remove from the heat; stir in cheese and vinegar. Serve vegetables over polenta. Sprinkle with paprika, if desired.

MAKES 4 SERVINGS, 1½ CUPS EACH.

372 calories;

11 g fat (3 g sat, 6 g mono);

15 mg cholesterol; 54 g carbohydrate;

14 g protein; 6 g fiber; 632 mg sodium;

790 mg potassium.

NUTRITION BONUS: Vitamin A (380% DAILY VALUE), Vitamin C (65% DV), Potassium (21% DV), Calcium (20% DV).

High ⬆ Fiber

ACTIVE TIME: 1 HOUR

TOTAL: 1 HOUR

CREAMY SQUASH RISOTTO

Winter squash, with its hearty, earthy flavors, is a reason to celebrate fall. Like any risotto, this takes a bit of time stirring at the stove, but it's otherwise simple and there's no reason to be daunted.

- **5 cups reduced-sodium chicken broth or vegetable broth**
- **2 tablespoons extra-virgin olive oil**
- **3 medium shallots, thinly sliced**
- **3 cups chopped peeled butternut, hubbard, red kuri or kabocha squash (1/2-inch pieces)**
- **2 cups shiitake mushroom caps, thinly sliced**
- **1/2 teaspoon dried thyme**
- **1/2 teaspoon salt**
- **1/4 teaspoon freshly ground pepper**
- **1/8 teaspoon crumbled saffron threads (optional)**
- **1 cup arborio rice**
- **1/2 cup dry white wine or dry vermouth**
- **1/2 cup finely grated Parmigiano-Reggiano cheese**

1. Place broth in a medium saucepan; bring to a simmer over medium-high heat. Reduce the heat so the broth remains steaming, but is not simmering.

2. Meanwhile, heat oil in a large saucepan over medium heat. Add shallots; cook, stirring, until fragrant, about 1 minute. Stir in squash and mushrooms; cook, stirring often, until the mushrooms give off their liquid, about 5 minutes. Add thyme, salt, pepper and saffron (if using); cook for 30 seconds. Add rice; stir until translucent, about 1 minute. Add wine (or vermouth) and cook, stirring, until almost absorbed by the rice, about 1 minute.

3. Stir in 1/2 cup of the hot broth; reduce heat to a gentle simmer and cook, stirring constantly, until the liquid has been absorbed. Continue adding the broth 1/2 cup at a time, stirring after each addition until all the liquid has been absorbed, until the rice is tender and creamy, 30 to 40 minutes total. (You may have some broth left.) Remove from the heat and stir in cheese.

MAKES 4 SERVINGS, ABOUT 1 1/2 CUPS EACH.

ATHENIAN PASTA PRIMAVERA

This Greek-inspired pasta dish also works well with cherry tomatoes and chopped kalamata olives.

2	teaspoons plus 1 tablespoon extra-virgin olive oil, divided
1	medium onion, sliced
1/2	teaspoon salt
1	yellow bell pepper, sliced
1	medium zucchini, trimmed, halved lengthwise and thinly sliced
3	cloves garlic, minced
1/2	cup dry white wine
	Freshly ground pepper to taste
1	pound whole-wheat penne
1 1/2	cups baby peas (if frozen, rinse under warm water and drain)
1/2	cup packed fresh mint leaves, chopped
3/4	cup crumbled feta cheese (4 ounces)

1. Put a large pot of water on to boil.

2. Heat 2 teaspoons oil in a large nonstick skillet over medium-high heat. Add onion and salt and cook, stirring occasionally, until the onion is beginning to brown, 3 to 5 minutes.

3. Add bell pepper and zucchini to the onion. Cook, stirring, until the vegetables are just beginning to soften, 3 minutes. Stir in garlic and continue cooking until fragrant, 1 minute more. Stir in wine and pepper; simmer until most of the wine has evaporated, 1 to 2 minutes.

4. Meanwhile, cook penne in the boiling water according to the package directions, until al dente. Drain, reserving 1/2 cup of the cooking liquid. Return the pasta to the pot.

5. Stir the reserved cooking liquid and the vegetables into the pasta along with the remaining 1 tablespoon oil, peas, mint and feta.

MAKES 8 SERVINGS, ABOUT 1 1/2 CUPS EACH.

PER SERVING:

305 calories;

6 g fat (3 g sat, 3 g mono);

13 mg cholesterol; 51 g carbohydrate;

10 g protein; 8 g fiber; 326 mg sodium;

236 mg potassium.

NUTRITION BONUS: Vitamin C (75% DAILY VALUE).

Healthy ⚖ Weight

High ⬆ Fiber

ACTIVE TIME: 30 MINUTES

TOTAL: 30 MINUTES

PER SERVING:

257 calories;

8 g fat (1 g sat, 3 g mono);

0 mg cholesterol; 29 g carbohydrate;

15 g protein; 10 g fiber; 520 mg sodium;

304 mg potassium.

NUTRITION BONUS: Vitamin C (90%
DAILY VALUE), Vitamin A (35% DV), Iron
(25% DV).

Healthy)(Weight

High ⬆ Fiber

ACTIVE TIME: 30 MINUTES

TOTAL: 30 MINUTES

EGYPTIAN EDAMAME STEW

A riff on the Egyptian classic ful medames, *a highly seasoned fava bean mash, this version is made with easier-to-find edamame. Edamame (fresh green soybeans) have been shown to lower LDL cholesterol. They can be found shelled in the freezer section of well-stocked supermarkets. This stew is great served with couscous, bulgur or warm whole-wheat pita bread to soak up the sauce.*

1¹/₂	**10-ounce packages frozen shelled edamame (about 3 cups), thawed**
1	**tablespoon extra-virgin olive oil**
1	**large onion, chopped**
1	**large zucchini, diced**
2	**tablespoons minced garlic**
2	**teaspoons ground cumin**
1	**teaspoon ground coriander**
¹/₈	**teaspoon cayenne pepper, or to taste**
1	**28-ounce can diced tomatoes**
¹/₄	**cup chopped fresh cilantro *or* mint**
3	**tablespoons lemon juice**

1. Bring a large saucepan of water to a boil. Add edamame and cook until tender, 4 to 5 minutes or according to package directions. Drain.

2. Heat oil in a large saucepan over medium heat. Add onion and cook, covered, stirring occasionally, until starting to soften, about 3 minutes. Add zucchini and cook, covered, until the onions are starting to brown, about 3 minutes more. Add garlic, cumin, coriander and cayenne and cook, stirring, until fragrant, about 30 seconds. Stir in tomatoes and bring to a boil; reduce heat to a simmer and cook until slightly reduced, about 5 minutes.

3. Stir in the edamame and cook until heated through, about 2 minutes more. Remove from the heat and stir in cilantro (or mint) and lemon juice.

MAKES 4 SERVINGS, ABOUT 2 CUPS EACH.

STIR-FRIED NOODLES WITH GREEN TEA

Many dishes cooked with tea come from China's Yangtze River Valley where there are countless tea farms. This is another way to get tea, which has been associated with heart health (see page 68), into your diet.

8	ounces udon *or* whole-wheat noodles
2	tablespoons canola oil
1	teaspoon loose green tea leaves, preferably gunpowder (optional)
2	teaspoons minced fresh ginger
2	cloves garlic, minced
8	ounces flavored baked tofu (see *Tip*), cut into matchsticks
1	small red bell pepper, cut into thin strips
1	small yellow bell pepper, cut into thin strips
4	scallions, cut diagonally into 2-inch pieces
2	tablespoons reduced-sodium soy sauce
2	tablespoons rice vinegar
1	teaspoon toasted sesame oil
¼	teaspoon freshly ground pepper

1. Bring a large pot of water to a boil. Cook noodles according to the package directions. Drain and rinse with cold water to prevent sticking. Set aside.

2. Heat a wok over medium heat. Add oil and swirl to coat. Add tea leaves (if using), ginger and garlic. Cook, stirring, until fragrant, about 30 seconds. Add tofu and cook, stirring, for 2 minutes. Add red and yellow bell peppers and cook, stirring, until the peppers soften, 1 to 2 minutes.

3. Stir in the noodles, scallions, soy sauce and vinegar. Cook, stirring occasionally, until the noodles are heated through, about 2 minutes. Stir in sesame oil and pepper. Toss to combine. Serve warm or cold.

MAKES 4 SERVINGS.

PER SERVING:

420 calories;

16 g fat (2 g sat, 5 g mono);

0 mg cholesterol; 47 g carbohydrate;

22 g protein; 5 g fiber; 593 mg sodium;

263 mg potassium.

NUTRITION BONUS: Vitamin C (100% DAILY VALUE), Vitamin A (40% DV), Iron (25% DV).

High ⬆ Fiber

ACTIVE TIME: 30 MINUTES

TOTAL: 30 MINUTES

SHOPPING TIP:

Precooked **"baked tofu"** is firmer than water-packed tofu and comes in a wide variety of flavors. Flavored baked tofu is also great on a sandwich or in a stir-fry.

PER SERVING:

272 calories;

12 g fat (1 g sat, 5 g mono);

0 mg cholesterol; 37 g carbohydrate;

10 g protein; 4 g fiber; 369 mg sodium;

556 mg potassium.

NUTRITION BONUS: Vitamin C (230% DAILY VALUE), Vitamin A (35% DV), Calcium (25% DV), Magnesium (17% DV), Iron (15% DV), Potassium (15% DV).

Healthy ⧓ Weight

ACTIVE TIME: 35 MINUTES

TOTAL: 40 MINUTES

TO MAKE AHEAD: The tofu can be marinated (Step 1) up to 30 minutes in advance.

♥ HEART-HEALTHY TIP

Because of their fiber and polyunsaturated-fat content, **tofu** and other soy products are heart-healthy, particularly when substituted for animal-based protein sources, which tend to be high in saturated fat and cholesterol.

SWEET & SOUR TOFU

To make this simple stir-fry a meal, serve it over brown rice and alongside Watercress & Pickled Ginger Salad (page 228). If you want to jazz it up, add a dash of crushed red pepper or chile-garlic sauce with the pineapple chunks and garnish with scallions.

- 1 **20-ounce can pineapple chunks or tidbits**
- 3 **tablespoons rice vinegar**
- 2 **tablespoons ketchup**
- 2 **tablespoons reduced-sodium soy sauce**
- 1 **tablespoon brown sugar**
- 1 **14-ounce package water-packed extra-firm tofu, drained, rinsed and cut into ½-inch cubes**
- 2 **teaspoons cornstarch**
- 2 **tablespoons canola oil, divided**
- 2 **tablespoons minced garlic**
- 1 **tablespoon minced ginger**
- 1 **large red bell pepper, cut into ½-by-2-inch strips**
- 1 **large green bell pepper, cut into ½-by-2-inch strips**

1. Drain pineapple and set aside, reserving ¼ cup of the juice. Whisk the reserved juice, vinegar, ketchup, soy sauce and brown sugar in a medium bowl until smooth. Place tofu in a large bowl; toss with 3 tablespoons of the sauce. Let marinate for at least 5 minutes and up to 30 minutes. Add cornstarch to the remaining sauce and whisk until smooth.

2. Heat 1 tablespoon oil in a large nonstick skillet over medium-high heat. Transfer the tofu to the pan using a slotted spoon; whisk any remaining marinade into the bowl of reserved sauce. Cook the tofu, stirring every 1 to 2 minutes, until golden brown, 7 to 9 minutes total. Transfer to a plate.

3. Add the remaining oil to the pan and heat over medium heat. Add garlic and ginger and cook, stirring constantly, until fragrant, about 30 seconds. Add red and green peppers and cook, stirring often, until just tender, 2 to 3 minutes. Pour in the reserved sauce and cook, stirring, until thickened, about 30 seconds. Add the tofu and pineapple and cook, stirring gently, until heated through, about 2 minutes more.

MAKES 4 SERVINGS, 1½ CUPS EACH.

GINGER FRIED RICE

This is a snap to pull together and can be made with whatever vegetables you have on hand—the more different colors, the better. Also, if you want to make it even "leaner," substitute an equivalent amount of Egg Beaters or 8 egg whites for the whole eggs.

3   **teaspoons peanut oil, divided**
4   **large eggs, beaten**
1   **bunch scallions, chopped**
2   **tablespoons minced fresh ginger**
3   **cups cold cooked long-grain brown rice**
1   **cup frozen peas**
1   **cup mung bean sprouts (see *Note*)**
3   **tablespoons prepared stir-fry *or* oyster sauce**

Heat 1 teaspoon oil in a wok or large nonstick skillet over high heat. Add eggs and cook, stirring, until scrambled. Transfer to a plate; set aside. Add the remaining 2 teaspoons oil to the wok. Add scallions and ginger and stir-fry until fragrant, about 1 minute. Add rice and peas and stir-fry until hot and beginning to stick to the pan, about 3 minutes. Add sprouts, stir-fry sauce (or oyster sauce) and the reserved eggs. Toss well, breaking up the eggs, until heated through, about 2 minutes. Serve immediately.

MAKES 4 SERVINGS, ABOUT 1½ CUPS EACH.

PER SERVING:

319 calories;

10 g fat (2 g sat, 4 g mono);

212 mg cholesterol; 45 g carbohydrate;

14 g protein; 5 g fiber; 520 mg sodium;

286 mg potassium.

NUTRITION BONUS: Vitamins A & C (25% DAILY VALUE), Folate (19% DV), Iron (15% DV).

Healthy ⤬ Weight

High ⬆ Fiber

ACTIVE TIME: 20 MINUTES

TOTAL: 20 MINUTES

INGREDIENT NOTE:

Mung bean sprouts are germinated mung beans, often simply labeled "bean sprouts" at the supermarket. They are white with a light yellow tip and are thicker than more common alfalfa sprouts.

225 calories;

13 g fat (2 g sat, 3 g mono);

4 mg cholesterol; 14 g carbohydrate;

18 g protein; 5 g fiber; 582 mg sodium;

849 mg potassium.

NUTRITION BONUS: Vitamin A (220% DAILY VALUE), Vitamin C (60% DV), Folate (55% DV), Calcium & Iron (30% DV), Magnesium (24% DV).

Healthy ⌇⌇ Weight

Lower ⬇ Carbs

High ⬆ Fiber

ACTIVE TIME: 30 MINUTES

TOTAL: 30 MINUTES

SAAG TOFU

Also known as palak paneer, saag paneer is an Indian classic composed mostly of spinach and paneer—*a cow's-milk cheese that is curdled then pressed until firm. Here, we substitute tofu for the cheese and incorporate low-fat yogurt and sliced onions for a healthier version that retains its authenticity.*

1	14-ounce package water-packed firm tofu, drained
4	teaspoons canola oil, divided
3/4	teaspoon salt, divided
1	onion, sliced 1/4 inch thick
2	medium cloves garlic, finely chopped
1	teaspoon freshly grated ginger
1	teaspoon mustard seeds
1	pound baby spinach
1	cup low-fat *or* nonfat plain yogurt
1 1/2	teaspoons curry powder
1/4	teaspoon cumin

1. Cut tofu into thirds lengthwise and eighths crosswise. Heat 2 teaspoons oil in a large nonstick skillet over medium-high heat. Add tofu and sprinkle with 1/4 teaspoon salt. Cook, stirring gently every 2 to 3 minutes, until browned on all sides, 6 to 8 minutes. Transfer to a plate.
2. Add the remaining 2 teaspoons oil to the pan and reduce heat to medium. Add onion, garlic, ginger and mustard seeds and cook until the onion is translucent, 4 to 6 minutes. Add spinach in batches small enough to fit in the pan and cook, stirring frequently, until all the spinach has been added and has wilted, 4 to 6 minutes more.
3. Meanwhile, combine yogurt, curry powder, cumin and the remaining 1/2 teaspoon salt in a small bowl. Add to the pan along with the tofu and cook until heated through, about 2 minutes.

MAKES 4 SERVINGS, ABOUT 1 1/4 CUPS EACH.

INDIAN-SPICED EGGPLANT & CAULIFLOWER STEW

Toasting the spices enhances the flavor in this one-pot vegetarian stew. Serve with brown basmati rice.

- 2 tablespoons curry powder, preferably hot Madras (see *Note, page 245*)
- 1 teaspoon garam masala (see *Tip*)
- 1 teaspoon mustard seeds
- 2 tablespoons canola oil
- 1 large onion, sliced
- 2 cloves garlic, minced
- 1 teaspoon finely grated fresh ginger
- 3/4 teaspoon salt
- 1 1-pound eggplant, cut into 1-inch chunks
- 3 cups cauliflower florets
- 1 15-ounce can diced tomatoes
- 1 15-ounce can chickpeas, rinsed
- 1/2 cup water
- 1/2 cup nonfat plain yogurt (optional)

1. Heat a Dutch oven over medium heat. Add curry powder, garam masala and mustard seeds and toast, stirring, until the spices begin to darken, about 1 minute. Transfer to a small bowl.

2. Add oil, onion, garlic, ginger and salt to the pot and cook, stirring, until softened, 3 to 4 minutes. Stir in eggplant, cauliflower, tomatoes, chickpeas, water and the reserved spices. Bring to a simmer. Cover, reduce heat and cook, stirring occasionally, until the vegetables are tender, 15 to 20 minutes. Top each serving with a dollop of yogurt, if desired.

MAKES 6 SERVINGS, ABOUT 1 1/3 CUPS EACH.

PER SERVING:

198 calories;

6 g fat (1 g sat, 3 g mono);

0 mg cholesterol; 31 g carbohydrate;

6 g protein; 8 g fiber; 605 mg sodium;

358 mg potassium.

NUTRITION BONUS: Vitamin C (60% DAILY VALUE), Folate (22% DV), Iron (15% DV).

Healthy ⚖ Weight

High ⬆ Fiber

ACTIVE TIME: 25 MINUTES

TOTAL: 40 MINUTES

SHOPPING TIP:

Garam masala is a flavorful, fragrant blend of dry-roasted ground spices. It's in the spice section of most supermarkets and specialty stores. To make your own, go to *eatingwell.com* for a recipe.

> ♥ **HEART-HEALTHY TIP**
>
> **Eggplant** contains important phytonutrients called phenolic compounds, which have strong antioxidant properties that can help fight the negative effects of LDL cholesterol.

228 calories;

10 g fat (1 g sat, 6 g mono);

0 mg cholesterol; 26 g carbohydrate;

9 g protein; 4 g fiber; 376 mg sodium;

418 mg potassium.

NUTRITION BONUS: Vitamin C (80% DAILY VALUE), Iron (25% DV), Vitamin A (20% DV), Magnesium (19% DV).

Healthy)(Weight

ACTIVE TIME: 25 MINUTES

TOTAL: 35 MINUTES

TO MAKE AHEAD: Store in an airtight container in the refrigerator for up to 1 day.

SHOPPING TIPS:

Quinoa is a delicately flavored, protein-rich grain. Rinsing removes any residue of saponin, quinoa's natural, bitter protective covering. Find it in natural-foods stores and the natural-foods sections of many supermarkets.

Precooked **"baked tofu"** is firmer than water-packed tofu and comes in a wide variety of flavors. You might also like flavored baked tofu on a sandwich or in a stir-fry.

QUINOA & SMOKED TOFU SALAD

We took the tangy fresh flavors of tabbouleh and paired them with smoky tofu and quinoa to create a main-dish salad that's perfect served on a bed of greens. This salad is jam-packed with heart-healthy ingredients—whole grains (quinoa), legumes (soy-based tofu) and plenty of vegetables.

- 2 **cups water**
- ³/₄ **teaspoon salt, divided**
- 1 **cup quinoa, rinsed well (see *Tip*)**
- ¼ **cup lemon juice**
- 3 **tablespoons extra-virgin olive oil**
- 2 **small cloves garlic, minced**
- ¼ **teaspoon freshly ground pepper**
- 1 **6- or 8-ounce package baked smoked tofu (see *Tip*), diced**
- 1 **small yellow bell pepper, diced**
- 1 **cup grape tomatoes, halved**
- 1 **cup diced cucumber**
- ½ **cup chopped fresh parsley**
- ½ **cup chopped fresh mint**

1. Bring water and ½ teaspoon salt to a boil in a medium saucepan. Add quinoa and return to a boil. Reduce to a simmer, cover and cook until the water has been absorbed, 15 to 20 minutes. Spread the quinoa on a baking sheet to cool for 10 minutes.

2. Meanwhile, whisk lemon juice, oil, garlic, the remaining ¼ teaspoon salt and pepper in a large bowl. Add the cooled quinoa, tofu, bell pepper, tomatoes, cucumber, parsley and mint; toss well to combine.

MAKES 6 SERVINGS, ABOUT 1¹/₃ CUPS EACH.

LENTIL & ALMOND BURGERS

These vegetarian burgers are just the thing for a summery picnic, on buns or on their own with sliced tomatoes and relish. Or try them with Oven-Fried Potatoes (page 232) and Roasted Broccoli with Lemon (page 230). Use a wide spatula to flip the delicate patties.

- **6 cups water**
- **1 cup brown or French green lentils (see *Note*)**
- **2 tablespoons extra-virgin olive oil, divided**
- **³/₄ cup finely chopped carrot**
- **¹/₃ cup finely chopped shallots (about 2 medium)**
- **¹/₃ cup finely chopped celery (about 1 stalk)**
- **¹/₄ cup sliced almonds**
- **1 teaspoon chopped fresh thyme**
- **¹/₂ teaspoon salt**
- **¹/₄ teaspoon freshly ground pepper**
- **1 large egg yolk, lightly beaten**
- **1 tablespoon lemon juice**

1. Bring water to a boil in a large saucepan. Stir in lentils, reduce heat to medium-low and simmer until very tender and beginning to break down, about 25 minutes for brown lentils or 30 minutes for green lentils. Drain in a fine-mesh sieve.

2. Meanwhile, heat 1 tablespoon oil in a large skillet over medium heat. Add carrot, shallots and celery and cook, stirring, until softened, about 3 minutes. Add almonds, thyme, salt and pepper; continue cooking until the almonds are lightly browned, about 2 minutes. Transfer the mixture to a food processor; add 1 cup of the cooked lentils. Pulse several times, scraping down the sides once or twice, until the mixture is coarsely ground. Transfer to a large bowl; stir in the remaining lentils. Let cool for 10 minutes. Mix in egg yolk and lemon juice. Cover and refrigerate for 1 hour.

3. Form the lentil mixture into 5 patties. Heat the remaining 1 tablespoon oil in a large nonstick skillet, preferably cast-iron, over medium-high heat. Add the patties and cook for 3 to 4 minutes. Turn gently and continue to cook until lightly browned and heated through, 3 to 4 minutes more. Serve immediately.

MAKES 5 SERVINGS.

PER SERVING:

228 calories;

9 g fat (1 g sat, 6 g mono);

41 mg cholesterol; 27 g carbohydrate;

11 g protein; 7 g fiber; 276 mg sodium;

467 mg potassium.

NUTRITION BONUS: Folate (53% DAILY VALUE), Vitamin A (50% DV), Fiber (40% DV), Iron (20% DV), Potassium (16% DV).

Healthy)(Weight

High ⬆ Fiber

ACTIVE TIME: 40 MINUTES

TOTAL: 2 HOURS (including 1 hour chilling time)

TO MAKE AHEAD: Prepare through Step 2 up to 6 hours in advance.

INGREDIENT NOTE:

French green lentils are smaller and firmer than brown lentils. They cook more quickly, too, in about 20 minutes. They can be found in natural-foods stores and some larger supermarkets.

Turkey Tenderloin with Whiskey-Cherry Sauce

Gorgonzola & Prune Stuffed Chicken

Pecan-Crusted Chicken

Chicken Cutlets with Grape-Shallot Sauce

CHICKEN, DUCK & TURKEY

MAKEOVER: Old-Fashioned
Chicken & Dumplings 154

Sofia's Chicken Paprikash 156

Grilled Orange Chicken Fingers 157

Pecan-Crusted Chicken 158

Balsamic Roasted Chicken Breasts 160

Chicken Cutlets with
Grape-Shallot Sauce 161

Gorgonzola & Prune Stuffed
Chicken 163

Snap Pea & Spring Herb Chicken 164

Sichuan-Style Chicken
with Peanuts 166

Five-Spice Roasted Duck Breasts 168

Sausage Gumbo 169

MAKEOVER: EATINGWELL'S
Pepperoni Pizza 170

Spicy Turkey Burgers with
Pickled Onions 172

Sweet Potato-Turkey Hash 174

Turkey Tenderloin with
Whiskey-Cherry Sauce 175

Additional poultry recipes:

MAKEOVER: Classic Lasagna 74

MAKEOVER: EatingWell's Oven-Fried Chicken 76

MAKEOVER: Chicken à la King 78

"I love chicken. I would eat chicken fingers on Thanksgiving
if it were socially acceptable."

TODD BERRY

	EatingWell's Old-Fashioned Chicken & Dumplings	Traditional Chicken & Dumplings
Calories	463	598
Fat	15 g	21 g
Saturated Fat	3 g	6 g
Sodium	629 mg	1,321 mg
Fiber	6 g	3 g

Many traditional recipes call for vegetable shortening, which adds either trans fat if it's made from partially hydrogenated oils or saturated fat if it's the newer "trans fat free" formulation. Both trans fat and saturated fat negatively impact heart health and add extra calories. We omit the vegetable shortening and add more buttermilk, which not only keeps the dumplings moist, but also ups the calcium.

Boneless, skinless chicken thighs replace the skin-on version to cut calories and fat.

We increase the amount of vegetables and decrease the amount of meat to keep the serving size generous with fewer calories and less fat.

Whole-wheat flour in the dumplings instead of all-purpose flour adds fiber and phytonutrients.

OLD-FASHIONED CHICKEN & DUMPLINGS

This is classic comfort food made healthy. Serve our tasty version of chicken and dumplings with a green salad and a cold beer. Try it with boneless, skinless chicken breasts if you prefer.

- 1³/₄ **pounds boneless, skinless chicken thighs, trimmed and cut into 1¹/₂-inch pieces**
- ²/₃ **cup all-purpose flour**
- 2 **tablespoons canola oil, divided**
- 2 **large carrots, diced**
- 2 **stalks celery, diced**
- 1 **large onion, diced**
- 1 **tablespoon poultry seasoning**
- ¹/₂ **teaspoon salt**
- ¹/₂ **teaspoon freshly ground pepper**
- 2 **14-ounce cans reduced-sodium chicken broth**
- 1 **cup water**
- 1¹/₂ **cups frozen peas, thawed**

DUMPLINGS
- 1 **cup whole-wheat pastry flour**
- ¹/₂ **cup all-purpose flour**
- 1 **teaspoon poultry seasoning**
- ¹/₂ **teaspoon baking soda**
- ¹/₄ **teaspoon salt**
- ³/₄ **cup nonfat buttermilk**

PER SERVING:

463 calories;

15 g fat (**3** g sat, 6 g mono);

91 mg cholesterol; 45 g carbohydrate;

34 g protein; 6 g fiber; 629 mg sodium;

412 mg potassium.

NUTRITION BONUS: Vitamin A (100% DAILY VALUE), Selenium (36% DV), Iron (20% DV), Vitamin C (15% DV).

High ↑ Fiber

ACTIVE TIME: 45 MINUTES

TOTAL: 1 HOUR

1. Toss chicken with ²/₃ cup all-purpose flour in a medium bowl until coated. Heat 1 tablespoon oil in a Dutch oven over medium-high heat. Reserving the remaining flour, add the chicken to the pot and cook, stirring occasionally, until lightly browned on the outside, 3 to 5 minutes. Remove the chicken to a plate.

2. Reduce heat to medium and add the remaining 1 tablespoon oil to the pot. Stir in carrots, celery, onion, 1 tablespoon poultry seasoning, ¹/₂ teaspoon salt and pepper. Cover and cook, stirring occasionally, until the vegetables are softened and the bottom of the pot is dark brown, 5 to 7 minutes. Sprinkle the reserved flour over the vegetables; stir to coat. Stir in broth, water, peas and the reserved chicken. Bring to a simmer, stirring often.

3. TO PREPARE DUMPLINGS: Meanwhile, stir together whole-wheat flour, ¹/₂ cup all-purpose flour, 1 teaspoon poultry seasoning, baking soda and ¹/₄ teaspoon salt in a medium bowl. Stir in buttermilk.

4. Drop the dough, 1 tablespoon at a time, over the simmering chicken stew, making about 18 dumplings. Adjust heat to maintain a gentle simmer, cover and cook undisturbed until the dumplings are puffed, the vegetables are tender and the chicken is cooked through, about 15 minutes.

MAKES 6 SERVINGS, 1¹/₃ CUPS STEW & 3 DUMPLINGS EACH.

263 calories;

7 g fat (2 g sat, 3 g mono);

72 mg cholesterol; 16 g carbohydrate;

30 g protein; 4 g fiber; 294 mg sodium;

804 mg potassium.

NUTRITION BONUS: Vitamin C (140% DAILY VALUE), Vitamin A (35% DV), Potassium (23% DV), Magnesium (16% DV).

Healthy ✕ Weight

Lower ⬇ Carbs

ACTIVE TIME: 40 MINUTES

TOTAL: 40 MINUTES

♥ HEART-HEALTHY TIP

Yellow **onions** are a good source of quercetin, a flavonoid that may stop the oxidation of LDL cholesterol and raise levels of HDL cholesterol.

SOFIA'S CHICKEN PAPRIKASH

This light version of chicken paprikash was passed along to our recipe developer Carolyn by her Aunt Sofia. Brilliant red paprika is the main seasoning in Hungarian cooking and this dish highlights its nuanced character. Vary the heat by using hot, sweet or a combination of paprikas. Serve over whole-wheat egg noodles with a side of steamed broccoli and a cool fruit salad for dessert.

1	**pound boneless, skinless chicken breasts, trimmed, cut into 2-inch pieces**
¼	**teaspoon kosher salt**
¼	**teaspoon freshly ground pepper**
1	**tablespoon canola oil**
2	**large green bell peppers, thinly sliced**
1	**large onion, halved and thinly sliced**
2	**teaspoons hot or sweet paprika**
½	**cup dry white wine**
1½	**cups canned crushed tomatoes**
½	**cup reduced-sodium chicken broth**
1	**tablespoon lemon juice**
¼	**cup reduced-fat sour cream**
2	**tablespoons chopped fresh parsley**

1. Sprinkle chicken with salt and pepper. Heat oil in a large skillet over medium-high heat. Add chicken and cook, turning occasionally, until browned, 3 to 5 minutes. Transfer to a plate.

2. Add bell peppers and onion to the pan and cook, covered, over medium heat, stirring occasionally, until softened, about 5 minutes. Add paprika and cook, stirring, until fragrant, about 30 seconds. Add wine; increase heat to medium-high and cook, stirring, until mostly evaporated, about 1½ minutes. Add tomatoes, broth and lemon juice; bring to a boil. Return the chicken and any accumulated juices to the pan; reduce heat to a lively simmer. Spoon some sauce over the chicken and cook, turning occasionally, until the sauce is reduced and the chicken is cooked through, 6 to 8 minutes.

3. Remove from the heat; stir in sour cream. Sprinkle with parsley.

MAKES 4 SERVINGS, ABOUT 1¼ CUPS EACH.

GRILLED ORANGE CHICKEN FINGERS

The simple, sweet glaze for the chicken can be whipped up fast; marinating time is just 15 minutes and the marinade caramelizes deliciously on the grill. Serve this with carrot sticks and baked potato wedges, tossed with herbs and olive oil.

1	**pound boneless, skinless chicken breasts, trimmed**
1½	**tablespoons Dijon mustard**
1½	**tablespoons frozen orange juice concentrate, thawed**
1½	**tablespoons honey**
1	**teaspoon sesame oil**
½	**teaspoon freshly ground pepper**
	Salt to taste

1. Cut chicken crosswise into ¾-inch-wide strips. Whisk mustard, orange juice concentrate, honey, sesame oil and pepper in a medium bowl until smooth. Add the chicken and toss to combine. Cover and marinate in the refrigerator for 15 minutes.

2. Meanwhile, prepare grill or preheat the broiler. Lightly oil the rack or coat with cooking spray. Remove the chicken strips from the marinade, discarding remaining marinade. Grill or broil the chicken until no longer pink in the center, 2 to 3 minutes per side. Season with salt and serve.

MAKES 4 SERVINGS.

PER SERVING:

173 calories;

4 g fat (1 g sat, 1 g mono);

63 mg cholesterol; 10 g carbohydrate;

23 g protein; 0 g fiber; 341 mg sodium;

249 mg potassium.

NUTRITION BONUS: Selenium (28% DAILY VALUE), Vitamin C (15% DV).

Healthy ⚖ Weight

Lower ⬇ Carbs

ACTIVE TIME: 10 MINUTES

TOTAL: 30 MINUTES

281 calories;

15 g fat (2 g sat, 8 g mono);

66 mg cholesterol; 7 g carbohydrate;

29 g protein; 2 g fiber; 430 mg sodium;

376 mg potassium.

NUTRITION BONUS: Selenium (34% DAILY VALUE), good source of omega-3s.

Healthy)(Weight

Lower ⬇ Carbs

ACTIVE TIME: 30 MINUTES

TOTAL: 30 MINUTES

KITCHEN TIP:

It can be hard to find individual chicken breasts small enough for our recommended 4-ounce (uncooked) portion size. If yours are closer to 5 ounces each, remove the tender (about 1 ounce) from the underside to get the correct portion size. Wrap and freeze the leftover tenders; when you have gathered enough, use them in a stir-fry, for chicken fingers or in soups (recipes at *eatingwell.com*).

PECAN-CRUSTED CHICKEN

Doctors and researchers suggest eating nuts because the phytonutrients and fiber they contain can help protect against heart disease. The EATINGWELL Test Kitchen recommends them because they're darned delicious. This recipe teams buttery pecans with spicy chipotle and zesty orange to coat tender chicken breasts. Serve with a spinach salad.

- 4 **boneless, skinless chicken breasts (1-1¼ pounds), trimmed (see *Tip*)**
- ½ **cup pecan halves *or* pieces**
- ¼ **cup plain dry breadcrumbs**
- 1½ **teaspoons freshly grated orange zest**
- ½ **teaspoon salt**
- ¼ **teaspoon ground chipotle pepper (see *Note*, page 244)**
- 1 **large egg white**
- 2 **tablespoons water**
- 1 **tablespoon canola oil, divided**

1. Working with one piece of chicken at a time, place between sheets of plastic wrap and pound with a meat mallet or heavy skillet until flattened to an even ¼-inch thickness.

2. Place pecans, breadcrumbs, orange zest, salt and ground chipotle in a food processor and pulse until the pecans are finely ground. Transfer the mixture to a shallow dish. Whisk egg white and water in a shallow dish until combined. Dip each chicken breast in the egg-white mixture, then dredge both sides in the pecan mixture.

3. Heat 1½ teaspoons oil in a large nonstick skillet over medium heat. Add half the chicken and cook until browned on the outside and no longer pink in the middle, 2 to 4 minutes per side. Transfer to a plate and cover to keep warm. Carefully wipe out the pan with a paper towel and add the remaining oil. Cook the remaining chicken, adjusting the heat as needed to prevent scorching. Serve immediately.

MAKES 4 SERVINGS.

305 calories;

3 g fat (1 g sat, 1 g mono);

132 mg cholesterol; 14 g carbohydrate;

52 g protein; 0 g fiber; 295 mg sodium;

587 mg potassium.

NUTRITION BONUS: Selenium (57% DAILY VALUE), Potassium (17% DV), Magnesium (16% DV).

Healthy)-(Weight

Lower ⬇ Carbs

ACTIVE TIME: 15 MINUTES

TOTAL: 40 MINUTES

BALSAMIC ROASTED CHICKEN BREASTS

Here's a simple way to prepare chicken breasts in the oven that delivers a ton of flavor. Bone-in chicken breasts retain more moisture than boneless, but take just a bit longer to cook. Look for small chicken breasts that yield a sensible 3-ounce portion of lean protein. If you can only find large ones, save some of the leftovers for a lunch salad the next day.

- **4** bone-in chicken breasts (about 2½ pounds), trimmed, skin removed
- **¼** teaspoon salt, divided
  Freshly ground pepper to taste
- **2** teaspoons dried thyme leaves, divided
- **¼** cup red currant jelly
- **2** tablespoons balsamic vinegar

1. Preheat oven to 400°F. Line a baking sheet with foil and lightly oil or coat it with cooking spray.

2. Season chicken on both sides with ⅛ teaspoon salt and pepper, then rub with 1½ teaspoons thyme. Place bone-side up in a single layer on the prepared baking sheet. Roast for 15 minutes.

3. Meanwhile, heat jelly, vinegar and the remaining ½ teaspoon thyme in a small saucepan over medium-low heat until the jelly is melted. Season with the remaining ⅛ teaspoon salt and pepper and remove from the heat.

4. Turn the chicken meat-side up. Brush liberally with the jelly glaze. Continue to roast, brushing twice with the remaining glaze, until the chicken is cooked through, about 15 minutes more.

MAKES 4 SERVINGS.

CHICKEN CUTLETS WITH GRAPE-SHALLOT SAUCE

This quick sauté pairs wine and grapes in a luscious sauce. Studies have linked grapes and especially their skin with a healthy heart and arteries. Serve with brown basmati rice or mashed sweet potatoes and sautéed Swiss chard.

- ¹/₄ **cup all-purpose flour**
- 4 **chicken breast cutlets, trimmed (about 1 pound)**
- 1 **teaspoon kosher salt**
- ¹/₄ **teaspoon freshly ground pepper**
- 5 **teaspoons canola oil, divided**
- 1 **cup thinly sliced shallots**
- 2 **cups halved seedless green or red grapes**
- 1 **cup white wine**
- 1 **cup reduced-sodium chicken broth**
- 2 **tablespoons chopped fresh parsley**

1. Place flour in a shallow dish. Sprinkle chicken with salt and pepper. Dredge the chicken in the flour (reserve excess flour). Heat 3 teaspoons oil in a large skillet over medium-high heat. Cook the chicken until golden on the first side, 2 to 4 minutes. Reduce heat to medium, turn the chicken and cook until the other side is golden, 2 to 4 minutes more. Transfer to a plate.

2. Add the remaining 2 teaspoons oil to the pan and heat over medium heat. Add shallots and cook, stirring, until just starting to brown, 2 to 3 minutes. Add grapes and cook, stirring occasionally, until just starting to brown, 2 to 3 minutes. Sprinkle with 5 teaspoons of the reserved flour; stir to coat. Add wine and broth; bring to a boil, stirring constantly. Reduce heat to a simmer and cook, stirring occasionally and scraping up any browned bits, until the sauce is reduced and thickened, about 8 minutes. Stir in parsley.

3. Return the chicken to the pan, turning to coat with sauce, and cook until heated through, about 2 minutes. Serve with the sauce.

MAKES 4 SERVINGS.

PER SERVING:

343 calories;

8 g fat (1 g sat, 4 g mono);

67 mg cholesterol; 29 g carbohydrate;

30 g protein; 1 g fiber; 399 mg sodium;

636 mg potassium.

NUTRITION BONUS: Selenium (33% DAILY VALUE), Vitamin C (25% DV), Potassium (18% DV).

Healthy)(Weight

ACTIVE TIME: 35 MINUTES

TOTAL: 35 MINUTES

GORGONZOLA & PRUNE STUFFED CHICKEN

Stuffing a chicken breast is relatively simple, but your guests need not know that. Try it with any favorite combination of dried fruit and flavorful cheese. Serve over quick-cooking barley with broccolini or a steamed artichoke on the side.

- 1/2 **cup chopped prunes, divided**
- 1/3 **cup crumbled Gorgonzola cheese**
- 1/4 **cup coarse dry whole-wheat breadcrumbs (see *Note*)**
- 1 **teaspoon minced fresh thyme, divided**
- 4 **boneless, skinless chicken breasts (1-1 1/4 pounds), trimmed (see *Tip, page 244*)**
- 1/2 **teaspoon salt**
- 1/2 **teaspoon freshly ground pepper**
- 1 **tablespoon plus 1 teaspoon extra-virgin olive oil, divided**
- 1 **shallot, minced**
- 1/2 **cup red wine**
- 1 **cup reduced-sodium chicken broth**
- 4 **teaspoons all-purpose flour**

1. Combine 1/4 cup prunes, Gorgonzola, breadcrumbs and 1/2 teaspoon thyme in a small bowl. Cut a horizontal slit along the thin edge of each chicken breast, nearly through to the opposite side. Stuff each breast with about 2 1/2 tablespoons filling. Use a couple of toothpicks to seal the opening. Season with salt and pepper.

2. Heat 1 tablespoon oil in a large nonstick skillet over medium-high heat. Add the chicken and cook until golden, about 4 minutes per side. Transfer to a plate.

3. Add the remaining 1 teaspoon oil, shallot and the remaining 1/2 teaspoon thyme to the pan; cook, stirring, until fragrant, about 1 minute. Add wine and the remaining 1/4 cup prunes. Reduce heat to medium; cook, scraping up any browned bits, until most of the wine evaporates, about 2 minutes. Whisk broth and flour in a small bowl until smooth; add to the pan and cook, stirring, until thickened, about 2 minutes.

4. Reduce heat to low, return the chicken and any juices to the pan and turn to coat with sauce. Cover and cook until the chicken is cooked through, 3 to 5 minutes more. Remove toothpicks, slice the chicken and top with the sauce.

MAKES 4 SERVINGS.

PER SERVING:

318 calories;

9 g fat (3 g sat, 4 g mono);

75 mg cholesterol; 21 g carbohydrate;

31 g protein; 2 g fiber; 541 mg sodium;

492 mg potassium.

NUTRITION BONUS: Selenium (30% DAILY VALUE).

Healthy ⚖ Weight

Lower ⬇ Carbs

ACTIVE TIME: 45 MINUTES

TOTAL: 45 MINUTES

INGREDIENT NOTE:

We like Ian's brand of coarse dry **whole-wheat breadcrumbs**, labeled "Panko breadcrumbs." Find them in the natural-foods section of large supermarkets. Or, make your own breadcrumbs: Trim crusts from firm sandwich bread. Tear the bread into pieces and process in a food processor until coarse crumbs form. One slice makes about 1/3 cup. Spread the breadcrumbs on a baking sheet and bake at 250°F until dry and crisp, about 15 minutes.

INGREDIENT NOTE:

Sprouted beans, not to be confused with bean sprouts, are beans that have just barely sprouted—they look like a bean with a tiny fiber attached (rather than the more fleshy-looking sprouts commonly used in Asian cooking). Eat raw in salads or add to cooked dishes; they're an excellent source of fiber and protein. Look for them in the produce section near other sprouts.

SNAP PEA & SPRING HERB CHICKEN

This is a model main course—you get just the right amount of lean protein, along with plenty of vegetables and fabulous flavor. It can be made without the sprouted beans, but is especially delicious with them— if you have extras, try them on a salad.

- 1   cup reduced-sodium chicken broth
- 1   teaspoon Dijon mustard
- ½   teaspoon salt
     Freshly ground pepper to taste
- 2   teaspoons plus 1 tablespoon flour, divided
- 1   pound thin-sliced chicken breast cutlets
- 1   tablespoon extra-virgin olive oil
- 8   ounces sugar snap peas, cut in half (2 cups)
- 1   14-ounce can quartered artichoke hearts, rinsed
- ¼   cup sprouted beans (see *Note*), optional
- 3   tablespoons minced fresh herbs, such as chives, tarragon *or* dill
- 2   teaspoons champagne vinegar *or* white-wine vinegar

1. Whisk broth, mustard, salt, pepper and 2 teaspoons flour in a small bowl until smooth.

2. Sprinkle both sides of the chicken with the remaining 1 tablespoon flour. Heat oil in a large nonstick skillet over medium-high heat. Cook the chicken in two batches, adjusting heat as necessary to prevent burning, until golden, about 2 minutes per side. Transfer the chicken to a plate; tent with foil to keep warm.

3. Increase heat to high; stir the broth mixture and add to the skillet along with snap peas, artichoke hearts and sprouted beans (if using). Bring to a simmer, stirring constantly. Reduce heat to maintain a gentle simmer and cook until the snap peas are tender-crisp, about 3 minutes.

4. Return the chicken to the pan, nestling it into the vegetables, and simmer until heated through, 1 to 2 minutes. Remove from heat; stir in herbs and vinegar.

MAKES 4 SERVINGS.

PER SERVING:

273 calories;

12 g fat (2 g sat, 6 g mono);

66 mg cholesterol; 11 g carbohydrate;

28 g protein; 3 g fiber; 177 mg sodium;

427 mg potassium.

NUTRITION BONUS: Vitamin C (30% DAILY VALUE), Iron (15% DV).

Healthy ⤬ Weight

Lower ⬇ Carbs

ACTIVE TIME: 25 MINUTES

TOTAL: 25 MINUTES

INGREDIENT NOTES:

Chinkiang is a dark, slightly sweet vinegar with a smoky flavor. It is available in many Asian specialty markets. If unavailable, balsamic vinegar is an acceptable substitute.

Shao Hsing (or Shaoxing) is a seasoned rice wine. It is available in most Asian specialty markets and some larger supermarkets in the Asian section. An acceptable substitute is **dry sherry**, sold with other fortified wines in your wine or liquor store. (We prefer it to the "cooking sherry" sold in many supermarkets, which can be surprisingly high in sodium.)

SICHUAN-STYLE CHICKEN WITH PEANUTS

When stir-frying chicken, always spread the pieces in the wok and let them cook undisturbed for 1 minute before stirring. This allows the chicken to sear and prevents sticking. To smash the ginger, use the side of a cleaver or chef's knife. The piquant Sichuan Sauce works well with almost any stir-fry but particularly enhances dishes with meat, fish and poultry. It doubles easily and keeps, covered, in the refrigerator for up to 1 week.

SICHUAN SAUCE

3	**tablespoons reduced-sodium chicken broth**
1	**tablespoon tomato paste**
2	**teaspoons Chinkiang rice vinegar (see *Note*) *or* balsamic vinegar**
1	**teaspoon sugar**
1	**teaspoon reduced-sodium soy sauce**
½	**teaspoon sesame oil**
¼	**teaspoon cornstarch**
¼	**teaspoon crushed red pepper, plus more to taste**

CHICKEN

1	**pound skinless, boneless chicken breast *or* thighs, trimmed and cut into 1-inch cubes**
1	**teaspoon Shao Hsing rice wine (see *Note*) *or* dry sherry**
1	**teaspoon reduced-sodium soy sauce**
1½	**teaspoons cornstarch**
½	**teaspoon minced garlic**
1	**tablespoon canola oil**
2	**½-inch-thick slices ginger, smashed**
2	**cups sugar snap peas (8 ounces)**
¼	**cup dry-roasted peanuts**
1	**scallion, minced**

1. TO PREPARE SICHUAN SAUCE: Whisk broth, tomato paste, vinegar, sugar, soy sauce, sesame oil, cornstarch and crushed red pepper to taste in a small bowl.

2. TO PREPARE CHICKEN: Combine chicken, rice wine (or sherry), soy sauce, cornstarch and garlic in a medium bowl; mix thoroughly.

3. Heat a 14-inch flat-bottomed wok or large skillet over high heat until a bead of water vaporizes within 1 to 2 seconds of contact. Swirl oil into the pan, add ginger and stir-fry for 10 seconds. Carefully add the chicken mixture, spreading it out. Cook until the chicken begins to brown, about 1 minute. Using a spatula, stir-fry for 30 seconds. Spread the chicken out again and cook for 30 seconds. Continue stir-frying until the chicken is lightly browned on all sides, 1 to 2 minutes. Add snap peas and stir-fry for 1 minute. Stir the Sichuan Sauce, swirl it into the pan and stir-fry until the chicken is just cooked through and the sauce is slightly thickened and glossy, 30 seconds to 1 minute. Transfer to a platter (discard the ginger) and sprinkle with peanuts and scallions. Serve immediately.

MAKES 4 SERVINGS, 1 CUP EACH.

152 calories;

2 g fat (O g sat, 1 g mono);

122 mg cholesterol; 8 g carbohydrate;

24 g protein; 0 g fiber; 309 mg sodium;

86 mg potassium.

NUTRITION BONUS: Vitamin C (45% DAILY VALUE), Selenium (36% DV), Iron (25% DV).

Healthy)(Weight

Lower ⬇ Carbs

ACTIVE TIME: 30 MINUTES

TOTAL: 45 MINUTES

INGREDIENT NOTE:

Boneless duck breast halves range widely in weight, from about ½ to 1 pound, depending on the breed of duck. They can be found in most supermarkets in the poultry or specialty-meat sections or online at *mapleleaffarms.com* or *dartagnan.com.*

FIVE-SPICE ROASTED DUCK BREASTS

You may be surprised to know that without the skin, duck is a great healthy choice, with no saturated fat in a 3-ounce serving. Starting duck breasts in a cool skillet, then heating, renders off most of the fat for a chic dinner with less mess.

2	pounds boneless duck breast (*see Note*)
1	teaspoon five-spice powder (*see Note, page 245*)
½	teaspoon kosher salt
	Zest & juice of 2 oranges
2	teaspoons honey
1	tablespoon reduced-sodium soy sauce
¼	teaspoon cornstarch dissolved in 1 teaspoon water

1. Preheat oven to 375°F.

2. Place duck skin-side down on a cutting board. Trim off all excess skin that hangs over the sides. Turn over and make three parallel, diagonal cuts in the skin of each breast, cutting through the fat but not into the meat. Sprinkle both sides with five-spice powder and salt.

3. Place the duck skin-side down in an ovenproof skillet over medium-low heat. Cook until the fat is melted and the skin is golden brown, about 10 minutes. Transfer the duck to a plate; pour off all the fat from the pan. Return the duck to the pan skin-side up and transfer to the oven.

4. Roast the duck for 10 to 15 minutes for medium, depending on the size of the breast, until a thermometer inserted into the thickest part registers 150°F. Transfer to a cutting board; let rest for 5 minutes.

5. Pour off any fat remaining in the pan (take care, the handle will still be hot); place the pan over medium-high heat and add orange juice and honey. Bring to a simmer, stirring to scrape up any browned bits. Add orange zest and soy sauce and continue to cook until the sauce is slightly reduced, about 1 minute. Stir cornstarch mixture then whisk into the sauce; cook, stirring, until slightly thickened, 1 minute. Remove the duck skin and thinly slice the breast meat. Drizzle with the orange sauce.

MAKES 4 SERVINGS.

SAUSAGE GUMBO

To keep it simple, we've opted for just the essential ingredients in this rendition of the hearty Creole favorite: sausage, okra, rice and a little spice. Okra is loaded with soluble fiber, which not only is important in keeping your digestive system working smoothly, but also may help lower LDL cholesterol. Look for Cajun seasoning, a spice blend that often includes cayenne, black pepper, paprika, onion powder, thyme and salt, in the spice section of the supermarket.

- 12 **ounces hot Italian turkey sausage links, removed from casings**
- 2 **teaspoons canola oil**
- 1 **large onion, diced**
- 4 **cloves garlic, minced**
- 1 **teaspoon Cajun seasoning**
- 2 **tablespoons all-purpose flour**
- 4 **cups chopped tomatoes**
- 4 **cups reduced-sodium chicken broth**
- 2¹/₂ **cups frozen chopped okra**
- ³/₄ **cup instant brown rice**
- 1 **bunch scallions, trimmed and sliced (optional)**

1. Cook sausage in a Dutch oven over medium-high heat, breaking it up into small pieces with a wooden spoon, until cooked through, about 5 minutes. Transfer to a medium bowl lined with paper towels.

2. Return the pan to medium-high heat and add oil. Add onion and cook, stirring often, until translucent, about 2 minutes. Add garlic and Cajun seasoning and cook, stirring often, until fragrant, about 30 seconds. Add flour and cook, stirring to coat the vegetables, until the flour browns, about 1 minute. Add tomatoes and cook, stirring occasionally, until they begin to release their juices, about 2 minutes. Stir in broth, cover, increase heat to high and bring to a boil.

3. Return the sausage to the pan, along with okra and rice; reduce the heat to a simmer. Cook until the okra is heated through and the rice is tender, about 10 minutes. Serve sprinkled with sliced scallions, if using.

MAKES 8 SERVINGS, ABOUT 1 CUP EACH.

PER SERVING:

168 calories;

6 g fat (2 g sat, 1 g mono);

25 mg cholesterol; 18 g carbohydrate;

11 g protein; 3 g fiber; 631 mg sodium;

448 mg potassium.

NUTRITION BONUS: Vitamin C (50% DAILY VALUE), Vitamin A (15% DV).

Healthy ⫶ Weight

Lower ⬇ Carbs

ACTIVE TIME: 30 MINUTES

TOTAL: 40 MINUTES

TO MAKE AHEAD: Cover and refrigerate for up to 3 days or freeze for up to 3 months.

♥ HEART-HEALTHY TIP

Tomatoes are a good source of folic acid, which helps break down homocysteine (an amino acid) in the blood. Too much homocysteine can harm the cells that line the heart and blood vessels, raising the risk of cardiovascular disease.

	EatingWell's Pepperoni Pizza	Regular Pepperoni Pizza
Calories	280	444
Fat	6 g	9 g
Saturated Fat	3 g	9 g
Sodium	602 mg	1,183 mg
Fiber	3 g	2 g

Whole-wheat pizza dough instead of regular dough adds fiber.

We replace regular pork-based pepperoni with turkey pepperoni to cut down on fat and saturated fat.

No-salt tomato sauce mixed with pumpkin puree stands in for pizza sauce. This cuts the sodium significantly. The pumpkin adds beta carotene and fiber.

Part-skim mozzarella replaces the full-fat version to keep calories and fat down.

By increasing the amount of sauce on our pizza and cutting back on the more calorie-dense ingredients, like cheese and pepperoni, our serving size comes up larger than a conventional slice with fewer calories, less fat and saturated fat.

EATINGWELL'S PEPPERONI PIZZA

Pizza is usually so high in saturated fat and sodium that it's earned a top spot on the "heart attack to go" food list. But our whole-wheat pizza, topped with a sauce that provides extra beta carotene and fiber (thanks to the addition of pumpkin puree), is both healthy and flavorful. We tested the recipe using low-fat turkey pepperoni, but try your favorite sliced vegetables or chicken sausage as optional toppings.

- 1 **pound prepared whole-wheat pizza dough (see _Tip_), thawed if frozen**
- 1 **cup canned unseasoned pumpkin puree**
- 1/2 **cup canned no-salt tomato sauce**
- 1/2 **teaspoon garlic powder**
- 1 **cup shredded part-skim mozzarella**
- 1/2 **cup grated Parmesan cheese**
- 2 **ounces turkey pepperoni (1/2 cup)**

1. Place oven rack in the lowest position; preheat to 450°F. Coat a large baking sheet with cooking spray.

2. Roll out dough on a lightly floured surface to the size of the baking sheet. Transfer to the baking sheet. Bake until puffed and lightly crisped on the bottom, 8 to 10 minutes.

3. Meanwhile, whisk pumpkin puree, tomato sauce and garlic powder in a small bowl until combined.

4. Spread sauce evenly over the baked crust. Top with mozzarella, Parmesan and pepperoni. Bake until the crust is crispy on the edges and the cheeses have melted, about 12 minutes.

MAKES 6 SERVINGS.

PER SERVING:

280 calories;

6 g fat (3 g sat, 2 g mono);

30 mg cholesterol; 35 g carbohydrate;

16 g protein; 3 g fiber; 602 mg sodium;

153 mg potassium.

NUTRITION BONUS: Vitamin A (120% DAILY VALUE), Calcium (25% DV).

Healthy)(Weight

ACTIVE TIME: 15 MINUTES

TOTAL: 35 MINUTES

TO MAKE AHEAD: Use leftover tomato sauce and pumpkin to make a second batch of pizza sauce. Store in an airtight container in the refrigerator for up to 5 days or freeze for 3 months.

SHOPPING TIP:

Look for balls of **whole-wheat pizza dough** at your supermarket, fresh or frozen and without any hydrogenated oils.

308 calories;

12 g fat (3 g sat, 1 g mono);

65 mg cholesterol; 30 g carbohydrate;

26 g protein; 4 g fiber; 738 mg sodium;

150 mg potassium.

NUTRITION BONUS: Selenium (30% DAILY VALUE), Iron (20% DV).

Healthy)(Weight

ACTIVE TIME: 35 MINUTES

TOTAL: 35 MINUTES

INGREDIENT NOTE:

Chipotle peppers are dried, smoked jalapeno peppers. **Ground chipotle** can be found in the specialty spice section of most supermarkets.

SPICY TURKEY BURGERS WITH PICKLED ONIONS

Spicy Southwest flavors pair with sweet and tangy pickled red onions to create a standout turkey burger. If you're used to having your burgers made of beef with plenty of melted cheese on top, don't worry. You won't be disappointed. What this burger lacks in bad-for-you saturated fat and calories it makes up for with huge flavor. Serve with corn on the cob and sweet potato fries.

PICKLED ONIONS
- 1 cup red-wine vinegar
- 2 tablespoons packed brown sugar
- 1/2 teaspoon salt
- 1/4 teaspoon ground allspice
- 1 small red onion, halved and very thinly sliced

BURGERS
- 1 pound 93%-lean ground turkey
- 2 tablespoons chopped fresh cilantro
- 1 1/2 teaspoons ground cumin
- 1/2 teaspoon ground chipotle pepper (see *Note*)
- 1/2 teaspoon salt
- 1/8 teaspoon ground allspice
- 1 teaspoon canola oil
- 4 whole-wheat buns, split
- 8 teaspoons reduced-fat mayonnaise

1. TO PREPARE PICKLED ONIONS: Whisk vinegar, brown sugar, salt and allspice in a medium glass bowl. Cover and microwave on High until the mixture boils, 2 to 3 minutes. (*Alternatively, bring the mixture to a boil in a small saucepan on the stove.*) Add onions and toss to coat.

2. TO PREPARE BURGERS: Preheat grill to high. Place turkey in a medium bowl and gently mix in cilantro, cumin, ground chipotle, salt and allspice until distributed throughout the meat. Form the mixture into 4 patties. Brush with oil.

3. Grill the burgers until cooked through and no longer pink in the center, 3 to 4 minutes per side. Toast buns on the grill, if desired.

4. Drain the onions, discarding the marinade. Spread 2 teaspoons mayonnaise on each bun; top with a burger and pickled onions.

MAKES 4 SERVINGS.

214 calories;

7 g fat (2 g sat, 2 g mono);

56 mg cholesterol; 15 g carbohydrate;

23 g protein; 3 g fiber; 262 mg sodium;

483 mg potassium.

NUTRITION BONUS: Vitamin A (150% DAILY VALUE), Selenium (33% DV), Vitamin C (20% DV).

Healthy ✝ Weight

Lower ⬇ Carbs

ACTIVE TIME: 45 MINUTES

TOTAL: 45 MINUTES

♥ HEART-HEALTHY TIP

Rich in potassium and beta carotene, **sweet potatoes** are also high in fiber, all of which help reduce the risk of chronic conditions like heart disease.

SWEET POTATO-TURKEY HASH

Hash is a flexible and easy way to transform leftover cooked meat into a distinctively different dish. This version brings together healthy sweet potatoes, apples and onions along with lean turkey or chicken.

- 2 **medium sweet potatoes, peeled and cut into ¹/₂-inch pieces**
- 1 **medium apple, washed, cored and cut into ¹/₂-inch pieces**
- ¹/₂ **cup reduced-fat sour cream**
- 1 **teaspoon lemon juice**
- 1 **tablespoon canola oil**
- 1 **medium onion, chopped**
- 3 **cups diced, cooked, skinless turkey *or* chicken**
- 1 **tablespoon chopped fresh thyme *or* 1 teaspoon dried**
- ¹/₂ **teaspoon salt**
  Freshly ground pepper to taste

1. Place sweet potatoes in a medium saucepan, cover with lightly salted water and bring to a boil. Reduce heat to medium, cover and cook for 3 minutes. Add apple and cook until everything is just tender, but not mushy, 2 to 3 minutes longer. Drain.

2. Transfer 1 cup of the mixture to a large bowl; mash. Stir in sour cream and lemon juice. Add the remaining unmashed mixture and stir gently to mix. Set aside.

3. Heat oil in a large nonstick skillet over medium-high heat. Add onion and cook, stirring often, until softened, 2 to 3 minutes. Add turkey (or chicken), thyme, salt and pepper; cook, stirring occasionally, until heated through, about 2 minutes.

4. Add the reserved sweet potato mixture to the skillet; stir to mix. Press on the hash with a wide metal spatula; cook until the bottom is lightly browned, about 3 minutes. Cut the hash into several rough sections; flip and cook until the undersides are browned, about 3 minutes longer. Serve immediately.

MAKES 6 SERVINGS, 1¹/₄ CUPS EACH.

TURKEY TENDERLOIN WITH WHISKEY-CHERRY SAUCE

Cherries and cranberries are terrific sources of heart-healthy poly-phenols. They make a luxurious pan sauce spiked with whiskey and cranberry juice that's luscious on turkey tenderloin (a lean but flavorful, quick-cooking cut you might have overlooked in the poultry case).

- **3 teaspoons extra-virgin olive oil, divided**
- **1½ pounds turkey tenderloin (see *Tip*)**
- **½ teaspoon salt, divided**
- **¼ teaspoon freshly ground pepper**
- **½ cup chopped onion**
- **2 cloves garlic, minced**
- **1 cup pitted and chopped fresh *or* frozen cherries**
- **1 cup cranberry juice, divided**
- **¼ cup whiskey**
- **2 teaspoons chopped fresh thyme *or* ½ teaspoon dried**
- **½ teaspoon dry mustard**
- **2 teaspoons cornstarch**

1. Preheat oven to 450°F.

2. Heat 2 teaspoons oil in a large ovenproof skillet over high heat. Season turkey with ¼ teaspoon salt and pepper and cook until golden brown on one side, about 3 minutes. Turn it over and transfer the pan to the oven. Roast until the turkey is no longer pink in the middle and registers 165°F on an instant-read thermometer, 15 to 20 minutes. Transfer the turkey to a clean cutting board and tent with foil to keep warm.

3. Heat the remaining 1 teaspoon oil in the pan over medium-high heat. (Be careful, the handle will still be hot.) Add onion and cook, stirring, until starting to soften, 2 to 3 minutes. Add garlic and cook, stirring, for 30 seconds. Add cherries, ¾ cup cranberry juice, whiskey, thyme, mustard and the remaining ¼ teaspoon salt. Cook, stirring occasionally and scraping up any browned bits, until reduced, about 4 minutes.

4. Meanwhile, stir together the remaining ¼ cup juice and cornstarch in a small bowl. Add to the pan and cook, stirring, until thickened, about 30 seconds. Slice the turkey and serve with the sauce.

MAKES 6 SERVINGS.

PER SERVING:

210 calories;

4 g fat (**0** g sat, 2 g mono);

45 mg cholesterol; 11 g carbohydrate;

29 g protein; 1 g fiber; 262 mg sodium;

121 mg potassium.

NUTRITION BONUS: Selenium (41% DAILY VALUE).

Healthy ⑂ Weight

Lower ⬇ Carbs

ACTIVE TIME: 40 MINUTES

TOTAL: 40 MINUTES

SHOPPING TIP:

Check the label to avoid turkey tenderloin "enhanced" with a sodium solution.

Tilapia & Summer Vegetable Packets

Scallops & Sweet Peas

Edamame Succotash with Shrimp

Grilled Salmon with Mustard & Herbs

FISH & SEAFOOD

Edamame Succotash
with Shrimp **179**

Shrimp & Plum Kebabs **180**

Shrimp & Pesto Pasta **182**

Spaghettini with Steamed Mussels **183**

Scallops & Sweet Peas **185**

Honey-Soy Broiled Salmon **186**

Grilled Rosemary-Salmon Skewers **188**

Poached Salmon with Creamy
Piccata Sauce **189**

Grilled Salmon with Mustard
& Herbs **190**

Salmon with Roasted
Chile-Mango Sauce **192**

Lemony Lentil & Salmon Salad **193**

Grilled Tuna with Olive Relish **194**

Fillet of Sole with Spinach
& Tomatoes **195**

Tilapia & Summer
Vegetable Packets **196**

Tilapia Ceviche **199**

Easy Sautéed Fish Fillets **200**

Avocado-Corn Salsa **200**

Quick Cajun Catfish **201**

Additional fish recipe:

MAKEOVER: Crispy Fish Sandwich with Pineapple Slaw **80**

❝I hope you end up thinking, as I do, that cooking and eating all kinds
of fish are two of life's greatest pleasures.❞

CHEF DAVE PASTERNACK, ESCA, NEW YORK CITY

EDAMAME SUCCOTASH WITH SHRIMP

We give succotash—traditionally a Southern dish made with corn, lima beans and peppers—an update using heart-healthy edamame instead of limas and turn it into a main dish by adding shrimp. To get it on the table even faster, purchase peeled, deveined shrimp from the fish counter instead of doing it yourself. Serve with a piece of warm cornbread to complete the meal.

2	slices bacon
1	tablespoon extra-virgin olive oil
1	bunch scallions, sliced, *or* 1 medium onion, diced
1	red bell pepper, diced
2	cloves garlic, minced
1½	teaspoons chopped fresh thyme
1	10-ounce package frozen shelled edamame (see *Tip*), thawed
1	10-ounce package frozen corn (about 2 cups), thawed
½	cup reduced-sodium chicken broth *or* vegetable broth
1	tablespoon cider vinegar
¼	teaspoon salt
1	pound raw shrimp (26-30 per pound), peeled and deveined
¼	teaspoon lemon pepper

1. Cook bacon in a large nonstick skillet over medium heat until crisp, about 5 minutes. Leaving the drippings in the pan, use tongs to transfer the bacon to a plate lined with paper towels; let cool.

2. Add oil to the pan. Add scallions (or onion), bell pepper, garlic and thyme and cook, stirring, until softened, about 3 minutes. Stir in edamame, corn, broth, vinegar and salt. Bring to a simmer; reduce heat to medium-low and cook for 5 minutes.

3. Meanwhile, sprinkle shrimp on both sides with lemon pepper. Scatter the shrimp on top of the vegetables, cover and cook until the shrimp are cooked through, about 5 minutes. Crumble the bacon and sprinkle it on top.

MAKES 4 SERVINGS, ABOUT 1½ CUPS EACH.

PER SERVING:

307 calories;

9 g fat (1 g sat, 4 g mono);

172 mg cholesterol; 26 g carbohydrate;

30 g protein; 7 g fiber; 491 mg sodium;

476 mg potassium.

NUTRITION BONUS: Vitamin C (120% DAILY VALUE), Selenium (53% DV), Vitamin A (40% DV), Iron (30% DV).

Healthy ✕ Weight

High ⬆ Fiber

ACTIVE TIME: 30 MINUTES

TOTAL: 30 MINUTES

SHOPPING TIP:

Edamame are found in the natural-foods freezer section of large supermarkets and natural-foods stores, sold both in and out of the "pods." For this recipe, you'll need the shelled edamame. One 10-ounce bag contains about 2 cups of shelled beans.

PER SERVING:

194 calories;

8 g fat (1 g sat, 4 g mono);

221 mg cholesterol; 5 g carbohydrate;

24 g protein; 1 g fiber; 446 mg sodium;

292 mg potassium.

NUTRITION BONUS: Selenium (64% DAILY VALUE), Iron & Vitamin C (20% DV).

Healthy ⨯ Weight

Lower ⬇ Carbs

ACTIVE TIME: 35 MINUTES

TOTAL: 35 MINUTES

EQUIPMENT: Four 10-inch skewers

SHRIMP & PLUM KEBABS

Toss quick-cooking shrimp, juicy summertime plums and zesty jalapeños with a simple cilantro-lime marinade for a deluxe meal in minutes. If you like, use peaches or nectarines in place of the plums and red or green bell peppers for the jalapeños.

- 3 **tablespoons canola oil *or* toasted sesame oil**
- 2 **tablespoons chopped fresh cilantro**
- 1 **teaspoon freshly grated lime zest**
- 3 **tablespoons lime juice**
- ½ **teaspoon salt**
- 12 **raw shrimp (8-12 per pound), peeled and deveined**
- 3 **jalapeño peppers, stemmed, seeded and quartered lengthwise**
- 2 **plums, pitted and cut into sixths**

1. Whisk oil, cilantro, lime zest, lime juice and salt in a large bowl. Set aside 3 tablespoons of the mixture in a small bowl to use as dressing. Add shrimp, jalapeños and plums to the remaining marinade; toss to coat.
2. Preheat grill to medium-high.
3. Make 4 kebabs, alternating shrimp, jalapeños and plums evenly among four 10-inch skewers. (Discard the marinade.) Grill the kebabs, turning once, until the shrimp are cooked through, about 8 minutes total. Drizzle with the reserved dressing.

MAKES 4 SERVINGS.

303 calories;

8 g fat (2 g sat, 4 g mono);

115 mg cholesterol; 32 g carbohydrate;

21 g protein; 6 g fiber; 284 mg sodium;

292 mg potassium.

NUTRITION BONUS: Iron (20% DAILY VALUE), Folate & Magnesium (16% DV), Calcium & Vitamin A (15% DV).

Healthy ⚖ Weight

High ⬆ Fiber

ACTIVE TIME: 35 MINUTES

TOTAL: 35 MINUTES

SHRIMP & PESTO PASTA

Choose whole-wheat pasta rather than regular white pasta because it's higher in fiber. To keep things streamlined, we add the asparagus to the pasta during the last few minutes of cooking. Serve with a tomato-and-arugula salad tossed with a red-wine vinaigrette.

8	**ounces whole-wheat fettuccine**
1	**pound asparagus, trimmed and cut into 1-inch pieces (about 4 cups)**
½	**cup sliced jarred roasted red peppers**
¼	**cup prepared pesto**
2	**teaspoons extra-virgin olive oil**
1	**pound raw shrimp (21-25 per pound), peeled and deveined**
1	**cup dry white wine**
	Freshly ground pepper to taste

1. Bring a large pot of water to a boil. Add fettuccine and cook for 3 minutes less than the package directions specify. Add asparagus and continue cooking until the pasta and asparagus are just tender, about 3 minutes more. Reserving ¼ cup of the cooking water, drain the fettuccine and asparagus and return to the pot. Stir in peppers and pesto. Cover to keep warm.

2. Heat oil in a large skillet over medium heat. Add shrimp and cook, stirring occasionally, until pink, about 3 minutes. Add wine, increase heat to high and continue cooking until the shrimp are curled and the wine is reduced, about 3 minutes. Add the shrimp and the reserved cooking water to the pasta; toss to coat. Season with pepper and serve immediately.

MAKES 6 SERVINGS, 1½ CUPS EACH.

SPAGHETTINI WITH STEAMED MUSSELS

Mussel lovers will enjoy this simple pasta preparation. Serve with an arugula salad and crusty whole-grain bread to soak up all the juices.

- **2 tablespoons extra-virgin olive oil, divided**
- **2 large shallots, finely chopped**
- **4 large cloves garlic, very finely chopped**
- **¼ teaspoon crushed red pepper**
- **½ cup dry white wine**
- **½ cup water**
- **2 pounds mussels, rinsed, scrubbed and debearded (see *Tip*)**
- **12 ounces whole-wheat spaghettini**
- **1 large ripe tomato, seeded and finely chopped**
- **¼ cup chopped fresh parsley, plus more for garnish**
- **¼ teaspoon salt**
- **Freshly ground pepper to taste**

1. Put a large pan of water on to boil for cooking pasta.

2. Heat 1 tablespoon oil in a large pot or Dutch oven over medium heat. Add shallots and cook, stirring, until softened, about 5 minutes. Add garlic and crushed red pepper and cook, stirring, until the garlic is fragrant, about 1 minute.

3. Add wine, water and mussels. Cover and cook for about 5 minutes. Check often and use tongs or a slotted spoon to transfer the mussels to a bowl as they open. (Discard any mussels that do not open.) Reserve the mussel-cooking liquid.

4. Meanwhile, cook pasta in the boiling water until al dente, about 5 minutes. Drain and return to the pot. Add the mussel-cooking liquid—pouring it slowly to leave any sand or grit behind. Stir in tomato, parsley and the remaining 1 tablespoon oil. Season with salt and pepper.

5. Divide the pasta among individual soup plates and top with the reserved mussels. Garnish with parsley and serve immediately.

MAKES 4 SERVINGS.

PER SERVING:

471 calories;

10 g fat (**2** g sat, 6 g mono);

21 mg cholesterol; 72 g carbohydrate;

22 g protein; 12 g fiber; 304 mg sodium;

627 mg potassium.

NUTRITION BONUS: Selenium (137% DAILY VALUE), Magnesium (40% DV), Iron (37% DV), Vitamin C (31% DV), Folate (24% DV), Zinc (23% DV), Vitamin A (20% DV), Potassium (18% DV).

High ⬆ Fiber

ACTIVE TIME: 35 MINUTES

TOTAL: 35 MINUTES

TEST KITCHEN TIP:

To clean **mussels**, use a stiff brush to scrub as you rinse them under running water. Discard any mussels with broken shells or any whose shells remain open after you tap them lightly. Use a blunt knife to scrape off any barnacles and pull off the "beard" as you wash them. Once you have debearded the mussels, cook them in short order because they don't live long afterward.

SCALLOPS & SWEET PEAS

Low in dietary cholesterol and saturated fat, scallops are a good heart-healthy choice. Their delicate flavor marries well with peas, and thyme adds a contrasting herbal note.

- 1 tablespoon dried thyme leaves
- 2 cups shelled fresh peas (3 pounds unshelled) **or** frozen peas
- 1½ pounds large dry sea scallops (about 12), tough muscle removed
- ½ teaspoon salt, divided
- ½ teaspoon freshly ground pepper, divided
- 2 cups pea shoots (optional; see *Tip*)
- 3 tablespoons extra-virgin olive oil
- 1 teaspoon freshly grated lemon zest
- 1 tablespoon lemon juice

1. Working over a small bowl, rub thyme leaves between your palms until finely powdered. Place a large steamer basket in a Dutch oven; add water to just below the steamer bottom. Add peas to the steamer; top with scallops in a single layer, touching each other as little as possible. Sprinkle with the powdered thyme, ¼ teaspoon salt and ¼ teaspoon pepper.

2. Cover the pot and place over high heat. When steam begins to escape, start timing. Steam for 3 minutes. Add pea shoots (if using), cover and continue steaming until the scallops are just cooked through, 2 to 3 minutes more. Remove from the heat.

3. Meanwhile, whisk oil, lemon zest, lemon juice and the remaining ¼ teaspoon salt and ¼ teaspoon pepper in a small bowl until combined. Spoon the scallops, peas and pea shoots (if using) onto a serving platter, drizzle with the dressing and serve immediately.

MAKES 4 SERVINGS.

PER SERVING:

305 calories;

12 g fat (2 g sat, 8 g mono);

56 mg cholesterol; 15 g carbohydrate;

32 g protein; 4 g fiber; 646 mg sodium;

669 mg potassium.

NUTRITION BONUS: Selenium (56% DAILY VALUE), Vitamin C (35% DV), Vitamin A (30% DV), Magnesium (29% DV), Potassium (19% DV), Iron (15% DV).

Healthy ⚖ Weight

Lower ⬇ Carbs

ACTIVE TIME: 30 MINUTES

TOTAL: 30 MINUTES

SHOPPING TIP:

Pea shoots, sometimes called "pea tendrils" or "pea sprouts," are the tender vines and leaves of pea plants. Sweet in flavor, with a delicate crisp texture, they can be found in the spring at farmers' markets, Asian markets and some supermarkets. They're best used immediately, but can be refrigerated for up to 2 days. Or use small sprouted pea plants (they resemble large, straight alfalfa sprouts), labeled "pea shoot" or "pea sprout," found with the produce in well-stocked supermarkets.

234 calories;

13 g fat (3 g sat, 5 g mono);

67 mg cholesterol; 6 g carbohydrate;

23 g protein; 0 g fiber; 335 mg sodium;

444 mg potassium.

NUTRITION BONUS: Selenium (60% DAILY VALUE), excellent source of omega-3s.

Healthy ✕ Weight

Lower ⬇ Carbs

ACTIVE TIME: 20 MINUTES

TOTAL: 40 MINUTES

HOW TO SKIN A SALMON FILLET:

Place skin-side down. Starting at the tail end, slip a long knife between the fish flesh and the skin, holding down firmly with your other hand. Gently push the blade along at a 30° angle, separating the fillet from the skin without cutting through either.

HONEY-SOY BROILED SALMON

One sweet, tangy and salty mixture doubles as both marinade and sauce. Toasted sesame seeds provide a nutty accent to the heart-healthy salmon. Serve with brown rice and sautéed red peppers and zucchini slices.

1	scallion, minced
2	tablespoons reduced-sodium soy sauce
1	tablespoon rice vinegar
1	tablespoon honey
1	teaspoon minced fresh ginger
1	pound center-cut salmon fillet, skinned (see *Tip*) and cut into 4 portions
1	teaspoon toasted sesame seeds (see *Tip*, page 244)

1. Whisk scallion, soy sauce, vinegar, honey and ginger in a medium bowl until the honey is dissolved. Place salmon in a sealable plastic bag, add 3 tablespoons of the sauce and refrigerate; let marinate for 15 minutes. Reserve the remaining sauce.

2. Preheat broiler. Line a small baking pan with foil and coat with cooking spray. Transfer the salmon to the pan, skinned-side down. (Discard the marinade.) Broil the salmon 4 to 6 inches from the heat source until cooked through, 6 to 10 minutes. Drizzle with the reserved sauce and garnish with sesame seeds.

MAKES 4 SERVINGS.

PER SERVING:

246 calories;

15 g fat (3 g sat, 6 g mono);

67 mg cholesterol; 4 g carbohydrate;

23 g protein; 1 g fiber; 211 mg sodium;

598 mg potassium.

NUTRITION BONUS: Selenium (60% DAILY VALUE), Vitamin C (25% DV), Potassium (17% DV), Vitamin A (15% DV), excellent source of omega-3s.

Healthy ⅓ Weight

Lower ⬇ Carbs

ACTIVE TIME: 30 MINUTES

TOTAL: 30 MINUTES

EQUIPMENT: Eight 12-inch skewers

TO MAKE AHEAD: Prepare the skewers (Step 2), cover and refrigerate for up to 8 hours. Proceed with grilling (Steps 1 & 3) when ready to serve.

TIP:

To oil the grill rack, oil a folded paper towel, hold it with tongs and rub it over the rack. (Don't use cooking spray on a hot grill.)

GRILLED ROSEMARY-SALMON SKEWERS

If you can find (or grow) them, use sturdy rosemary branches, stripped of leaves, as skewers for these Italian kebabs; they'll add a subtle, smoky flavor that hints of pine. Oil your grill well to prevent sticking, don't move the kebabs around unnecessarily and keep a close eye on the fire to avoid flare-ups.

- 2 teaspoons minced fresh rosemary
- 2 teaspoons extra-virgin olive oil
- 2 cloves garlic, minced
- 1 teaspoon freshly grated lemon zest
- 1 teaspoon lemon juice
- ½ teaspoon kosher salt
- ¼ teaspoon freshly ground pepper
- 1 pound center-cut salmon fillet, skinned (see *Tip*, page 189) and cut into 1-inch cubes
- 1 pint cherry tomatoes

1. Preheat grill to medium-high.

2. Combine rosemary, oil, garlic, lemon zest, lemon juice, salt and pepper in a medium bowl. Add salmon; toss to coat. Alternating the salmon and tomatoes, divide among eight 12-inch skewers.

3. Oil the grill rack (*see Tip*). Grill the skewers, carefully turning once, until the salmon is cooked through, 4 to 6 minutes total. Serve immediately.

MAKES 4 SERVINGS, 2 SKEWERS EACH.

POACHED SALMON WITH CREAMY PICCATA SAUCE

Poaching salmon gives it a velvety, luscious texture and moistness. It's wonderful on its own, but you can't go wrong with a creamy caper-and-lemon sauce that takes just 5 minutes to make. Snow peas, roasted asparagus and a whole grain like quinoa or brown rice are healthy choices to accompany this dish.

- 1 **pound center-cut salmon fillet, skinned (see *Tip*) and cut into 4 portions**
- 1 **cup dry white wine, divided**
- 2 **teaspoons extra-virgin olive oil**
- 1 **large shallot, minced**
- 2 **tablespoons lemon juice**
- 4 **teaspoons capers, rinsed**
- ¼ **cup nonfat sour cream**
- ¼ **teaspoon salt**
- 1 **tablespoon chopped fresh dill**

1. Place salmon in a large skillet. Add ½ cup wine and enough water to just cover the salmon. Bring to a boil over high heat. Reduce to a simmer, turn the salmon over, cover and cook for 5 minutes. Remove from the heat.

2. Meanwhile, heat oil in a medium skillet over medium-high heat. Add shallot and cook, stirring, until fragrant, about 30 seconds. Add the remaining ½ cup wine; boil until slightly reduced, about 1 minute. Stir in lemon juice and capers; cook 1 minute more. Remove from the heat; stir in sour cream and salt. To serve, top the salmon with the sauce and garnish with dill.

MAKES 4 SERVINGS.

PER SERVING:

294 calories;

15 g fat (3 g sat, 6 g mono);

67 mg cholesterol; 5 g carbohydrate;

23 g protein; 0 g fiber; 321 mg sodium;

481 mg potassium.

NUTRITION BONUS: Selenium (60% DAILY VALUE), Vitamin C (15% DV), excellent source of omega-3s.

Healthy ✝ Weight

Lower ⬇ Carbs

ACTIVE TIME: 20 MINUTES

TOTAL: 20 MINUTES

HOW TO SKIN A SALMON FILLET:

Place skin-side down. Starting at the tail end, slip a long knife between the fish flesh and the skin, holding down firmly with your other hand. Gently push the blade along at a 30° angle, separating the fillet from the skin without cutting through either.

Healthy ⫝ Weight

Lower ⬇ Carbs

ACTIVE TIME: 15 MINUTES

TOTAL: 40 MINUTES

HOW TO SKIN A SALMON FILLET:

Place skin-side down. Starting at the tail end, slip a long knife between the fish flesh and the skin, holding down firmly with your other hand. Gently push the blade along at a 30° angle, separating the fillet from the skin without cutting through either.

GRILLED SALMON WITH MUSTARD & HERBS

Fatty fish like salmon are loaded with heart-healthy omega-3 fatty acids. Cooking salmon over a bed of lemon and fresh herbs infuses it with flavor and keeps the fish tender and moist. We like a blend of thyme, tarragon and oregano, but any of your favorite herbs will work.

2	**lemons, thinly sliced, plus 1 lemon cut into wedges for garnish**
20-30	**sprigs mixed fresh herbs plus 2 tablespoons chopped, divided**
1	**clove garlic**
¼	**teaspoon salt**
1	**tablespoon Dijon mustard**
1	**pound center-cut salmon, skinned (see *Tip*)**

1. Preheat grill to medium-high.

2. Lay two 9-inch pieces of heavy-duty foil on top of each other and place on a rimless baking sheet. Arrange lemon slices in two layers in the center of the foil. Spread herb sprigs over the lemons. With the side of a chef's knife, mash garlic with salt to form a paste. Transfer to a small dish and stir in mustard and the remaining 2 tablespoons chopped herbs. Spread the mixture over both sides of the salmon. Place the salmon on the herb sprigs.

3. Slide the foil and salmon off the baking sheet onto the grill without disturbing the salmon-lemon stack. Cover the grill; cook until the salmon is opaque in the center, 18 to 24 minutes. Wearing oven mitts, carefully transfer foil and salmon back onto the baking sheet. Cut the salmon into 4 portions and serve with lemon wedges (discard herb sprigs and lemon slices).

MAKES 4 SERVINGS.

271 calories;

12 g fat (2 g sat, 6 g mono);

72 mg cholesterol; 14 g carbohydrate;

27 g protein; 2 g fiber; 352 mg sodium;

810 mg potassium.

NUTRITION BONUS: Selenium (70% DAILY VALUE), Potassium (23% DV).

Healthy ⊬ Weight

Lower ⬇ Carbs

ACTIVE TIME: 30 MINUTES

TOTAL: 30 MINUTES

♥ HEART-HEALTHY TIP

Mangoes are high in soluble fiber and an excellent source of antioxidant carotenoids, such as beta carotene. A diet rich in antioxidants is linked to a reduced risk of cardiovascular disease.

SALMON WITH ROASTED CHILE-MANGO SAUCE

Pungent red chiles and sweet mango flavor this robust sauce, which accents simply broiled salmon wonderfully. Broiling salmon will perfume your kitchen, so if you prefer, cook the salmon on the grill, over direct heat, 8 to 12 minutes total.

3	teaspoons extra-virgin olive oil, divided
½	cup thinly sliced shallot (about 1 medium)
2	teaspoons coriander seed
1-2	dried red chiles, such as Thai, cayenne *or* chile de arbol, stem end removed (see *Note, page 244*)
1	medium ripe, slightly soft mango, peeled (see *page 244*) and diced (about 1 cup)
2	tablespoons finely chopped fresh cilantro, divided
4	medium cloves garlic, minced
½	teaspoon salt
1	pound salmon fillet, skin removed (see *Tip, page 244*)

1. Position oven rack in upper third of oven; preheat broiler. Coat a broiler pan with cooking spray.

2. Heat 1 teaspoon oil in a small skillet over medium heat. Add shallot, coriander and chile(s); cook, stirring, until the shallot begins to brown and the spices smell fragrant, 2 to 3 minutes. Transfer the shallot mixture to a food processor or blender. Add the remaining 2 teaspoons oil and mango. Process until almost smooth (it will be slightly gritty from the bruised coriander seed). Transfer the sauce to a small bowl; stir in 1 tablespoon cilantro.

3. Combine garlic and salt in a small bowl. Spread the salted garlic on top of the salmon. Place the salmon, garlic side up, on the prepared broiling pan. Broil, 3 to 4 inches from heat, until opaque in the center, 8 to 14 minutes, depending on the thickness. Serve the salmon topped with the sauce and sprinkled with the remaining 1 tablespoon cilantro.

MAKES 4 SERVINGS.

LEMONY LENTIL & SALMON SALAD

Salmon and lentils are a familiar combo in French bistro cooking. For the best presentation, flake the salmon with a fork, then stir gently into the salad to keep it in chunks, not tiny bits.

1/3   **cup lemon juice**
1/3   **cup chopped fresh dill**
2   **teaspoons Dijon mustard**
1/4   **teaspoon salt**
     Freshly ground pepper to taste
1/3   **cup extra-virgin olive oil**
1   **medium red bell pepper, seeded and diced**
1   **cup diced seedless cucumber**
1/2   **cup finely chopped red onion**
2   **15-ounce cans lentils, rinsed, *or* 3 cups cooked brown or green lentils (*see Tip*)**
2   **7-ounce cans salmon, drained and flaked, *or* 1½ cups flaked cooked salmon**

Whisk lemon juice, dill, mustard, salt and pepper in a large bowl. Gradually whisk in oil. Add bell pepper, cucumber, onion, lentils and salmon; toss to coat.

MAKES 6 SERVINGS, 1 CUP EACH.

PER SERVING:

354 calories;

18 g fat (**3** g sat, 12 g mono);

31 mg cholesterol; 25 g carbohydrate;

24 g protein; 9 g fiber; 194 mg sodium;

743 mg potassium.

NUTRITION BONUS: Vitamin C (80% DAILY VALUE), Folate (49% DV), Selenium (40% DV), Iron (25% DV), Potassium (21% DV), Calcium (20% DV).

High ⬆ Fiber

ACTIVE TIME: 30 MINUTES

TOTAL: 30 MINUTES

TO MAKE AHEAD: Store in an airtight container in the refrigerator for up to 8 hours.

TO COOK LENTILS:

Place in a saucepan, cover with water and bring to a boil. Reduce heat to a simmer and cook until just tender, about 20 minutes for green lentils and 30 minutes for brown. Drain and rinse under cold water.

PER SERVING:

184 calories;

5 g fat (1 g sat, 3 g mono);

60 mg cholesterol; 1 g carbohydrate;

31 g protein; 1 g fiber; 266 mg sodium;

636 mg potassium.

NUTRITION BONUS: Selenium (69% DAILY VALUE), Potassium (18% DV), Magnesium (17% DV), Vitamin C (16% DV).

Healthy ♓ Weight

Lower ⬇ Carbs

ACTIVE TIME: 25 MINUTES

TOTAL: 25 MINUTES

TO MAKE AHEAD: The Olive Relish will keep for up to 1 hour.

♥ HEART-HEALTHY TIP

Albacore tuna is an oily fish rich in beneficial omega-3s. These fatty acids have been shown to block dangerous irregular heart rhythms, called arrhythmias, slow the growth of arterial plaque and lower triglyceride levels.

GRILLED TUNA WITH OLIVE RELISH

Pay attention once you get the tuna on the grill. Although it is considered a fatty fish (and does have plenty of omega-3s), tuna dries out when it is overcooked.

OLIVE RELISH
- ½ cup finely chopped fresh parsley
- ⅓ cup chopped pitted imported black olives, such as kalamata
- ¼ cup finely chopped celery
- 1 small clove garlic, minced
- ½ teaspoon dried oregano
- 1 tablespoon lemon juice
- 1 teaspoon extra-virgin olive oil
- ⅛ teaspoon salt
  Freshly ground pepper to taste

GRILLED TUNA
- 1¾ pounds tuna steak, trimmed and cut into 6 portions
- 1 tablespoon extra-virgin olive oil
- ¼ teaspoon salt
  Freshly ground pepper to taste
  Lemon wedges for garnish

1. TO PREPARE OLIVE RELISH: Combine parsley, olives, celery, garlic, oregano, lemon juice, oil, salt and pepper in a small bowl.

2. TO GRILL TUNA: Preheat grill to medium-high.

3. Rub tuna all over with oil and season with salt and pepper. Grill the tuna until seared on both sides and just cooked through, about 4 minutes per side. Serve with Olive Relish and lemon wedges.

MAKES 6 SERVINGS.

FILLET OF SOLE WITH SPINACH & TOMATOES

A number of flatfish are marketed as sole or flounder. Eco-friendly choices include U.S. and Canadian Pacific-caught English, Dover and petrale sole as well as sand dabs and flounder, according to the Monterey Bay Aquarium's Seafood Watch program. Pacific halibut is a good option if you can't find Pacific sole or flounder.

- 12 **cups spinach (1¼ pounds), trimmed and washed thoroughly**
- 2 **cloves garlic, minced**
- ¼ **teaspoon salt**
  Freshly ground pepper to taste
- 1 **pound Pacific sole fillets, divided into 4 portions**
- 4 **small plum tomatoes, sliced**

1. Preheat oven to 400°F.

2. Put spinach, with water still clinging to its leaves, into a large pot. Cover; steam the spinach over medium-high heat, stirring occasionally, until just wilted, about 5 minutes. Drain; when cool enough to handle, press out excess liquid. Chop and place in a small bowl. Stir in garlic. Season with salt and pepper.

3. To make a packet, lay two 20-inch sheets of foil on top of each other (the double layers will help protect the contents from burning); generously coat the top piece with cooking spray. Place one-quarter of the spinach mixture in the center of the foil. Lay a portion of sole over the spinach and arrange tomato slices over the sole. Season with salt and pepper.

4. Bring the short ends of the foil together, leaving enough room in the packet for steam to gather and cook the food. Fold the foil over and pinch to seal. Pinch seams together along the sides. Make sure all the seams are tightly sealed to keep steam from escaping. Repeat with more foil, cooking spray and the remaining ingredients.

5. Place the packets on a baking sheet. Bake the packets until the fish is cooked through and the vegetables are just tender, 10 to 12 minutes. To serve, carefully open both ends of the packets and allow the steam to escape. Use a spatula to slide the contents onto plates.

MAKES 4 SERVINGS.

PER SERVING:

138 calories;

2 g fat (0 g sat, 0 g mono);

53 mg cholesterol; 8 g carbohydrate;

24 g protein; 4 g fiber; 343 mg sodium;

1,213 mg potassium.

NUTRITION BONUS: Vitamin A (280% DAILY VALUE), Vitamin C (80% DV), Folate (73% DV), Potassium (35% DV), Iron (25% DV), Calcium (15% DV).

Healthy ⬥ Weight

Lower ⬇ Carbs

ACTIVE TIME: 30 MINUTES

TOTAL: 40 MINUTES

♥ **HEART-HEALTHY TIP**

Spinach is an excellent source of folic acid, which helps break down homocysteine, an amino acid in the blood that can harm the cells that line the heart and blood vessels.

181 calories;

7 g fat (1 g sat, 4 g mono);

57 mg cholesterol; 8 g carbohydrate;

24 g protein; 2 g fiber; 435 mg sodium;

591 mg potassium.

NUTRITION BONUS: Selenium (68% DAILY VALUE), Vitamin C (30% DV), Potassium (17% DV).

Healthy ⊬ Weight

Lower ⬇ Carbs

ACTIVE TIME: 35 MINUTES

TOTAL: 35 MINUTES

OVEN VARIATION:

Preheat oven to 425°F. Place green beans in a microwavable bowl with 1 tablespoon water. Cover and microwave on High until the beans are just beginning to cook, about 30 seconds. Drain and add to the other vegetables (Step 2). Assemble packets (Steps 3-4). Bake the packets directly on an oven rack until the tilapia is cooked through and the vegetables are just tender, about 20 minutes.

TILAPIA & SUMMER VEGETABLE PACKETS

Wrapping vegetables and fish in a foil packet for grilling or baking is a foolproof way to get moist, tender results. Tilapia and summer vegetables pair with olives and capers for a Mediterranean flair.

- 1 cup quartered cherry or grape tomatoes
- 1 cup diced summer squash
- 1 cup thinly sliced red onion
- 12 green beans, trimmed and cut into 1-inch pieces
- ¼ cup pitted and coarsely chopped black olives
- 2 tablespoons lemon juice
- 1 tablespoon chopped fresh oregano
- 1 tablespoon extra-virgin olive oil
- 1 teaspoon capers, rinsed
- ½ teaspoon salt, divided
- ½ teaspoon freshly ground pepper, divided
- 1 pound tilapia fillets, cut into 4 equal portions

1. Preheat grill to medium. (*No grill? See Oven Variation.*)

2. Combine tomatoes, squash, onion, green beans, olives, lemon juice, oregano, oil, capers, ¼ teaspoon salt and ¼ teaspoon pepper in a large bowl.

3. To make a packet, lay two 20-inch sheets of foil on top of each other (the double layers will help protect the contents from burning); generously coat the top piece with cooking spray. Place one portion of tilapia in the center of the foil. Sprinkle with some of the remaining ¼ teaspoon salt and pepper, then top with about ¾ cup of the vegetable mixture.

4. Bring the short ends of the foil together, leaving enough room in the packet for steam to gather and cook the food. Fold the foil over and pinch to seal. Pinch seams together along the sides. Make sure all the seams are tightly sealed to keep steam from escaping. Repeat with more foil, cooking spray and the remaining fish, salt, pepper and vegetables.

5. Grill the packets until the fish is cooked through and the vegetables are just tender, about 5 minutes. To serve, carefully open both ends of the packets and allow the steam to escape. Use a spatula to slide the contents onto plates.

MAKES 4 SERVINGS.

TILAPIA CEVICHE

U.S. farmed tilapia provides a heart-healthy lean source of protein, it's a good choice from an environmental perspective and it's relatively inexpensive. Traditionally, ceviche is raw fish that's "cooked" by marinating it in citrus juice. In this version we quickly poach tilapia then marinate it with fresh herbs, lime juice and crunchy vegetables for an easy dinner. Serve it with warm corn tortillas.

1	pound tilapia fillets, cut into 2-inch pieces
1-2	jalapeño peppers, minced
½	cup lime juice
½	cup chopped fresh cilantro, divided
1	teaspoon chopped fresh oregano
¼	teaspoon salt
1	large green bell pepper, halved crosswise and thinly sliced
1	large tomato, chopped
½	cup very thinly sliced white onion
¼	cup quartered green olives
1	avocado, chopped

1. Place tilapia in a medium skillet. Cover with water. Bring to a boil over high heat, remove from the heat, cover and let stand for 5 minutes.
2. Meanwhile, place jalapeño(s) to taste in a small bowl and whisk in lime juice, 2 tablespoons cilantro, oregano and salt. Transfer the tilapia to a large, shallow, nonreactive dish with a slotted spoon and pour the lime juice mixture over the top. Add bell pepper, tomato, onion and olives; gently mix to combine. (It's OK if the tilapia breaks apart.) Cover and chill for at least 20 minutes.
3. Sprinkle with the remaining cilantro and avocado just before serving.

MAKES 4 SERVINGS, ABOUT 1½ CUPS EACH.

PER SERVING:

236 calories;

11 g fat (**2** g sat, 7 g mono);

57 mg cholesterol; 13 g carbohydrate;

25 g protein; 5 g fiber; 378 mg sodium;

831 mg potassium.

NUTRITION BONUS: Vitamin C (80% DAILY VALUE), Potassium (24% DV), Folate (22% DV), Vitamin A (15% DV).

Healthy ⚖ Weight

Lower ⬇ Carbs

High ⬆ Fiber

ACTIVE TIME: 20 MINUTES

TOTAL: 40 MINUTES

TO MAKE AHEAD: Store in an airtight container in the refrigerator for up to 2 hours.

♥**HEART-HEALTHY TIP**

Avocados boast heart-healthy mono- and poly-unsaturated fats as well as beta-sitosterol, a natural plant sterol that may help maintain healthy cholesterol levels.

175 calories;

5 g fat (1 g sat, 3 g mono);

54 mg cholesterol; 9 g carbohydrate;

23 g protein; 0 g fiber; 383 mg sodium;

421 mg potassium.

NUTRITION BONUS: Selenium (53% DAILY VALUE).

━━━━━━━━━━━━━━━━━━━

Healthy ⚖ Weight

Lower ⬇ Carbs

ACTIVE TIME: 15 MINUTES

TOTAL: 15 MINUTES

EASY SAUTEED FISH FILLETS

Here's an easy method for quickly cooking fish fillets. Pair them with prepared sauces like pesto or salsa or make your own creation like Avocado-Corn Salsa (below) or Fresh Tomato & Herb Sauce (page 229).

- 1/3 **cup all-purpose flour**
- 1/2 **teaspoon salt**
  Freshly ground pepper to taste
- 1 **pound sole, haddock *or* other white fish fillets, cut into 4 portions**
- 1 **tablespoon extra-virgin olive oil**

1. Combine flour, salt and pepper in a shallow dish; thoroughly dredge fillets (discard any leftover flour).
2. Heat oil in a large nonstick skillet over medium-high heat. Add the fish, working in batches if necessary, and cook until lightly browned and just opaque in the center, 3 to 4 minutes per side. Serve immediately.

MAKES 4 SERVINGS.

PER SERVING:

101 calories;

7 g fat (1 g sat, 4 g mono);

0 mg cholesterol; 11 g carbohydrate;

2 g protein; 4 g fiber; 75 mg sodium;

339 mg potassium.

━━━━━━━━━━━━━━━━━━━

ACTIVE TIME: 10 MINUTES

TOTAL: 10 MINUTES

AVOCADO-CORN SALSA

This fresh salsa is great with simple sautéed fish or serve it with just about anything Mexican inspired—huevos rancheros, a quick quesadilla or atop rice and beans.

- 1 **medium avocado, diced**
- 3/4 **cup frozen corn, thawed**
- 1/2 **cup quartered grape tomatoes**
- 1 **tablespoon chopped fresh cilantro**
- 2 **teaspoons lime juice**
- 1/4 **teaspoon kosher salt**

Toss avocado, corn, tomatoes, cilantro, lime juice and salt in a medium bowl.

MAKES 4 SERVINGS.

QUICK CAJUN CATFISH

The catfish-farming industry has grown in the U.S. and the quality of the fish has improved. Farmers raise catfish sustainably in closed pens and feed them a mostly vegetarian diet. If you're wary of fish but enjoy bold flavors, this is a good recipe to help you get more heart-healthy fish into your diet.

- ¼ **cup nonfat buttermilk**
- 2 **teaspoons Dijon mustard**
- ½ **cup cornmeal**
- 1 **teaspoon salt**
- 1 **teaspoon paprika**
- 1 **teaspoon onion powder**
- ½ **teaspoon garlic powder**
- ½ **teaspoon dried thyme**
- ½ **teaspoon cayenne pepper**
- ½ **teaspoon freshly ground pepper**
- 4 **catfish fillets (1¼ pounds)**
- 4 **lemon wedges**

1. Preheat broiler. Lightly oil a wire rack large enough to hold fish in a single layer. Place the rack on a baking sheet.

2. Whisk buttermilk and mustard in a medium bowl until smooth. Combine cornmeal, salt and paprika, onion powder, garlic powder, thyme, cayenne pepper and black pepper in a shallow dish. Dip each fillet in the buttermilk mixture, turning to coat. Transfer to the cornmeal mixture, turning to coat completely. Place the fillets on the prepared rack; they should not touch.

3. Broil 4 inches from the heat source until the fish is opaque in the center, about 3 minutes per side. Serve hot with lemon wedges.

MAKES 4 SERVINGS.

PER SERVING:

239 calories;

11 g fat (3 g sat, 5 g mono);

67 mg cholesterol; 10 g carbohydrate;

24 g protein; 1 g fiber; 546 mg sodium;

452 mg potassium.

NUTRITION BONUS: Selenium (25% DAILY VALUE).

Healthy ⨝ Weight

Lower ⬇ Carbs

ACTIVE TIME: 20 MINUTES

TOTAL: 20 MINUTES

Maple-Mustard Pork Tenderloin

Filet Mignon with Blueberry-Bourbon Barbecue Sauce

Louisiana Red Beans & Rice

Oven-Barbecued Pork Chops

BEEF & PORK

MAKEOVER: Hamburger Buddy 204

MAKEOVER: The EatingWell Taco 206

MAKEOVER: EatingWell's
Chicken-Fried Steak 208

Brazilian Grilled Flank Steak 210

Bistro Beef Tenderloin 211

Filet Mignon with Blueberry-Bourbon
Barbecue Sauce 212

Oven-Barbecued Pork Chops.................215

Tangelo Pork Stir-Fry.............................216

Maple-Mustard Pork Tenderloin.............218

Roast Pork with Sweet Onion-
Rhubarb Sauce 221

Pork Medallions with Prune-
Ginger Sauce 222

Louisiana Red Beans & Rice..................223

Ham & Swiss Rösti.................................225

Additional beef recipe:

MAKEOVER: Blue Ribbon Meatloaf..82

"If God did not intend for us to eat animals, then why
did he make them out of meat?"

JOHN CLEESE

	EatingWell's Hamburger Buddy	Hamburger "Helper" Stroganoff
Calories	297	320
Fat	7 g	14 g
Saturated Fat	3 g	5 g
Sodium	442 mg	670 mg
Fiber	4 g	1 g

We chop vegetables in a food processor to sneak them into this take on the classic Hamburger Helper. With more vegetables we are able to use less beef and get a serving that's one-third larger than the original, with less fat and saturated fat.

Replacing regular white noodles with whole-wheat noodles, along with adding vegetables, quadruples the fiber. Plus you squeeze in a serving of vegetables.

HAMBURGER BUDDY

Much better for you than the convenience meals that inspired it, this one-skillet supper is loaded with vegetables but, thanks to a quick spin in the food processor, picky eaters will hardly notice them. Round out the meal with a crisp green salad.

- 3 **cloves garlic, crushed and peeled**
- 2 **medium carrots, cut into 2-inch pieces**
- 10 **ounces white mushrooms, large ones cut in half**
- 1 **large onion, cut into 2-inch pieces**
- 1 **pound 93%-lean ground beef**
- 2 **teaspoons dried thyme**
- 3/4 **teaspoon salt**
- 1/4 **teaspoon freshly ground pepper**
- 2 **cups water**
- 1 **14-ounce can reduced-sodium beef broth, divided**
- 8 **ounces whole-wheat elbow noodles (2 cups)**
- 2 **tablespoons Worcestershire sauce**
- 2 **tablespoons all-purpose flour**
- 1/3 **cup reduced-fat sour cream**
- 1 **tablespoon chopped fresh parsley or chives for garnish**

1. Fit a food processor with the steel blade attachment. With the motor running, drop garlic through the feed tube and process until minced, then add carrots and mushrooms and process until finely chopped. Turn it off, add onion, and pulse until roughly chopped.

2. Cook beef in a large straight-sided skillet or Dutch oven over medium-high heat, breaking it up with a wooden spoon, until no longer pink, 3 to 5 minutes. Stir in the chopped vegetables, thyme, salt and pepper and cook, stirring often, until the vegetables start to soften and the mushrooms release their juices, 5 to 7 minutes.

3. Stir in water, 1½ cups broth, noodles and Worcestershire sauce; bring to a boil. Cover, reduce heat to medium and cook, stirring occasionally, until the pasta is tender, 8 to 10 minutes.

4. Whisk flour with the remaining ¼ cup broth in a small bowl until smooth; stir into the hamburger mixture. Stir in the sour cream. Simmer, stirring often, until the sauce is thickened, about 2 minutes. Serve sprinkled with parsley (or chives).

MAKES 6 SERVINGS, ABOUT 1⅓ CUPS EACH.

PER SERVING:

297 calories;

7 g fat (3 g sat, 2 g mono);

48 mg cholesterol; 38 g carbohydrate;

24 g protein; 4 g fiber; 442 mg sodium;

483 mg potassium.

NUTRITION BONUS: Vitamin A (70% DAILY VALUE), Zinc (33% DV), Iron (20% DV).

Healthy ⚖ Weight

ACTIVE TIME: 40 MINUTES

TOTAL: 40 MINUTES

	The EatingWell Taco	Traditional Taco
Calories	**261**	**340**
Fat	**5 g**	**19 g**
Saturated Fat	**1 g**	**7 g**
Sodium	**582 mg**	**710 mg**
Fiber	**5 g**	**5 g**

To "oven fry" the taco shells we spray them with cooking spray then bake them until they're crisp. We use this technique instead of deep-frying to reduce fat and saturated fat. Also, we avoid the trans fats found in most store-bought brands of taco shells.

Using lean ground beef and turkey cuts out much of the fat and saturated fat.

Adding vegetables in place of extra meat and cheese helps keep calories and saturated fat down.

THE EATINGWELL TACO

This is like the tacos with crispy shells and ground beef that many Americans were first introduced to. Try with Tomato Salsa (page 229).

CRISPY TACO SHELLS
- **12 6-inch corn tortillas**
-    **Canola oil cooking spray**
- **³/₄ teaspoon chili powder, divided**
- **¹/₄ teaspoon salt, divided**

LEAN & SPICY TACO MEAT
- **8 ounces 93%-lean ground beef**
- **8 ounces 99%-lean ground turkey breast**
- **¹/₂ cup chopped onion**
- **1 10-ounce can diced tomatoes with green chiles, preferably Rotel, or 1¹/₄ cups petite-diced tomatoes**
- **¹/₂ teaspoon ground cumin**
- **¹/₂ teaspoon ground chipotle chile *or* 1 teaspoon chili powder (see *Note, page 244*)**
- **¹/₂ teaspoon dried oregano**

TOPPINGS
- **3 cups shredded romaine lettuce**
- **³/₄ cup shredded reduced-fat Cheddar cheese**
- **³/₄ cup diced tomatoes**
- **³/₄ cup prepared salsa**
- **¹/₄ cup diced red onion**

1. TO PREPARE TACO SHELLS: Preheat oven to 375°F.

2. Wrap 4 tortillas in a barely damp cloth or paper towel and microwave on High until steamed, about 30 seconds. (*Alternatively, wrap in foil and heat in the preheated oven until steaming, 5 to 7 minutes.*) Coat both sides with cooking spray; sprinkle a little chili powder and salt on one side.

3. Drape each tortilla over a panel on a baked-taco rack and bake until crispy and brown, 7 to 10 minutes. (*Or see Tip, page 244.*)

4. Remove the shells from the rack and repeat Steps 2 and 3 with the remaining 8 tortillas.

5. TO PREPARE TACO MEAT: Place beef, turkey and onion in a large nonstick skillet over medium heat. Cook, breaking up the meat with a wooden spoon, until cooked through, about 10 minutes. Transfer to a colander to drain off fat. Wipe out the pan. Return the meat to the pan and add tomatoes, cumin, ground chipotle (or chili powder) and oregano. Cook over medium heat, stirring occasionally, until most of the liquid has evaporated, 3 to 6 minutes.

6. TO ASSEMBLE: Fill each taco shell with (in any order): a generous 3 tablespoons taco meat, ¼ cup lettuce, 1 tablespoon cheese, 1 tablespoon tomato, 1 tablespoon salsa, 1 teaspoon onion.

MAKES 6 SERVINGS, 2 FILLED TACOS EACH.

PER SERVING:

261 calories;

5 g fat (**1** g sat, 1 g mono);

38 mg cholesterol; 31 g carbohydrate;

24 g protein; 5 g fiber; 582 mg sodium;

272 mg potassium.

NUTRITION BONUS: Vitamin A (40% DAILY VALUE), Vitamin C (25% DV), Zinc (17% DV), Iron (15% DV).

=====

Healthy ⚖ Weight

High ⬆ Fiber

ACTIVE TIME: 50 MINUTES

TOTAL: 50 MINUTES

TO MAKE AHEAD: Store taco shells in an airtight container for up to 2 days. Reheat at 375°F for 1 to 2 minutes before serving. Refrigerate taco meat in an airtight container for up to 1 day. Reheat just before serving.

EQUIPMENT: Baked-taco rack (*or see Tip, page 244*)

	EatingWell's Chicken-Fried Steak	Traditional Chicken-Fried Steak
Calories	316	817
Fat	13 g	44 g
Saturated Fat	3 g	12 g
Sodium	312 mg	1,124 mg
Fiber	1 g	2 g

We start the steak on the stovetop and finish it in the oven. This gives it a crispy, delicious texture without frying and eliminates a significant amount of calories and fat.

Instead of using white crackers as part of the crispy outer crust, we use a combination of whole-wheat flour and yellow cornmeal, which has significantly less sodium.

Using egg whites instead of whole eggs cuts down on total fat, saturated fat and calories.

Opt for reduced-sodium beef broth rather than regular beef broth to reduce sodium.

Most gravy recipes rely on heavy cream for a rich, full flavor and velvety texture. We use a combination of cornstarch and a small amount of half-and-half. This leaves us with a similar richness and creamy mouthfeel, while keeping the total fat, saturated fat and calorie levels in check.

EATINGWELL'S CHICKEN-FRIED STEAK

This American classic is named for its similarity in technique to fried chicken. We skip the deep frying, but with rich country gravy as consolation, you won't miss it. Serve with steamed carrots and a green salad.

- ¼ cup all-purpose flour
- 2 egg whites, lightly beaten
- ¼ cup cornmeal
- ¼ cup whole-wheat flour
- ¼ cup plus 1 tablespoon cornstarch, divided
- 1 teaspoon paprika
- 1 pound cube steak, cut into 4 portions
- ¾ teaspoon kosher salt
- ½ teaspoon freshly ground pepper
- 2 tablespoons canola oil, divided
- 1 14-ounce can reduced-sodium beef broth
- 1 tablespoon water
- ¼ cup half-and-half

1. Preheat oven to 350°F. Coat a baking sheet with cooking spray.

2. Place all-purpose flour on a large plate. Place egg whites in a shallow dish. Whisk cornmeal, whole-wheat flour, ¼ cup cornstarch and paprika in another shallow dish. Season both sides of steak with ½ teaspoon each salt and pepper. Dredge the steak in the flour, shaking off excess; dip in the egg whites, then dredge in the cornmeal mixture.

3. Heat 1 tablespoon oil in a large nonstick skillet over medium-high heat. Reduce heat to medium and add 2 pieces of the steak; cook until browned on both sides, turning once, 3 to 5 minutes total. Transfer the steak to the prepared baking sheet and repeat with the remaining 1 tablespoon oil and 2 pieces of steak. Transfer the baking sheet to the oven and bake until cooked through, about 10 minutes.

4. Meanwhile, add broth to the pan and boil over medium-high heat, stirring occasionally, until reduced to about 1 cup, 3 to 5 minutes. Whisk water and the remaining 1 tablespoon cornstarch until smooth. Remove the pan from the heat and stir in the cornstarch mixture. Return to the heat and cook, stirring, until thickened, 1 to 2 minutes. Stir in half-and-half; season with the remaining ¼ teaspoon salt and pepper. Serve the steak topped with the gravy.

MAKES 4 SERVINGS.

PER SERVING:

316 calories;

13 g fat (3 g sat, 7 g mono);

57 mg cholesterol; 14 g carbohydrate;

33 g protein; 1 g fiber; 312 mg sodium;

379 mg potassium.

NUTRITION BONUS: Selenium (50% DAILY VALUE), Potassium & Zinc (15% DV).

Healthy Weight

Lower Carbs

ACTIVE TIME: 35 MINUTES

TOTAL: 35 MINUTES

215 calories;

8 g fat (3 g sat, 4 g mono);

37 mg cholesterol; 7 g carbohydrate;

29 g protein; 2 g fiber; 341 mg sodium;

627 mg potassium.

NUTRITION BONUS: Zinc (36% DAILY VALUE), Vitamin C (25% DV), Iron (20% DV), Potassium (18% DV), Vitamin A (15% DV).

Healthy ⚖ Weight

Lower ⬇ Carbs

ACTIVE TIME: 30 MINUTES

TOTAL: 30 MINUTES

BROILING VARIATION:

Instead of grilling, in Step 1 position oven rack 6 inches from the heat source and preheat broiler. In Step 4, cook steak on a broiler pan under the broiler until medium-rare, turning once, about 10 minutes total.

BRAZILIAN GRILLED FLANK STEAK

Barbecued meats (churrasco) *are served in* churrascarias, *Brazilian barbecued-meat restaurants, with a salsa-like sauce as an accompaniment. Since hearts of palm show up at every salad bar in these restaurants, we've added them to the sauce to give it a tasty twist.*

STEAK

- 6 cloves garlic, minced
- ½ small hot pepper, such as jalapeño *or* serrano, minced
- 2 teaspoons extra-virgin olive oil
- ¼ teaspoon kosher salt
- 2 pounds flank steak

SALSA

- 1 14-ounce can hearts of palm, drained, halved lengthwise and thinly sliced
- 4 medium tomatoes, chopped
- ½ cup chopped red onion
- ½ small hot chile, such as jalapeño *or* serrano, minced
- ¼ cup chopped fresh cilantro
- 2 tablespoons red-wine vinegar
- ¼ teaspoon kosher salt

1. Preheat grill to high (*see Broiling Variation*).

2. TO PREPARE STEAK: Combine garlic, hot pepper, oil and salt in a small bowl. Rub the mixture on both sides of steak.

3. TO PREPARE SALSA: Combine hearts of palm, tomatoes, onion, hot pepper, cilantro, vinegar and salt in a medium bowl.

4. Reduce grill heat to medium and grill the steak 4 to 6 minutes per side for medium-rare. Transfer to a cutting board, tent with foil and let rest for 5 minutes. Cut the steak across the grain into thin pieces. Serve with the salsa.

MAKE 8 SERVINGS.

BISTRO BEEF TENDERLOIN

Tenderloin is one of the leanest cuts of beef, so it can certainly be part of a heart-healthy diet. It's fantastic for a dinner party, and leftovers the next day are pure heaven. Trim off any visible silver skin—the translucent, tough membrane lying along the outside curve of the tenderloin.

- **1 3-pound beef tenderloin, trimmed**
- **2 tablespoons extra-virgin olive oil**
- **1 teaspoon kosher salt**
- **1/2 teaspoon freshly ground pepper**
- **2/3 cup chopped mixed fresh herbs, such as chives, parsley, chervil, tarragon, thyme**
- **2 tablespoons Dijon mustard**

1. Preheat oven to 400°F.

2. Tie kitchen string around tenderloin in three places so it doesn't flatten while roasting. Rub the tenderloin with oil; pat on salt and pepper. Place in a large roasting pan.

3. Roast until a thermometer inserted into the thickest part of the tenderloin registers 140°F (*see Note*) for medium-rare, about 45 minutes, turning two or three times during roasting to ensure even cooking. Transfer to a cutting board; let rest for 10 minutes. Remove the string.

4. Place herbs on a large plate. Coat the tenderloin evenly with mustard; then roll in the herbs, pressing gently to adhere. Slice and serve.

MAKES ABOUT 12 SERVINGS.

PER 3-OZ. SERVING:

185 calories;

9 g fat (3 g sat, 4 g mono);

67 mg cholesterol; 1 g carbohydrate;

24 g protein; 0 g fiber; 178 mg sodium;

325 mg potassium.

NUTRITION BONUS: Selenium (40% DAILY VALUE), Zinc (30% DV).

Healthy ⬥ Weight

Lower ⬇ Carbs

ACTIVE TIME: 25 MINUTES

TOTAL: 1 HOUR 10 MINUTES

EQUIPMENT: Kitchen string

NOTE:

The internal temperature of roasted meat rises as it rests—how much depends on the size of the meat, how long it rests and the temperature at which it was cooking. Our rule of thumb is that the internal temperature will rise 5° to 10° per 10 minutes of resting.

309 calories;

12 g fat (3 g sat, 6 g mono);

67 mg cholesterol; 16 g carbohydrate;

25 g protein; 1 g fiber; 430 mg sodium;

462 mg potassium.

NUTRITION BONUS: Selenium (40% DAILY VALUE), Zinc (30% DV), Vitamin C (15% DV).

Healthy ⋈ Weight

Lower ⬇ Carbs

ACTIVE TIME: 45 MINUTES

TOTAL: 45 MINUTES

♥ HEART-HEALTHY TIP

Blueberries contain fiber and anthocyanin, a compound with strong antioxidant and anti-inflammatory properties.

FILET MIGNON WITH BLUEBERRY-BOURBON BARBECUE SAUCE

Blueberries, loaded with antioxidants, have a balance of sweet and sour, which makes them an excellent base for a rich, tangy barbecue sauce. Fresh thyme rubbed on the steak dovetails wonderfully with the blueberries. Serve with fresh tomato wedges.

BLUEBERRY-BOURBON BARBECUE SAUCE

- 1½ teaspoons canola oil
- ½ small red onion, chopped
- 2 cloves garlic, chopped
- 1 jalapeño pepper, seeded and chopped
- ¼ cup bourbon
- 1 cup fresh *or* frozen (*not* thawed) blueberries
- ¼ cup ketchup
- 3 tablespoons cider vinegar
- 1 tablespoon brown sugar
- 1½ teaspoons molasses
- Pinch of ground allspice

FILET MIGNON

- 1 tablespoon chopped fresh thyme
- 1 tablespoon extra-virgin olive oil
- ¾ teaspoon kosher salt
- ½ teaspoon coarsely ground pepper
- 1 pound filet mignon, 1½ to 2 inches thick, trimmed and cut into 4 portions

1. TO PREPARE SAUCE: Heat oil in a small saucepan over medium heat. Add onion and cook, stirring occasionally, until tender and just starting to brown, 2 to 4 minutes. Add garlic and jalapeño and cook, stirring, until fragrant, about 30 seconds. Add bourbon, increase heat to high and bring to a boil; cook until most of the liquid has evaporated, 2 to 5 minutes. Stir in blueberries, ketchup, vinegar, brown sugar, molasses and allspice; return to a boil. Reduce the heat and simmer, stirring occasionally, until thickened, 15 to 20 minutes.

2. Preheat grill to high.

3. Combine thyme, oil, salt and pepper in a small bowl. Rub the mixture on all sides of steaks. Grill the steaks 3 to 5 minutes per side for medium-rare. Let the steaks rest for 5 minutes before serving with the sauce.

MAKES 4 SERVINGS.

OVEN-BARBECUED PORK CHOPS

Try this swift recipe and enjoy a "barbecue" indoors. Serve with Savoy Cabbage Slaw (page 228) and cornbread.

1½-1¾ **pounds bone-in, ¾-inch-thick pork rib chops, trimmed**
  ¼ **teaspoon salt**
  ¼ **teaspoon freshly ground pepper**
  3 **teaspoons canola oil, divided**
  1 **medium onion, diced**
  1 **clove garlic, minced**
  ⅓ **cup orange juice**
  ½ **cup barbecue sauce (see *Tip*)**

1. Preheat oven to 400°F.

2. Sprinkle pork chops with salt and pepper. Heat 2 teaspoons oil in a large ovenproof skillet over high heat. Add the pork chops and cook until beginning to brown, 1 to 2 minutes per side. Transfer to a plate.

3. Add the remaining 1 teaspoon oil to the pan. Add onion and cook, stirring, until softened, 3 to 4 minutes. Stir in garlic and cook, stirring, until fragrant, 30 seconds. Add orange juice and cook until most of the liquid has evaporated, 30 seconds to 1 minute. Stir in barbecue sauce. Return the pork chops to the pan, turning several times to coat with the sauce.

4. Transfer the pan to the oven and bake until the pork chops are barely pink in the middle and an instant-read thermometer registers 145°F, 6 to 10 minutes. Serve the sauce over the pork chops.

MAKES 4 SERVINGS.

PER SERVING:

270 calories;

10 g fat (**3** g sat, 5 g mono);

69 mg cholesterol; 17 g carbohydrate;

26 g protein; 1 g fiber; 547 mg sodium;

473 mg potassium.

NUTRITION BONUS: Selenium (57% DAILY VALUE), Vitamin C (25% DV).

Healthy ⟩⟨ Weight

Lower ⬇ Carbs

ACTIVE TIME: 20 MINUTES

TOTAL: 30 MINUTES

SHOPPING TIP:

Check the sodium content of your favorite barbecue sauce—some can be quite high. This recipe was developed with Annie's Natural Hot Chipotle BBQ Sauce, which has only 240 mg sodium per 2-tablespoon serving.

PER SERVING:

226 calories;

8 g fat (2 g sat, 3 g mono);

63 mg cholesterol; 16 g carbohydrate;

25 g protein; 3 g fiber; 329 mg sodium;

562 mg potassium.

NUTRITION BONUS: Vitamin C (220% DAILY VALUE), Selenium (56% DV), Vitamin A (40% DV), Potassium (16% DV), Zinc (15% DV).

Healthy ✕ Weight

Lower ⬇ Carbs

ACTIVE TIME: 45 MINUTES

TOTAL: 45 MINUTES

TANGELO PORK STIR-FRY

This stir-fry is complex with strips of tangelo zest and bright tangelo juice, a little sunshine on a midwinter night. Tangelos, hybrids of tangerines and pummelos (or grapefruit), are often labeled as Minneolas or Honeybells.

- 2 **tangelos, such as Minneolas or Honeybells**
- 3 **teaspoons toasted sesame oil, divided**
- 1 **pound pork tenderloin, trimmed and cut into thin strips**
- 2 **medium shallots, thinly sliced**
- 2 **cloves garlic, minced**
- 2 **tablespoons minced fresh ginger**
- ¼ **teaspoon crushed red pepper**
- 2 **red bell peppers, thinly sliced**
- 2 **stalks celery, thinly sliced**
- 2 **tablespoons reduced-sodium soy sauce**
- 1 **tablespoon rice vinegar**
- 2 **teaspoons cornstarch**

1. Using a vegetable peeler, remove zest from tangelos in long strips. Cut the strips lengthwise into very thin pieces. Cut the tangelos in half and squeeze enough juice from them to get ½ cup.

2. Heat a large wok or skillet over medium-high heat. Swirl in 2 teaspoons oil, then add pork and cook, stirring, until just cooked, 2 to 3 minutes. Transfer to a plate.

3. Add the remaining 1 teaspoon oil to the pan along with shallots, garlic, ginger, crushed red pepper and the zest. Cook, stirring, for 1 minute. Add bell peppers and celery and cook, stirring constantly, until crisp-tender, about 2 minutes. Stir in the tangelo juice and soy sauce; bring to a simmer. Cook for 1 minute.

4. Whisk vinegar and cornstarch in a small bowl, then pour it into the pan along with the pork and its juices. Cook, stirring often, until thickened and bubbling and the pork is heated through, about 1 minute.

MAKES 4 SERVINGS, ABOUT 1¼ CUPS EACH.

225 calories;

7 g fat (2 g sat, 3 g mono);

78 mg cholesterol; 9 g carbohydrate;

28 g protein; 0 g fiber; 479 mg sodium;

489 mg potassium.

NUTRITION BONUS: Selenium (68% DAILY VALUE), Zinc (21% DV).

Healthy)(Weight

Lower ⬇ Carbs

ACTIVE TIME: 30 MINUTES

TOTAL: 45 MINUTES

MAPLE-MUSTARD PORK TENDERLOIN

Pork tenderloin is about as lean as it comes so it's a great healthy option, but it shouldn't be overcooked as it can dry out. This sweet-and-savory mahogany-colored sauce has a delicate note of sage that gives it a wintery touch. Fresh thyme or rosemary also work if you prefer. Serve with barley, roasted squash and a Pinot Noir.

3	tablespoons Dijon mustard, divided
1/2	teaspoon kosher salt
1/2	teaspoon freshly ground pepper
1	pound pork tenderloin, trimmed
2	teaspoons canola oil
1/4	cup cider vinegar
2	tablespoons maple syrup
1 1/2	teaspoons chopped fresh sage

1. Preheat oven to 425°F.

2. Combine 1 tablespoon mustard, salt and pepper in a small bowl; rub all over pork. Heat oil in a large ovenproof skillet over medium-high heat. Add pork and brown on all sides, 3 to 5 minutes. Transfer the pan to the oven and roast until an instant-read thermometer inserted in the center registers 145°F, about 15 minutes. Transfer to a cutting board and let rest for 5 minutes.

3. Place the skillet over medium-high heat (take care, the handle will still be hot), add vinegar, and boil, scraping up any browned bits with a wooden spoon, about 30 seconds. Whisk in maple syrup and the remaining 2 tablespoons mustard; bring to a boil, reduce heat to a simmer and cook until the sauce is thickened, about 5 minutes.

4. Slice the pork. Add any accumulated juices to the sauce along with sage. Serve the pork topped with the sauce.

MAKES 4 SERVINGS.

ROAST PORK WITH SWEET ONION-RHUBARB SAUCE

Tart rhubarb, which contains vitamin C and fiber, is a natural complement to pork. If you can't find fresh rhubarb for this, use frozen (no need to thaw it first). For dinner in a hurry, try two quick sides like whole-wheat couscous and steamed broccoli.

4	teaspoons extra-virgin olive oil, divided
1½	teaspoons ground coriander
1	teaspoon kosher salt, divided
¼	teaspoon freshly ground pepper
1-1¼	pounds pork tenderloin, trimmed
1	large sweet onion, sliced
2-4	tablespoons water
2	cups diced rhubarb
¼	cup red-wine vinegar
¼	cup brown sugar
¼	cup minced fresh chives

1. Preheat oven to 450°F.

2. Mix 1 teaspoon oil, coriander, ½ teaspoon salt and pepper in a small bowl. Rub the mixture into pork. Heat 1 teaspoon oil in a large oven-proof skillet over medium-high heat. Add the pork and cook, turning occasionally, until brown on all sides, 5 to 7 minutes. Transfer the pan to the oven and roast the pork until an instant-read thermometer registers 145°F, 15 to 17 minutes. Let rest 5 minutes before slicing.

3. Meanwhile, heat the remaining 2 teaspoons oil in a large nonstick skillet over medium heat. Add onion and the remaining ½ teaspoon salt; cook, stirring occasionally, until browned, 7 to 8 minutes. Add 2 tablespoons water; continue cooking, stirring often, until the onion is soft, 5 to 7 minutes more, adding water a tablespoon at a time if necessary to prevent burning. Stir in rhubarb, vinegar and brown sugar and cook, stirring often, until the rhubarb has broken down, about 5 minutes. Spoon the sauce over the sliced pork and sprinkle with chives.

MAKES 4 SERVINGS.

PER SERVING:

261 calories;

8 g fat (2 g sat, 5 g mono);

68 mg cholesterol; 23 g carbohydrate;

23 g protein; 2 g fiber; 348 mg sodium;

715 mg potassium.

NUTRITION BONUS: Selenium (45% DAILY VALUE), Potassium & Vitamin C (20% DV), Zinc (16% DV).

Healthy ⅜ Weight

ACTIVE TIME: 35 MINUTES

TOTAL: 40 MINUTES

♥ HEART-HEALTHY TIP

Prunes are a good source of soluble fiber, which binds to fatty substances and helps remove them from the body, thereby lowering cholesterol.

PORK MEDALLIONS WITH PRUNE-GINGER SAUCE

Prunes, ginger and curry make an exotic spicy sweet sauce for pork tenderloin. Look for a spicy version of ginger beer—it gives the most nuanced flavor to this recipe. Prunes contain pectin, a type of soluble fiber, which is important for heart health. Serve with rice pilaf and roasted green beans.

- **2** tablespoons all-purpose flour
- **3** teaspoons curry powder, preferably hot Madras (see Note, page 245), divided
- **½** teaspoon salt
  Pinch of cayenne pepper
- **1** pound pork tenderloin, trimmed and cut into 12 medallions
- **3** teaspoons extra-virgin olive oil, divided
- **1** clove garlic, minced
- **1** 1½-inch piece fresh ginger, peeled and cut into fine julienne
- **1¼** cups ginger beer *or* ginger ale
- **⅓** cup pitted prunes, quartered
- **¼** cup reduced-fat sour cream
  Freshly ground pepper to taste

1. Combine flour, 2½ teaspoons curry powder, salt and cayenne in a shallow pan. Dredge pork lightly in the flour mixture. (Discard any remaining flour mixture.)

2. Heat 1½ teaspoons oil in a large skillet over medium-high heat. Add pork and cook until golden outside and faintly pink inside, about 3 minutes per side. Transfer to a plate and tent with foil to keep warm.

3. Add the remaining 1½ teaspoons oil to the pan. Add garlic and ginger and cook, stirring, until fragrant, about 1 minute. Add ginger beer (or ginger ale), prunes and the remaining ½ teaspoon curry powder; bring to a boil, scraping up any browned bits. Reduce heat to medium and cook until the prunes are tender and the liquid is reduced by half, about 4 minutes. Remove from the heat and whisk in sour cream and any accumulated juices from the pork. Gently heat through. Season with salt and pepper.

4. Arrange the pork on plates and spoon the sauce over it. Serve immediately.

MAKES 4 SERVINGS.

LOUISIANA RED BEANS & RICE

This quick version of red beans and rice gets its smoky goodness from super-lean Canadian bacon and a hit of ground chipotle pepper. It's delicious as a leftover but will thicken as it stands. To keep it properly syrupy, just thin with a little water and reheat.

4¹/₃   cups water, divided
1¹/₂   cups brown basmati rice
¹/₂   teaspoon salt
1   tablespoon extra-virgin olive oil
1   cup diced onion
2   teaspoons minced garlic
2   15-ounce cans red kidney beans *or* pink beans, rinsed
6   ounces sliced Canadian bacon, chopped
¹/₂   cup chopped celery plus 1 tablespoon finely chopped celery leaves
¹/₂   cup diced green bell pepper
¹/₄-¹/₂   teaspoon ground chipotle pepper (see *Note, page 244*) *or* cayenne pepper

1. Combine 3⅓ cups water, rice and salt in a large saucepan. Bring to a simmer; reduce heat to low, cover and cook until all the water has been absorbed, about 45 minutes.

2. About 10 minutes before the rice is ready, heat oil in a large skillet over medium-high heat. Add onion and garlic and cook, stirring, until the onion is lightly colored and tender, about 3 minutes.

3. Place 1 cup beans in a small bowl and mash with a fork. Add the mashed and whole beans, the remaining 1 cup water, Canadian bacon, celery, celery leaves, bell pepper and ground chipotle (or cayenne) to taste to the skillet. Simmer, stirring occasionally, until the liquid has thickened into a gravy and the vegetables are crisp-tender, about 6 minutes. Serve in shallow bowls, spooned over the rice.

MAKES 6 SERVINGS, 1¹/₃ CUPS EACH.

PER SERVING:

342 calories;

5 g fat (1 g sat, 3 g mono);

14 mg cholesterol; 57 g carbohydrate;

17 g protein; 8 g fiber; 645 mg sodium;

196 mg potassium.

NUTRITION BONUS: Fiber (33% DAILY VALUE), Vitamin C (20% DV), Iron (15% DV).

Healthy ⊁ Weight

High ⬆ Fiber

ACTIVE TIME: 25 MINUTES

TOTAL: 50 MINUTES

> **♥ HEART-HEALTHY TIP**
>
> **Beans** (legumes) are an excellent source of soluble fiber, which helps lower heart disease risk by reducing the absorption of cholesterol in the bloodstream.

HAM & SWISS RÖSTI

Rösti is a traditional Swiss potato pancake typically served as a side dish but we added ham and cheese to transform it into an easy weeknight supper. Enjoy with steamed asparagus and chunky applesauce on the side.

- 1 **large egg**
- 1 **cup diced ham (about 5 ounces)**
- 1 **cup shredded part-skim Jarlsberg *or* Swiss cheese, divided**
- 1 **shallot, minced**
- 1 **teaspoon chopped fresh rosemary *or* ¼ teaspoon dried**
- ½ **teaspoon freshly ground pepper**
- ¼ **teaspoon salt**
- 4 **cups frozen hash brown potatoes**
- 2 **tablespoons extra-virgin olive oil, divided**

1. Beat egg in a large bowl. Stir in ham, ½ cup cheese, shallot, rosemary, pepper and salt. Add frozen potatoes and stir to combine.

2. Heat 1 tablespoon oil in a large nonstick skillet over medium heat. Pat the potato mixture into an even round in the pan. Cover and cook until browned and crispy on the bottom, 4 to 6 minutes.

3. Remove the pan from the heat. Place a rimless baking sheet on top. Wearing oven mitts, grasp the pan and baking sheet together and carefully invert, unmolding the rösti onto the baking sheet. Wipe out any browned bits from the pan. Return it to the heat and add the remaining 1 tablespoon oil. Slide the rösti back into the pan. Top with the remaining ½ cup cheese, cover and cook the second side until crispy and browned, 4 to 6 minutes. Slide onto a platter, cut into wedges and serve.

MAKES 4 SERVINGS.

PER SERVING:

262 calories;

13 g fat (3 g sat, 8 g mono);

94 mg cholesterol; 15 g carbohydrate;

21 g protein; 2 g fiber; 276 mg sodium;

174 mg potassium.

NUTRITION BONUS: Selenium (34% DAILY VALUE), Calcium (25% DV), Zinc (15% DV).

Healthy Weight

Lower Carbs

ACTIVE TIME: 25 MINUTES

TOTAL: 25 MINUTES

QUICK SIDES

Left to right: Cucumber & Black-Eyed Pea Salad, Creamed Corn, Brussels Sprouts with Walnut-Lemon Vinaigrette, Green Papaya Salad

SIDE SALADS
Arugula & Strawberry Salad 227
Baby Spinach Salad with Raspberry
    Vinaigrette...227
Cucumber & Black-Eyed Pea Salad 227
Curried Waldorf Salad...227
Green Papaya Salad..227
Red & White Salad...227
Romaine & Fresh Herb Salad 227
Savoy Cabbage Slaw 228
Snap Pea Salad with Radish & Lime..................228
Watercress & Pickled Ginger Salad....................228

SALAD DRESSINGS & SAUCES
Champagne Vinaigrette..228
Raspberry Vinaigrette 228
Homemade Buttermilk Mayonnaise...................228
Fresh Tomato & Herb Sauce 229
Tomato Salsa 229

BEANS & GRAINS
Chile-Spiced Black Beans 229
Caribbean Rice & Beans......................................229
15 ways to spice your brown rice 229
Rice & Peas with Feta 230

Parsley Tabbouleh..230

VEGETABLES
Roasted Asparagus with Caper Dressing...........230
Roasted Broccoli with Lemon 230
Brussels Sprouts with Walnut-Lemon
    Vinaigrette...230
Roasted Savoy Cabbage with Black Bean-
    Garlic Sauce 230
Chard with Pancetta & Walnuts 231
Creamed Corn 231
Green Bean & Cherry Tomato Sauté.................231
Indian-Style Green Beans....................................231
Kale with Apples & Mustard...............................231
Garlic-Rosemary Mushrooms.............................232
Sesame-Roasted Mushrooms
    & Scallions..232
New Potato & Pea Salad......................................232
Oven-Fried Potatoes 232
Roasted Snap Peas with Shallots........................232
Mexican Sautéed Summer Squash 232
Coconut Mashed Sweet Potatoes 233
Oven-Fried Zucchini Sticks................................233
Roasted Zucchini & Pesto...................................233

VEGETABLE-COOKING GUIDE 234   GRAIN-COOKING GUIDE 236

SIDE SALADS

ARUGULA & STRAWBERRY SALAD

Lower ⬇ Carbs

Put 4 cups baby arugula in a salad bowl. Add 2 cups sliced strawberries, ½ cup toasted chopped walnuts (*see Tip, page 244*), ¼ cup shaved and crumbled Parmesan cheese, ¼ teaspoon pepper and ⅛ teaspoon salt. Sprinkle 2 tablespoons aged balsamic vinegar and 1 tablespoon olive oil over the salad; toss gently.

MAKES 4 SERVINGS, 1½ CUPS EACH.

PER SERVING: 181 calories; 15 g fat (2 g sat, 4 g mono); 4 mg cholesterol; 10 g carbohydrate; 5 g protein; 3 g fiber; 166 mg sodium; 258 mg potassium. **NUTRITION BONUS:** Vitamin C (70% DAILY VALUE).

BABY SPINACH SALAD WITH RASPBERRY VINAIGRETTE

Healthy ⋈ Weight   Lower ⬇ Carbs

Thinly slice 1 small red bell pepper and cut 1 nectarine into 1-inch chunks. Combine with 6 cups baby spinach in a large bowl; toss with 3 tablespoons Raspberry Vinaigrette (*page 228*).

MAKES 4 SERVINGS, 1½ CUPS EACH.

PER SERVING: 70 calories; 5 g fat (0 g sat, 3 g mono); 0 mg cholesterol; 6 g carbohydrate; 2 g protein; 2 g fiber; 74 mg sodium; 348 mg potassium. **NUTRITION BONUS:** Vitamin A (100% DAILY VALUE), Vitamin C (70% DV), Folate (24% DV).

CUCUMBER & BLACK-EYED PEA SALAD

Healthy ⋈ Weight   Lower ⬇ Carbs

Whisk 3 tablespoons olive oil, 2 tablespoons lemon juice, 2 teaspoons chopped fresh oregano (*or 1 teaspoon dried*) and pepper to taste in a large bowl. Add 4 cups diced peeled cucumbers, one 14-ounce can black-eyed peas (*or white beans*), ⅔ cup diced red bell pepper, ½ cup crumbled reduced-fat feta, ¼ cup slivered red onion and 2 tablespoons chopped black olives; toss. Serve room temperature or chilled.

MAKES 6 SERVINGS, ABOUT 1 CUP EACH.

PER SERVING: 149 calories; 9 g fat (2 g sat, 6 g mono); 4 mg cholesterol; 12 g carbohydrate; 6 g protein; 3 g fiber; 294 mg sodium; 266 mg potassium. **NUTRITION BONUS:** Vitamin C (50% DAILY VALUE), Vitamin A (15% DV).

CURRIED WALDORF SALAD

Healthy ⋈ Weight   Lower ⬇ Carbs

Whisk ¼ cup nonfat plain yogurt, 3 tablespoons reduced-fat mayonnaise, ½ teaspoon curry powder, ⅛ teaspoon salt and a pinch of cayenne pepper in a medium bowl. Grate 2 teaspoons zest from 1 orange and add to the dressing. Segment the orange (*see Tip, page 244*) over the bowl (to catch the juice) and add the segments along with 2 diced tart-sweet red apples, 1 cup chopped celery, ⅓ cup golden raisins and ⅓ cup chopped toasted walnuts (*see Tip, page 244*); toss.

MAKES 6 SERVINGS, ¾ CUP EACH.

PER SERVING: 152 calories; 6 g fat (1 g sat, 1 g mono); 2 mg cholesterol; 25 g carbohydrate; 2 g protein; 4 g fiber; 116 mg sodium; 230 mg potassium. **NUTRITION BONUS:** Vitamin C (25% DAILY VALUE), Fiber (16% DV).

GREEN PAPAYA SALAD

Healthy ⋈ Weight   Lower ⬇ Carbs

Whisk ¼ teaspoon freshly grated lime zest, ¼ cup lime juice, 2 tablespoons packed brown sugar, 2 tablespoons fish sauce and minced hot chiles to taste in a large bowl. Add 3 cups matchstick-cut green papaya (*see Note, page 245*), ½ cup very thinly sliced sweet onion and ½ cup pea shoots (*or bean sprouts*); toss to combine. Sprinkle with pepper to taste before serving.

MAKES 6 SERVINGS, ⅔ CUP EACH.

PER SERVING: 59 calories; 0 g fat (0 g sat, 0 g mono); 0 mg cholesterol; 15 g carbohydrate; 1 g protein; 1 g fiber; 403 mg sodium; 65 mg potassium. **NUTRITION BONUS:** Vitamin C (60% DAILY VALUE).

RED & WHITE SALAD

Healthy ⋈ Weight   Lower ⬇ Carbs

Thinly slice hearts of romaine to make 4 cups. Core and thinly slice 2 heads Belgian endive. Trim and core 1 fennel bulb, then quarter and thinly slice it. Drain one 15-ounce can hearts of palm; halve lengthwise and thinly slice. Core, quarter and thinly slice ½ head radicchio. Cut 1 red apple into matchsticks. Thinly slice radishes to make 1 cup. Combine everything in a large salad bowl and toss. Add Champagne Vinaigrette (*page 228*) and toss to coat. Season with pepper to taste.

MAKES 8 SERVINGS, ABOUT 1¾ CUPS EACH.

PER SERVING: 111 calories; 7 g fat (1 g sat, 5 g mono); 0 mg cholesterol; 11 g carbohydrate; 2 g protein; 3 g fiber; 424 mg sodium; 324 mg potassium. **NUTRITION BONUS:** Vitamin C (30% DAILY VALUE).

ROMAINE & FRESH HERB SALAD

Healthy ⋈ Weight   Lower ⬇ Carbs

Mix 3 tablespoons balsamic vinegar, 2 tablespoons olive oil, ⅛ teaspoon salt and pepper to taste and 2 teaspoons ouzo (if desired) in a small bowl or jar. Cut 1 garlic clove in half and rub a large salad bowl with the cut sides. Place 12 cups torn romaine lettuce, 1 small bunch sliced scallions, ⅔ cup finely chopped fresh parsley, ⅓ cup finely chopped fresh dill and 1 tablespoon finely chopped fresh mint in the bowl. Drizzle the dressing over the salad and toss.

PER SERVING: 46 calories; 3 g fat (0 g sat, 2 g mono); 0 mg cholesterol; 4 g carbohydrate; 1 g protein; 2 g fiber; 40 mg sodium; 225 mg potassium. **NUTRITION BONUS:** Vitamin A (90% DAILY VALUE), Vitamin C (40% DV), Folate (26% DV).

SAVOY CABBAGE SLAW

Healthy)(Weight   Lower ↓ Carbs

Whisk 2 tablespoons olive oil, 2 tablespoons red-wine vinegar, 1 teaspoon sugar, ½ teaspoon crushed caraway seeds, a pinch of salt and pepper to taste in a large bowl. Add 3 cups finely shredded Savoy cabbage, 3 cups finely shredded red cabbage and ⅓ cup coarsely grated onion. Toss to coat. Serve within 2 hours.

MAKES 6 SERVINGS, 1 CUP EACH.

PER SERVING: 69 calories; 5 g fat (1 g sat, 4 g mono); 0 mg cholesterol; 6 g carbohydrate; 1 g protein; 2 g fiber; 44 mg sodium; 181 mg potassium. **NUTRITION BONUS:** Vitamin C (50% DAILY VALUE), Vitamin A (15% DV).

SNAP PEA SALAD WITH RADISH & LIME

Healthy)(Weight   Lower ↓ Carbs

Steam 8 ounces sugar snap peas over boiling water, stirring once, until crisp-tender, 4 to 5 minutes. Transfer to a baking sheet lined with paper towels. Steam 8 ounces halved yellow wax beans until crisp-tender, about 5 minutes. Transfer to the baking sheet. Refrigerate until chilled, about 20 minutes. Whisk ½ cup chopped fresh cilantro, 3 tablespoons lime juice, 2 tablespoons olive oil, ¼ teaspoon salt and pepper to taste in a large bowl. Add 10 thinly sliced radishes, the peas and beans; toss to coat with the dressing. Serve chilled.

MAKES 4 SERVINGS, ABOUT 1 CUP EACH.

PER SERVING: 110 calories; 7 g fat (1 g sat, 5 g mono); 0 mg cholesterol; 9 g carbohydrate; 2 g protein; 3 g fiber; 157 mg sodium; 140 mg potassium. **NUTRITION BONUS:** Vitamin A (20% DAILY VALUE).

WATERCRESS & PICKLED GINGER SALAD

Healthy)(Weight   Lower ↓ Carbs

Mash 1 garlic clove with ⅛ teaspoon kosher salt using the side of a chef's knife. Place in a small bowl. Add 1 tablespoon liquid from a jar of pickled ginger, 1 tablespoon rice vinegar, 1 tablespoon canola oil, 1 teaspoon honey and pepper to taste; whisk until blended. Place 6 cups stemmed watercress, 4 chopped scallions and ⅓ cup pickled ginger in a large bowl. Just before serving, toss with the dressing.

MAKES 4 SERVINGS, ABOUT 1 CUP EACH.

PER SERVING: 76 calories; 4 g fat (0 g sat, 2 g mono); 0 mg cholesterol; 9 g carbohydrate; 2 g protein; 1 g fiber; 192 mg sodium; 231 mg potassium. **NUTRITION BONUS:** Vitamin A (50% DAILY VALUE), Vitamin C (45% DV).

SALAD DRESSINGS & SAUCES

CHAMPAGNE VINAIGRETTE

Peel and quarter 1 shallot. Place in a blender and add ¼ cup champagne vinegar (or white-wine vinegar), ¼ cup olive oil, 1 tablespoon Dijon mustard, ¾ teaspoon salt and pepper to taste. Puree until smooth. (*Cover and refrigerate for up to 1 week.*)

MAKES ²⁄₃ CUP.

PER TABLESPOON: 53 calories; 5 g fat (1 g sat, 4 g mono); 0 mg cholesterol; 1 g carbohydrate; 0 g protein; 0 g fiber; 182 mg sodium; 4 mg potassium.

RASPBERRY VINAIGRETTE

Combine ⅓ cup canola oil, ¼ cup raspberry vinegar (or red-wine vinegar), 3 tablespoons orange juice, ¼ teaspoon salt and pepper to taste in a jar with a tight-fitting lid; shake well to combine. Refrigerate for up to 1 week. Shake before using.

MAKES ³⁄₄ CUP.

PER TABLESPOON: 58 calories; 6 g fat (0 g sat, 4 g mono); 0 mg cholesterol; 0 g carbohydrate; 0 g protein; 0 g fiber; 50 mg sodium; 8 mg potassium.

HOMEMADE BUTTERMILK MAYONNAISE

Whisk 1 tablespoon cornstarch, 1½ teaspoons dry mustard (preferably Colman's), 1 teaspoon sugar, ½ teaspoon salt and a pinch of cayenne pepper in a medium saucepan. Whisk in ¼ cup buttermilk to make a smooth paste. Whisk in 1 large egg and another ½ cup buttermilk until smooth. Cook over medium-low heat, whisking, until the mixture comes to a simmer and thickens. Whisk for 15 seconds more, then remove from the heat. Whisk in 2 tablespoons lemon juice and 1 tablespoon olive oil. Transfer the mayonnaise to a small bowl and press a piece of plastic wrap directly on the surface to prevent a skin from forming. Let cool. (*Refrigerate for up to 3 days. Whisk before using.*)

MAKES ABOUT 1 CUP.

PER TABLESPOON: 21 calories; 1 g fat (0 g sat, 1 g mono); 14 mg cholesterol; 1 g carbohydrate; 1 g protein; 0 g fiber; 89 mg sodium; 24 mg potassium.

FRESH TOMATO & HERB SAUCE

Place 3 rinsed and chopped anchovy fillets in a food processor. Add 1 chopped garlic clove, ⅓ cup chopped fresh flat-leaf parsley, ¼ cup chopped celery leaves, 2 tablespoons packed chopped fresh basil, ¼ cup olive oil and 1 tablespoon balsamic vinegar; pulse until blended. Transfer to a bowl and stir in 1 cup diced seeded tomatoes. Season with ¼ teaspoon kosher salt and pepper to taste.

MAKES ABOUT 1 CUP, FOR 8 SERVINGS.

PER SERVING: 73 calories; 7 g fat (1 g sat, 5 g mono); 1 mg cholesterol; 1 g carbohydrate; 1 g protein; 0 g fiber; 94 mg sodium; 74 mg potassium. **NUTRITION BONUS:** Vitamin C (15% DAILY VALUE).

TOMATO SALSA

Healthy)(Weight   Lower ⬇ Carbs

Combine 5 diced medium tomatoes, 1 finely diced small red onion, ¼ cup red-wine vinegar, 1 to 2 seeded and minced jalapeño peppers, ½ cup chopped fresh cilantro, ½ teaspoon salt and a pinch of cayenne pepper in a medium bowl. Refrigerate until ready to serve.

MAKES 10 SERVINGS, ½ CUP EACH.

PER SERVING: 21 calories; 0 g fat (0 g sat, 0 g mono); 0 mg cholesterol; 5 g carbohydrate; 1 g protein; 1 g fiber; 124 mg sodium; 185 mg potassium. **NUTRITION BONUS:** Vitamin C (35% DAILY VALUE).

BEANS & GRAINS

CHILE-SPICED BLACK BEANS

Healthy)(Weight   Lower ⬇ Carbs   High ⬆ Fiber

Heat 2 teaspoons olive oil in a medium saucepan over medium-high heat. Add 1 diced medium yellow onion and cook, stirring, until translucent, 4 to 5 minutes. Add 2 minced garlic cloves and cook, stirring constantly, for 30 seconds. Add 2 teaspoons ground ancho chile pepper, ½ teaspoon ground cumin and ½ teaspoon dried oregano and cook, stirring, until fragrant, about 30 seconds more. Add two 15-ounce cans black beans (rinsed), 1 cup water and 1 tablespoon tomato paste; stir to combine. Bring to a simmer, reduce heat to medium-low and cook, stirring occasionally, until the beans are heated through and the sauce is slightly thickened, 8 to 10 minutes. Serve warm. (*Alternatively, cover and refrigerate for up to 2 days.*)

MAKES 8 SERVINGS, SCANT ½ CUP EACH.

PER SERVING: 117 calories; 1 g fat (0 g sat, 1 g mono); 0 mg cholesterol; 21 g carbohydrate; 6 g protein; 5 g fiber; 84 mg sodium; 69 mg potassium. **NUTRITION BONUS:** Folate (41% DAILY VALUE), Magnesium (19% DV), Iron (15% DV).

---

15 WAYS TO SPICE YOUR **BROWN RICE**

Cook 1 cup rice (*see Grain-Cooking Guide, page 236*) **with:**

- 2½ cups chicken broth and a pinch of saffron threads
- 2½ cups water, ½ teaspoon salt, 1 cinnamon stick and 1 bay leaf
- 2½ cups water, ½ teaspoon salt and 2 crushed coins of fresh ginger
- 2½ cups chicken broth, 1 teaspoon curry powder and ¼ cup shredded coconut
- 1¾ cups water, ¾ cup tomato juice and ½ teaspoon salt
- 2½ cups water, ½ teaspoon salt and a wide strip of fresh lemon *or* orange zest
- 2½ cups chicken broth, 1 teaspoon ground cumin and 1 clove crushed garlic

Or into 3 cups plain cooked rice stir:

- 1 cup thawed frozen peas and ¼ cup chopped smoked ham
- 2 tablespoons basil pesto and 1 cup diced tomatoes
- ½ cup freshly grated Parmesan and 2 teaspoons freshly grated lemon zest
- One 4-ounce can chopped mild green chiles and 1 cup thawed frozen corn
- 2 teaspoons freshly grated lemon *or* orange zest and ¼ cup chopped olives
- 2 tablespoons toasted poppy *or* sunflower seeds and 1 cup caramelized onions
- One 15-ounce can black beans, rinsed, and 3 tablespoons chopped fresh cilantro
- ½ cup currants (*or* raisins) and ¼ cup toasted pine nuts

CARIBBEAN RICE & BEANS

Healthy)(Weight   High ⬆ Fiber

Heat 1½ teaspoons olive oil in a large skillet over medium-high heat. Add 1 large pimiento (*or* roasted red bell pepper) and ½ green bell pepper, both cut into short strips, and 2 minced garlic cloves; sauté for 2 minutes. Add two 16-ounce cans black beans, 2 tablespoons white vinegar and 5 to 10 dashes of hot sauce. Bring to a boil; reduce heat to low, cover and simmer for 5 minutes. Stir in 3 cups cooked brown rice and 3 tablespoons chopped fresh cilantro. Season with ⅛ teaspoon salt and pepper. Serve accompanied by additional hot sauce.

MAKES 6 SERVINGS.

PER SERVING: 236 calories; 1 g fat (0 g sat, 1 g mono); 0 mg cholesterol; 46 g carbohydrate; 9 g protein; 7 g fiber; 168 mg sodium; 70 mg potassium. **NUTRITION BONUS:** Vitamin C (30% DAILY VALUE), Folate (20% DV), Iron (15% DV).

RICE & PEAS WITH FETA

Healthy)(Weight   Lower ⬇ Carbs

Bring 1¼ cups reduced-sodium chicken broth to a boil in a large saucepan over high heat. Add ¾ cup instant brown rice and bring to a simmer; cover, reduce heat to medium-low and cook for 4 minutes. Stir in 1½ cups frozen peas and return to a simmer over high heat. Cover, reduce heat to medium-low and continue to cook until the peas are hot and the rice has absorbed most of the liquid, about 6 minutes. Remove from heat and stir in ¾ cup sliced scallions, ¼ cup finely crumbled feta cheese, ¼ cup sliced fresh mint and pepper to taste. Cover and let stand until the liquid is absorbed, 3 to 5 minutes.

MAKES 4 SERVINGS, ¾ CUP EACH.

PER SERVING: 134 calories; 3 g fat (1 g sat, 0 g mono); 8 mg cholesterol; 22 g carbohydrate; 7 g protein; 4 g fiber; 321 mg sodium; 203 mg potassium. **NUTRITION BONUS:** Vitamin A (30% DAILY VALUE), Iron (15% DV).

PARSLEY TABBOULEH

Healthy)(Weight   Lower ⬇ Carbs   High ⬆ Fiber

Prepare ½ cup bulgur according to package directions; drain. Transfer to a large bowl and let cool for 15 minutes. Add 2 cups finely chopped flat-leaf parsley, ¼ cup chopped fresh mint, 2 diced tomatoes, 1 peeled, seeded and diced small cucumber and 4 thinly sliced scallions. Combine ¼ cup lemon juice, 2 tablespoons olive oil, ½ teaspoon minced garlic, ¼ teaspoon salt and pepper to taste in a small bowl; add to the bulgur and toss. Serve room temperature or chilled.

MAKES 4 SERVINGS, GENEROUS 1 CUP EACH.

PER SERVING: 165 calories; 8 g fat (1 g sat, 6 g mono); 0 mg cholesterol; 22 g carbohydrate; 4 g protein; 6 g fiber; 175 mg sodium; 555 mg potassium. **NUTRITION BONUS:** Vitamin C (100% DAILY VALUE), Vitamin A (70% DV), Folate (21% DV), Iron (20% DV).

VEGETABLES

ROASTED ASPARAGUS WITH CAPER DRESSING

Healthy)(Weight   Lower ⬇ Carbs   High ⬆ Fiber

Preheat oven to 450°F. Trim tough ends from 2 bunches asparagus (about 2 pounds); place on a baking sheet. Drizzle the asparagus with 1 tablespoon olive oil, ¼ teaspoon salt and ¼ teaspoon pepper. Spread in a single layer and roast, turning once halfway through, until the asparagus begins to brown, 12 to 14 minutes. Transfer to a serving platter. Meanwhile, place ⅓ cup chopped shallot, ¼ cup flat-leaf parsley leaves and 3 tablespoons rinsed capers on a cutting board and chop together to make a coarse mixture. Transfer to a small bowl; combine with 2 tablespoons white-wine vinegar, 2 teaspoons olive oil and ¼ teaspoon pepper. Serve the asparagus topped with the dressing.

MAKES 4 SERVINGS.

PER SERVING: 122 calories; 6 g fat (1 g sat, 5 g mono); 0 mg cholesterol; 12 g carbohydrate; 6 g protein; 5 g fiber; 346 mg sodium; 526 mg potassium. **NUTRITION BONUS:** Vitamin A (45% DAILY VALUE), Folate (33% DV), Iron & Vitamin C (30% DV).

ROASTED BROCCOLI WITH LEMON

Healthy)(Weight   Lower ⬇ Carbs

Preheat oven to 450°F. Toss 4 cups broccoli florets with 1 tablespoon olive oil, ¼ teaspoon salt and pepper to taste. Place on a large baking sheet and roast until the broccoli is tender and blackened on the bottom, 10 to 12 minutes. Serve immediately, with lemon wedges.

MAKES 4 SERVINGS, 1 CUP EACH.

PER SERVING: 54 calories; 4 g fat (1 g sat, 3 g mono); 0 mg cholesterol; 4 g carbohydrate; 2 g protein; 2 g fiber; 165 mg sodium; 240 mg potassium. **NUTRITION BONUS:** Vitamin C (120% DAILY VALUE), Vitamin A (45% DV).

BRUSSELS SPROUTS WITH WALNUT-LEMON VINAIGRETTE

Healthy)(Weight   Lower ⬇ Carbs

Trim and quarter 1 pound Brussels sprouts. Place in a steamer basket and steam in a large saucepan over 1 inch of boiling water until tender, 7 to 8 minutes. Meanwhile, whisk 2 tablespoons walnut oil, 1 tablespoon minced shallot, ¼ teaspoon freshly grated lemon zest, 1 tablespoon lemon juice, 1 teaspoon whole-grain (or Dijon) mustard, ¼ teaspoon salt and pepper to taste in a medium bowl. Add the sprouts to the dressing; toss to coat.

MAKES 4 SERVINGS, ABOUT ¾ CUP EACH.

PER SERVING: 108 calories; 7 g fat (1 g sat, 2 g mono); 0 mg cholesterol; 10 g carbohydrate; 3 g protein; 3 g fiber; 188 mg sodium; 405 mg potassium. **NUTRITION BONUS:** Vitamin K (216% DAILY VALUE), Vitamin C (130% DV), Vitamin A (20% DV), Folate (19% DV).

ROASTED SAVOY CABBAGE WITH BLACK BEAN-GARLIC SAUCE

Healthy)(Weight   Lower ⬇ Carbs   High ⬆ Fiber

Preheat oven to 500°F. Core 1 head Savoy cabbage (1½ pounds) and cut into 1-inch squares. Toss with 4 teaspoons canola oil in a large roasting pan and spread out in an even layer. Roast until beginning to wilt and brown, about 15 minutes. Combine 2 tablespoons Shao

Hsing rice wine (*or dry sherry; see Note, page 245*) and 4 teaspoons black bean-garlic sauce; drizzle over the cabbage and toss. Continue roasting until tender, about 5 minutes more. Toss with 1 bunch minced scallions, 2 teaspoons distilled white vinegar, 2 teaspoons toasted sesame oil and 5 dashes hot sauce, or to taste, until combined.

MAKES 4 SERVINGS, ³/₄ CUP EACH.

PER SERVING: 123 calories; 8 g fat (1 g sat, 4 g mono); 0 mg cholesterol; 12 g carbohydrate; 4 g protein; 5 g fiber; 485 mg sodium; 406 mg potassium. **NUTRITION BONUS:** Vitamin C (80% DAILY VALUE), Vitamin A (35% DV), Folate (32% DV), high omega-3s.

CHARD WITH PANCETTA & WALNUTS

Healthy ⚖ Weight   Lower ⬇ Carbs

Separate stems and leaves from 1 pound chard; chop both. Dice 2 thin slices of pancetta; cook in a Dutch oven over medium heat, stirring, until it begins to brown, 4 to 6 minutes. Transfer to a paper towel. Add 2 thinly sliced medium shallots, the chard stems and 1 teaspoon chopped fresh thyme to the pan drippings and cook, stirring, until the shallots begin to brown, 4 to 5 minutes. Add the chard leaves, ¼ cup water and 1 tablespoon lemon juice and cook, stirring, until wilted, about 2 minutes. Cover and cook until tender, 2 to 4 minutes more. Remove from the heat; stir in the pancetta, 2 tablespoons toasted chopped walnuts (*see Tip, page 244*) and ¼ teaspoon pepper.

MAKES 6 SERVINGS, ²/₃ CUP EACH.

PER SERVING: 62 calories; 4 g fat (1 g sat, 1 g mono); 5 mg cholesterol; 5 g carbohydrate; 3 g protein; 2 g fiber; 252 mg sodium; 452 mg potassium. **NUTRITION BONUS:** Vitamin K (346% DAILY VALUE), Vitamin A (90% DV), Vitamin C (25% DV), Magnesium (18% DV).

CREAMED CORN

Healthy ⚖ Weight

Place 2 cups fresh corn kernels (*see Tip, page 244*), ¾ cup low-fat milk, 1 tablespoon cornstarch and ¼ teaspoon salt in a blender; blend until smooth. Transfer the puree to a saucepan, and add an additional 1 cup corn. Cook over medium-high heat, stirring constantly, until the mixture simmers and thickens and the corn is tender, 5 to 7 minutes.

MAKES 4 SERVINGS, ¹/₂ CUP EACH.

PER SERVING: 131 calories; 2 g fat (1 g sat, 0 g mono); 4 mg cholesterol; 26 g carbohydrate; 5 g protein; 3 g fiber; 186 mg sodium; 312 mg potassium. **NUTRITION BONUS:** Vitamin C (15% DAILY VALUE).

GREEN BEAN & CHERRY TOMATO SAUTE

Healthy ⚖ Weight   Lower ⬇ Carbs   High ⬆ Fiber

Heat 1 teaspoon olive oil in a large skillet over medium-high heat. Add 1 pound trimmed green beans; cook, stirring often, until seared in

spots, 2 to 3 minutes. Add ½ cup water, cover, reduce heat to medium and cook, stirring occasionally, about 3 minutes for tender-crisp or 6 minutes for tender. Push the beans aside; add 1 teaspoon olive oil and 2 minced garlic cloves and cook until fragrant, about 30 seconds. Stir in 1½ cups halved cherry tomatoes and cook until the tomatoes begin to break down, 2 to 3 minutes. Remove from heat; stir in 1 tablespoon balsamic vinegar, ¼ teaspoon salt and pepper to taste.

MAKES 4 SERVINGS, 1 CUP EACH.

PER SERVING: 71 calories; 3 g fat (0 g sat, 2 g mono); 0 mg cholesterol; 11 g carbohydrate; 3 g protein; 5 g fiber; 157 mg sodium; 379 mg potassium. **NUTRITION BONUS:** Vitamin C (45% DAILY VALUE), Vitamin K (26% DV), Vitamin A (18% DV).

INDIAN-STYLE GREEN BEANS

Healthy ⚖ Weight   Lower ⬇ Carbs   High ⬆ Fiber

Heat 1½ teaspoons canola oil in a large nonstick skillet over medium-high heat. Add 1 teaspoon mustard seeds and sauté for 30 seconds, or until they start to pop. Stir in 1 pound halved green beans, 2 sliced medium carrots and 1 chopped small onion and cook, stirring constantly, for 5 minutes. Stir in 1 teaspoon salt, 1 teaspoon ground coriander and ⅛ teaspoon ground ginger. Reduce heat to low, cover and cook, stirring often, until the beans are tender-crisp, 8 to 10 minutes. Stir in 2 tablespoons lemon juice.

MAKES 4 SERVINGS.

PER SERVING: 76 calories; 2 g fat (0 g sat, 1 g mono); 0 mg cholesterol; 14 g carbohydrate; 3 g protein; 5 g fiber; 610 mg sodium; 376 mg potassium. **NUTRITION BONUS:** Vitamin A (120% DAILY VALUE), Vitamin C (40% DV).

KALE WITH APPLES & MUSTARD

Healthy ⚖ Weight   Lower ⬇ Carbs

Remove ribs from 1 to 1½ pounds kale; coarsely chop the kale. Heat 1 tablespoon olive oil in a Dutch oven over medium heat. Add the kale and cook, tossing, until bright green, about 1 minute. Add ⅔ cup water, cover and cook, stirring occasionally, for 3 minutes. Stir in 2 sliced Granny Smith apples; cover and cook, stirring occasionally, until the kale is tender, 8 to 10 minutes more. Meanwhile, whisk 2 tablespoons cider vinegar, 4 teaspoons whole-grain mustard, 2 teaspoons brown sugar and a pinch of salt in a small bowl. Add the mixture to the kale, increase heat to high and boil, uncovered, until most of the liquid evaporates, 3 to 4 minutes.

MAKES 4 SERVINGS, ABOUT ³/₄ CUP EACH.

PER SERVING: 107 calories; 4 g fat (1 g sat, 3 g mono); 0 mg cholesterol; 18 g carbohydrate; 2 g protein; 3 g fiber; 134 mg sodium; 399 mg potassium. **NUTRITION BONUS:** Vitamin A (170% DAILY VALUE), Vitamin C (100% DV).

GARLIC-ROSEMARY MUSHROOMS

Healthy ⊁ Weight   **Lower ↓ Carbs**

Cook 1½ slices chopped bacon in a large skillet over medium heat until just beginning to brown, about 4 minutes. Add 1½ pounds thinly sliced mixed mushrooms, such as cremini, shiitake or portobello, 2 minced garlic cloves, 1½ teaspoons chopped fresh rosemary (*or* ½ teaspoon dried), ¼ teaspoon salt and pepper to taste and cook, stirring occasionally, until almost dry, 8 to 10 minutes. Add ¼ cup dry white wine and cook until most of the liquid has evaporated, 30 seconds to 1 minute.

MAKES 4 SERVINGS, ABOUT ¾ CUP EACH.

PER SERVING: 95 calories; 3 g fat (1 g sat, 1 g mono); 8 mg cholesterol; 8 g carbohydrate; 7 g protein; 1 g fiber; 316 mg sodium; 795 mg potassium. **NUTRITION BONUS:** Potassium (23% DAILY VALUE).

SESAME-ROASTED MUSHROOMS & SCALLIONS

Healthy ⊁ Weight   **Lower ↓ Carbs**

Preheat oven to 450°F. Combine 2 tablespoons toasted sesame oil, 2 tablespoons reduced-sodium soy sauce, 1 tablespoon grated fresh ginger, 1 tablespoon minced garlic, 4 teaspoons rice vinegar and ½ teaspoon pepper in a large bowl. Add 1½ pounds thickly sliced mixed mushrooms, such as shiitake, oyster or white, and 2 bunches scallions, cut into 2-inch pieces; toss to coat. Transfer to a roasting pan. Roast, stirring once or twice, until browned and cooked through, about 25 minutes. Sprinkle with 1 tablespoon toasted sesame seeds (*see Tip, page 244*).

MAKES 6 SERVINGS, ABOUT ⅔ CUP EACH.

PER SERVING: 109 calories; 6 g fat (1 g sat, 2 g mono); 0 mg cholesterol; 12 g carbohydrate; 5 g protein; 4 g fiber; 205 mg sodium; 606 mg potassium. **NUTRITION BONUS:** Iron (25% DAILY VALUE), Potassium (17% DV), Vitamin C (15% DV).

NEW POTATO & PEA SALAD

Healthy ⊁ Weight

TO MAKE DRESSING: Whisk ¼ cup dry white wine, 2 tablespoons canola oil and 3 tablespoons coarse-grained mustard in a small bowl. Stir in ½ cup finely chopped shallots and ¼ cup chopped fresh dill and season with ⅛ teaspoon salt and pepper to taste.

TO MAKE SALAD: Place 2 pounds small red-skinned potatoes, quartered, in a large pot and cover with cold water. Bring to a boil, reduce heat to medium-low and cook, partially covered, until almost tender, 8 to 10 minutes. Add 2 cups fresh (*or* frozen) peas and cook until heated through, 1 to 3 minutes. Drain and transfer to a large bowl. Add 2 tablespoons lemon juice and toss to coat. Toss the potato mixture with the

dressing; season with salt and pepper. Serve within 1 hour.

MAKES 8 SERVINGS.

PER SERVING: 170 calories; 5 g fat (0 g sat, 3 g mono); 0 mg cholesterol; 27 g carbohydrate; 5 g protein; 4 g fiber; 85 mg sodium; 640 mg potassium. **NUTRITION BONUS:** Vitamin C (30% DAILY VALUE), Vitamin A (20% DV), Potassium (18% DV).

OVEN-FRIED POTATOES

Healthy ⊁ Weight   **Lower ↓ Carbs**

Preheat oven to 450°F. Cut 2 large Yukon Gold potatoes into wedges. Toss with 4 teaspoons olive oil, ½ teaspoon salt and ½ teaspoon dried thyme (optional). Spread the wedges out on a rimmed baking sheet. Bake until browned and tender, turning once, about 20 minutes total.

MAKES 4 SERVINGS.

PER SERVING: 103 calories; 5 g fat (1 g sat, 4 g mono); 0 mg cholesterol; 13 g carbohydrate; 2 g protein; 1 g fiber; 291 mg sodium; 407 mg potassium.

ROASTED SNAP PEAS WITH SHALLOTS

Healthy ⊁ Weight   **Lower ↓ Carbs**

Preheat oven to 475°F. Toss 1 pound trimmed sugar snap peas, 1 halved and thinly sliced large shallot, 2 teaspoons olive oil, ¼ teaspoon salt and pepper to taste in a medium bowl. Spread in a single layer on a baking sheet. Roast, stirring once halfway through, until the peas are tender and beginning to brown slightly, 12 to 14 minutes. If desired, sprinkle with 2 pieces cooked bacon, crumbled. Serve warm.

MAKES 4 SERVINGS, ½ CUP EACH.

PER SERVING: 83 calories; 2 g fat (0 g sat, 2 g mono); 0 mg cholesterol; 11 g carbohydrate; 3 g protein; 3 g fiber; 147 mg sodium; 212 mg potassium. **NUTRITION BONUS:** Vitamin C (20% DAILY VALUE).

MEXICAN SAUTEED SUMMER SQUASH

Healthy ⊁ Weight   **Lower ↓ Carbs**

Heat 1 tablespoon olive oil in a large nonstick skillet over medium heat. Add 1 chopped medium onion and 1 seeded and diced poblano (*or* Anaheim) pepper; cook, stirring, until soft, about 4 minutes. Add 2 cups diced zucchini, 2 cups diced summer squash and ½ teaspoon salt; cover and cook, stirring once or twice, until tender, about 3 minutes. Stir in 2 tablespoons chopped fresh cilantro (optional).

MAKES 6 SERVINGS, ABOUT ⅔ CUP EACH.

PER SERVING: 40 calories; 2 g fat (0 g sat, 2 g mono); 0 mg cholesterol; 4 g carbohydrate; 1 g protein; 1 g fiber; 199 mg sodium; 201 mg potassium. **NUTRITION BONUS:** Vitamin C (30% DV).

COCONUT MASHED SWEET POTATOES

Healthy)(Weight

Prick 3 medium sweet potatoes with a fork in several places. Microwave on High until tender all the way to the center, 10 to 15 minutes. (*Alternatively, place in a baking dish and bake at 425°F until tender all the way to the center, about 1 hour.*) When cool enough to handle, peel off and discard skin. Transfer the sweet potatoes to a medium microwavable bowl and mash thoroughly with a potato masher. Add ¾ cup "lite" coconut milk, 1 tablespoon minced fresh ginger and ½ teaspoon salt; stir well. Reheat in the microwave for 1 to 2 minutes, or in the oven for 8 to 10 minutes. Serve warm.

MAKES 4 SERVINGS, GENEROUS ½ CUP EACH.

PER SERVING: 130 calories; 3 g fat (2 g sat, 0 g mono); 0 mg cholesterol; 23 g carbohydrate; 3 g protein; 3 g fiber; 339 mg sodium; 498 mg potassium. **NUTRITION BONUS:** Vitamin A (400% DAILY VALUE), Vitamin C (35% DV), Fiber & Potassium (14% DV).

OVEN-FRIED ZUCCHINI STICKS

Healthy)(Weight   Lower ⬇ Carbs

Preheat oven to 475°F. Coat a large baking sheet with cooking spray. Cut 3 medium zucchini into ½-by-3-inch sticks. Combine ½ cup whole-wheat flour, ½ cup all-purpose flour, 2 tablespoons cornmeal, 1 teaspoon salt and ½ teaspoon pepper in a large sealable plastic bag. Lightly beat 2 egg whites in a shallow dish. Dip the zucchini in egg white, shake in the bag to coat, and arrange, not touching, on the baking sheet. Coat all exposed sides with cooking spray. Bake on the center rack for 7 minutes. Turn the zucchini and coat any floury spots with cooking spray. Continue to bake until golden and just tender, about 5 minutes more. Serve hot.

MAKES 4 SERVINGS.

PER SERVING: 108 calories; 1 g fat (0 g sat, 0 g mono); 0 mg cholesterol; 22 g carbohydrate; 6 g protein; 4 g fiber; 427 mg sodium; 524 mg potassium. **NUTRITION BONUS:** Vitamin C (48% DAILY VALUE), Potassium (15% DV).

ROASTED ZUCCHINI & PESTO

Healthy)(Weight   Lower ⬇ Carbs

Place a baking sheet on the middle rack of the oven. Preheat oven to 500°F. Cut 4 medium zucchini into 1-inch chunks. Toss with 1 tablespoon olive oil in a large bowl. Spread the zucchini on the preheated baking sheet in a single layer. Roast until beginning to brown, 5 to 7 minutes. Turn the zucchini and continue roasting until just tender, 7 to 9 minutes more. Return the zucchini to the bowl. Add 2 tablespoons prepared pesto, salt and pepper to taste; toss to coat.

MAKES 4 SERVINGS, ABOUT 1 CUP EACH.

PER SERVING: 107 calories; 7 g fat (2 g sat, 5 g mono); 3 mg cholesterol; 8 g carbohydrate; 4 g protein; 3 g fiber; 119 mg sodium; 617 mg potassium. **NUTRITION BONUS:** Vitamin C (70% DAILY VALUE), Potassium (18% DV), Folate (16% DV).

Roasted Asparagus with Caper Dressing

Garlic-Rosemary Mushrooms

VEGETABLE-COOKING GUIDE

Start with 1 pound untrimmed raw vegetables for 4 servings.

Artichokes, Baby

LOOK FOR: Tight, small heads, no browning or bruising. PREP: Snip off tough outer leaves; cut off top quarter and trim off woody stem. GRILL: Halve artichokes, scoop out the choke if necessary, then toss with 1 tablespoon olive oil and ½ teaspoon kosher salt. Preheat grill. Place the artichokes over direct, medium-high heat and cook, turning once or twice, until tender, about 8 minutes. MICROWAVE: Place artichokes in a large glass baking dish, add ½ cup white wine (or dry vermouth), ½ teaspoon salt and 1 teaspoon dried thyme. Cover tightly and microwave on High until tender, about 8 minutes. STEAM: Place artichokes in a steamer basket over 1 inch of water in a large pot set over high heat. Cover and steam until tender, about 15 minutes.

Asparagus

LOOK FOR: Sturdy spears with tight heads; cut ends not desiccated or woody. Fresh asparagus snaps when bent. PREP: Trim off stem ends; shave down any woody bits with a vegetable peeler. BRAISE: Place a large skillet over high heat. Add asparagus, ½ cup water and a slice of lemon. Cover, bring to a simmer, and cook until tender, about 5 minutes. GRILL: Preheat grill; lightly oil rack. Place asparagus over direct, medium heat; cook until browned, turning occasionally, about 6 minutes. MICROWAVE: Place asparagus in a large glass baking dish; add ¼ cup water, drizzle with 1 teaspoon olive oil, and cover tightly. Microwave on High until tender, about 3 minutes. ROAST: Preheat oven to 500°F. Spread asparagus on a baking sheet or in a pan large enough to hold it in a single layer. Coat with 2 teaspoons olive oil. Roast, turning once halfway through cooking, until wilted and browned, about 10 minutes.

Beets

LOOK FOR: Small; firm, richly colored. PREP: Peel. MICROWAVE: Cut beets into ¼-inch-thick rings; place in a large glass baking dish. Add ¼ cup water, cover tightly and microwave on High for 10 minutes. Let stand, covered, for 5 minutes before serving. ROAST: Preheat oven to 500°F. Cut beets into 1½-inch chunks. Spread on a baking sheet or in a pan large enough to hold them in a single layer. Coat with 2 teaspoons olive oil. Roast, turning once halfway through cooking, until tender, about 30 minutes. STEAM: Cut beets into quarters. Place in a steamer basket over 1 inch of water in a large pot set over high heat. Cover and steam until tender, about 15 minutes.

Broccoli

LOOK FOR: Sturdy, dark-green spears with tight buds, no yellowing and a high floret-to-stem ratio. PREP: Cut off florets; cut stalks in half lengthwise and then into 1-inch-thick half-moons. MICROWAVE: Place stems and florets in a large glass baking dish. Cover tightly and microwave on High until tender, about 4 minutes. ROAST: Preheat oven to 500°F. Spread on a baking sheet or in a pan large enough to hold them in a single layer. Coat with 1 tablespoon olive oil. Roast, turning once halfway through cooking, until tender and browned in places, 10 to 12 minutes. STEAM: Place stems in a steamer basket over 1 inch of water (with 1 tablespoon lemon juice added to it) in a large pot set over high heat. Cover and steam for 2 minutes. Add florets; cover and continue steaming until tender, about 5 minutes more.

Carrots

LOOK FOR: Orange, firm; no gray, white or desiccated residue on skin; greens preferably still attached. PREP: Peel; cut off greens. MICROWAVE: Cut carrots into ⅛-inch-thick rounds. Place in a large glass baking dish. Add ¼ cup broth (or white wine). Cover tightly and microwave on High until tender, about 3 minutes. ROAST: Preheat oven to 500°F. Cut carrots in half lengthwise then slice into 1½-inch-long pieces. Spread on a baking sheet or in a pan large enough to hold them in a single layer. Coat with 2 teaspoons olive oil. Roast, turning once halfway through cooking, until beginning to brown, about 15 minutes. SAUTÉ: Cut carrots into ⅛-inch-thick rounds. Heat 1 tablespoon olive oil in a large skillet over medium-low heat. Add carrots; stir and cook until tender, about 4 minutes. Add 1 teaspoon sugar; stir until glazed. STEAM: Cut carrots into ⅛-inch thick rounds. Place in a steamer basket over 1 inch of water in a large pot set over high heat. Cover and steam for 4 minutes.

Cauliflower

LOOK FOR: Tight white or purple heads without brown or yellow spots; the green leaves at the stem should still be attached firmly to the head, not limp or withered. PREP: Cut into 1-inch-wide florets; discard core and thick stems. MICROWAVE: Place florets in a large glass baking dish. Add ¼ cup dry white wine (or dry vermouth). Cover tightly and microwave on High until tender, about 4 minutes. ROAST: Preheat oven to 500°F. Spread florets on a baking sheet or in a pan large enough to hold them in a single layer. Coat with 1 tablespoon olive oil. Roast, turning once halfway through cooking, until tender and beginning to brown, about 15 minutes. STEAM: Place florets in a steamer basket over 1 inch of water in a large pot set over high heat. Cover and steam for 5 minutes.

Corn

LOOK FOR: Pale to dark green husks with moist silks; ears should feel heavy, the cob filling the husk well. GRILL: Pull back the husks without removing them; pull out the silks. Replace the husks; soak the ears in water for 20 minutes. Preheat grill. Place corn (in husks) over high heat and grill, turning occasionally, until lightly browned, about 5 minutes. Remove husks before serving. MICROWAVE: Husk corn and cut ears in thirds; place in a large glass baking dish. Cover tightly and microwave on High until tender, about 4 minutes. SAUTÉ: Remove kernels from cobs. Heat 2 teaspoons olive oil in a large skillet over medium heat. Add corn kernels; cook, stirring constantly, until tender, about 3 minutes. Stir in ½ teaspoon white-wine vinegar before serving. STEAM: Husk corn, then break or cut ears in half to fit in a steamer basket. Set over 1 inch of water in a large pot over high heat. Cover and steam until tender, about 4 minutes.

Eggplant
LOOK FOR: Smooth, glossy skins without wrinkles or spongy spots; each should feel heavy for its size. PREP: Slice into ½-inch-thick rounds (peeling is optional). GRILL: Preheat grill. Brush eggplant slices lightly with 2 teaspoons olive oil. Place over medium-high heat and grill, turning once, until browned, about 8 minutes. ROAST: Preheat oven to 500°F. Brush both sides of eggplant slices with 2 teaspoons olive oil and arrange on a baking sheet or pan large enough to hold them in a single layer. Roast, turning once halfway through cooking, until tender, about 15 minutes.

Green Beans
LOOK FOR: Small, thin, firm beans. PREP: Snip off stem ends. MICROWAVE: Place beans in a large glass baking dish. Add ¼ cup broth (or water). Cover tightly and microwave on High for 4 minutes. ROAST: Preheat oven to 500°F. Spread beans on a baking sheet or in a pan large enough to hold them in a single layer. Coat with 1 tablespoon olive oil. Roast, turning once halfway through cooking, until tender and beginning to brown, about 10 minutes. SAUTÉ: Heat 2 teaspoons walnut oil in a large skillet. Add beans; cook, stirring constantly, for 2 minutes. STEAM: Place beans in a steamer basket over 1 inch of water in a large pot set over high heat. Cover and steam for 5 minutes.

Peas
LOOK FOR: If fresh, look for firm, vibrant green pods without blotches and with the stem end still attached. PREP: If fresh, zip open the hull, using the stem end as a tab. If frozen, do not defrost before using. MICROWAVE: Place peas in a large glass baking dish; add 2 tablespoons broth (or unsweetened apple juice). Cover tightly and microwave on High for 2 minutes. SAUTÉ: Heat 2 teaspoons olive oil in a large skillet over medium heat. Add peas; cook, stirring often, until bright green, about 3 minutes. STEAM: Place peas in a steamer basket over 1 inch of water in a large pot set over high heat. Cover and steam for 2 minutes.

Potatoes, Red or Yukon Gold
LOOK FOR: Small potatoes with firm skins that are not loose, papery or bruised. PREP: Scrub off any dirt (peeling is optional; the skin is fiber-rich and the nutrients are clustered about ½ inch below the skin). ROAST: Preheat oven to 500°F. Halve potatoes then cut into ½-inch wedges. Spread on a baking sheet or in a pan large enough to hold them in a single layer. Coat with 2 teaspoons olive oil. Roast,

stirring once halfway through cooking, until crispy and browned on the outside and tender on the inside, 20 to 25 minutes. STEAM: Place potatoes in a steamer basket over 2 inches of water in a large pot set over high heat. Cover and steam until tender when pierced with a fork, about 10 minutes.

Spinach & Swiss Chard
LOOK FOR: Supple, deeply colored leaves without mushy spots. PREP: Rinse thoroughly to remove sand; remove thick stems and shred leaves into 2-inch pieces. Rinse leaves again but do not dry. BRAISE: Heat 2 teaspoons walnut oil (or canola oil) in a large skillet over medium heat. Add spinach or chard and toss until wilted. Add ½ cup dry white wine (or dry vermouth). Cover, reduce heat and cook, about 5 minutes. Uncover and cook until liquid is reduced to a glaze. Sprinkle 2 teaspoons balsamic vinegar (or rice vinegar) over the greens.

Squash, Acorn
LOOK FOR: Green, orange or white varietals with firm, smooth skins and no spongy spots. PREP: Cut in quarters and scoop out the seeds. BRAISE: Place squash in a pot with 2 cups unsweetened apple juice. Set over medium-high heat and bring to a simmer. Cover, reduce heat and cook until tender when pierced with a fork, about 20 minutes. MICROWAVE: Place squash in a large glass baking dish; add ½ cup water. Cover tightly and microwave on High for 15 minutes; let stand, covered, for 10 minutes.

Squash, Delicata
LOOK FOR: Small, firm squash with bright yellow or orange skins that have green veins branching like lightning through them. PREP: Cut squash in half lengthwise, scoop out seeds and slice into thin half-moons (peeling is optional). MICROWAVE: Place squash in a large glass baking dish with ¼ cup broth (or water). Cover tightly and microwave on High for 10 minutes. SAUTÉ: Heat 2 teaspoons olive oil in a large skillet over medium heat. Add squash slices; cook, stirring frequently, until tender, about 10 minutes. Stir in a pinch of grated nutmeg before serving. STEAM: Place squash slices in a steamer basket over 1 inch of water in a large pot set over high heat. Cover and cook until tender, about 6 minutes.

Squash, Summer & Zucchini
LOOK FOR: No breaks, gashes or soft spots; smaller squash (under 8 inches) are sweeter and have fewer seeds. PREP: Do not peel, but scrub off dirt; cut off stem ends. GRILL: Cut squash lengthwise into ¼-inch strips. Preheat grill; brush strips lightly with 1 tablespoon olive oil. Place over direct, medium heat; grill, turning once, until marked and lightly browned, 3 to 4 minutes. ROAST: Preheat oven to 500°F. Cut squash lengthwise into ¼-inch-thick slices. Spread on a baking sheet or in a pan large enough to hold them in a single layer. Coat with 2 teaspoons olive oil. Roast, turning once halfway through cooking, until tender, about 10 minutes. SAUTÉ: Cut squash into ¼-inch-

thick rings. Heat 1 tablespoon olive oil in a large skillet over medium heat. Add 1 minced garlic clove and squash; cook, stirring frequently, until tender, about 7 minutes. STEAM: Cut squash into ½-inch-thick rings. Place in a steamer basket with 1 thinly sliced small onion. Place over 1 inch of water in a large pot set over high heat. Cook until tender, about 5 minutes.

Sweet Potatoes

LOOK FOR: Taut if papery skins with tapered ends. PREP: Scrub. BRAISE: Peel sweet potatoes and cut into 1-inch pieces. Place in a large skillet with 1 cup broth, 1 teaspoon honey and ½ teaspoon dried thyme. Bring to a simmer over high heat; reduce heat, cover and cook until almost tender, about 15 minutes. Uncover, increase heat and cook until the liquid is reduced to a glaze, about 2 minutes. MICRO-WAVE: Place sweet potatoes in a large glass baking dish; pierce with a knife. Microwave on High until soft, 8 to 12 minutes. Let stand for 5 minutes. ROAST: Preheat oven to 500°F. Halve sweet potatoes, then slice into ½-inch wedges. Spread on a baking sheet or in a pan large enough to hold them in a single layer. Coat with 2 teaspoons olive oil. Roast, turning once halfway through cooking, until browned and tender, 20 to 25 minutes.

Roasted Sweet Potatoes

GRAIN-COOKING GUIDE

Serving size is ½ cup cooked.

Barley

Bring **1¾ cups liquid** to a boil; add **1 cup quick-cooking barley**. Reduce heat to low and simmer, covered, 10 to 12 minutes.
YIELD: 2 CUPS

Bring **2½ cups liquid** and **1 cup pearl barley** to a boil. Reduce heat to low and simmer, covered, 35 to 50 minutes.
YIELD: 3-3½ CUPS

Couscous

Bring **1¾ cups liquid** to a boil; stir in **1 cup whole-wheat couscous**. Remove from heat and let stand, covered, 5 minutes. Fluff with a fork.
YIELD: 3-3½ CUPS

Quinoa

Rinse in several changes of cold water. Bring **2 cups liquid** and **1 cup quinoa** to a boil. Reduce heat to low and simmer, covered, until tender and most of the liquid has been absorbed, 15 to 20 minutes. Fluff with a fork.
YIELD: 3 CUPS

Rice

Bring **2½ cups liquid** and **1 cup long-grain brown rice** to a boil. Reduce heat to low and simmer, covered, until tender and most of the liquid has been absorbed, 40 to 50 minutes. Let stand 5 minutes, then fluff with a fork.
YIELD: 3 CUPS

Bring **at least 4 cups lightly salted water** to a boil. Add **1 cup wild rice** and cook until tender, 45 to 55 minutes. Drain.
YIELD: 2-2½ CUPS

Wheat Berries

Sort through **1 cup hard red winter-wheat berries** (*see Tip, page 245*), discarding any stones. Rinse well. Place in a large heavy saucepan. Add **3½ cups cold water** and **½ teaspoon salt**. Bring to a boil over high heat, then reduce heat, cover, and simmer gently for 1 hour, stirring occasionally. Drain and rinse. (*If not using immediately, store in an airtight container and refrigerate for up to 2 days or freeze for up to 1 month.*)
YIELD: 2¼ CUPS

DESSERTS

(Left to right): Warm Chocolate Pudding, Pear Crumble, Dark Fudgy Brownies, Strawberry-Raspberry Sundaes

Lemon Poppy-Seed Cake **238**

Dark Fudgy Brownies **239**

Warm Chocolate Pudding....................................**240**

Amazing No-Butter Apple Cranberry Pie.......**241**

Pear Crumble **242**

QUICK DESSERTS
Broiled Mango **243**

Cherries with Ricotta &
  Toasted Almonds **243**

Chocolate & Nut-Butter Bites **243**

"Cocoa-Nut" Bananas..**243**

Nutty Baked Apples **243**

Strawberry-Mango Margarita Compote **243**

Strawberry-Raspberry Sundaes **243**

> " What you see before you, my friend, is the result of
> a lifetime of chocolate... "
>
> KATHARINE HEPBURN

215 calories;

6 g fat (1 g sat, 2 g mono);

27 mg cholesterol; 38 g carbohydrate;

5 g protein; 2 g fiber; 146 mg sodium;

70 mg potassium.

Healthy ⚓ Weight

ACTIVE TIME: 30 MINUTES

TOTAL: 1¼ HOURS

EQUIPMENT: 10-inch (12-cup) Bundt pan, preferably nonstick

TIPS:

Toast **poppy seeds** in a small dry skillet over medium heat, stirring constantly, until fragrant, 3 to 4 minutes. Transfer to a plate to cool.

To **bring cold eggs to room temperature** quickly, place in a mixing bowl and set it in a larger bowl of warm water for a few minutes; the eggs will beat to a greater volume.

To **separate eggs** safely: Use an egg separator, an inexpensive gadget found in cookware stores; separating eggs by passing the yolk back and forth between pieces of eggshell or your hands can expose the eggs to bacteria.

LEMON POPPY-SEED CAKE

We love that Bundt cakes don't demand frosting—just let a sweet lemon glaze run over the warm cake and you've got perfection.

- 1½ **cups whole-wheat pastry flour (see *Note*, page 245)**
- 1 **cup all-purpose flour**
- ¼ **cup poppy seeds, toasted (see *Tip*)**
- 1½ **teaspoons baking powder**
- ½ **teaspoon baking soda**
- ¼ **teaspoon salt**
- 1 **cup buttermilk (see *Tip*, page 244)**
- ¼ **cup canola oil**
- 1 **teaspoon vanilla extract**
- 2 **tablespoons freshly grated lemon zest**
- 2 **tablespoons lemon juice**
- 2 **large eggs, at room temperature (see *Tip*)**
- 2 **large egg whites, at room temperature**
- 1¼ **cups sugar**

LEMON GLAZE
- ¾ **cup confectioners' sugar, plus more for dusting**
- 3 **tablespoons lemon juice**
- 1 **tablespoon water**

1. Preheat oven to 350°F. Coat a 12-cup Bundt pan, preferably nonstick, with cooking spray and dust with flour (or use cooking spray with flour).
2. Whisk whole-wheat flour, all-purpose flour, poppy seeds, baking powder, baking soda and salt in a medium bowl. Combine buttermilk, oil, vanilla, lemon zest and lemon juice in a glass measuring cup.
3. Beat eggs, egg whites and sugar in a large bowl with an electric mixer on high speed until thickened and pale, about 5 minutes.
4. Fold the dry ingredients into the egg mixture with a rubber spatula, a third at a time, alternating with 2 additions of the buttermilk mixture. Scrape the batter into the prepared pan, spreading evenly.
5. Bake the cake until the top springs back when touched lightly and a toothpick inserted in the center comes out clean, 35 to 40 minutes. Let cool in the pan for 5 minutes, then turn out onto a wire rack.
6. TO PREPARE GLAZE: Sift ¾ cup confectioners' sugar into a small bowl; mix with lemon juice and water to create a thin glaze. Poke 1-inch-deep holes all over the cake with a skewer. Coat the warm cake with the glaze using a pastry brush. Let cool completely. To serve, set the cake on a serving plate and dust with confectioners' sugar.

MAKES 16 SERVINGS.

DARK FUDGY BROWNIES

We like to use chocolate with 60-72% cacao content in these rich, fudgelike brownies, as it imparts a deeper, fuller flavor than less-chocolaty choices.

- **³/₄ cup all-purpose flour**
- **²/₃ cup confectioners' sugar**
- **3 tablespoons unsweetened cocoa powder, American-style *or* Dutch-process**
- **3 ounces semisweet *or* bittersweet chocolate (50-72% cacao), coarsely chopped, plus 2¹/₂ ounces chopped into mini chip-size pieces, divided**
- **1¹/₂ tablespoons canola oil**
- **¹/₄ cup granulated sugar**
- **1¹/₂ tablespoons light corn syrup blended with 3 tablespoons lukewarm water**
- **2 teaspoons vanilla extract**
- **¹/₈ teaspoon salt**
- **1 large egg**
- **¹/₃ cup chopped toasted walnuts (see *Tip, page 244*), optional**

1. Position rack in center of oven; preheat to 350°F. Line an 8-inch-square baking pan with foil, letting it overhang on two opposing sides. Coat with cooking spray.

2. Sift flour, confectioners' sugar and cocoa together into a small bowl. Combine the 3 ounces coarsely chopped chocolate and oil in a heavy medium saucepan; place over the lowest heat, stirring, until just melted and smooth, being very careful the chocolate does not overheat. Remove from the heat and stir in granulated sugar, corn syrup mixture, vanilla and salt until the sugar dissolves. Vigorously stir in egg until smoothly incorporated. Gently stir in the dry ingredients. Fold in the walnuts (if using) and the remaining 2¹/₂ ounces chopped chocolate just until well blended. Turn out the batter into the pan, spreading evenly.

3. Bake the brownies until almost firm in the center and a toothpick inserted comes out with some moist batter clinging to it, 20 to 24 minutes. Let cool completely on a wire rack, about 2¹/₂ hours.

4. Using the overhanging foil as handles, carefully lift the brownie slab from the pan. Peel the foil from the bottom; set the slab right-side up on a cutting board. Using a large, sharp knife, trim off any dry edges. Mark and then cut the slab crosswise into fifths and lengthwise into fourths. Wipe the blade with a damp cloth between cuts.

MAKES 20 BROWNIES.

PER BROWNIE:

86 calories;

3 g fat (1 g sat, 1 g mono);

11 mg cholesterol; 15 g carbohydrate;

2 g protein; 0 g fiber; 19 mg sodium;

25 mg potassium.

Healthy ⟩⟨ Weight

Lower ⬇ Carbs

ACTIVE TIME: 30 MINUTES

TOTAL: 3 HOURS 20 MINUTES (including cooling time)

TO MAKE AHEAD: Store in an airtight container for up to 3 days or in the freezer for up to 2 weeks.

♥ HEART-HEALTHY TIP

The omega-3 fatty acids (in the form of plant-based alpha-linolenic acid) in **walnuts** can help improve arterial functioning. Their high mono- and polyunsaturated-fat content also helps reduce total and LDL cholesterol levels while maintaining healthy HDL cholesterol levels.

164 calories;

2 g fat (1 g sat, 1 g mono);

37 mg cholesterol; 34 g carbohydrate;

6 g protein; 3 g fiber; 110 mg sodium;

311 mg potassium.

Healthy ⅜ Weight

ACTIVE TIME: 20 MINUTES

TOTAL: 20 MINUTES

TO MAKE AHEAD: Pour the pudding into a bowl and place a piece of plastic wrap directly on the surface. Refrigerate for up to 3 days; serve cold.

WARM CHOCOLATE PUDDING

This warm pudding has a marvelous deep chocolaty flavor, but it's low in fat and super-quick to make. Don't skimp on the quality of cocoa with this one—treat yourself to the good stuff.

1	**large egg**
2¼	**cups nonfat *or* low-fat milk, divided**
⅔	**cup sugar, divided**
⅛	**teaspoon salt**
⅔	**cup unsweetened cocoa powder**
2	**tablespoons cornstarch**
1	**teaspoon vanilla extract**

1. Lightly beat egg with a fork in a medium bowl.

2. Combine 1½ cups milk, ⅓ cup sugar and salt in a medium saucepan; bring to a simmer over medium heat, stirring occasionally.

3. Meanwhile, whisk the remaining ⅓ cup sugar, cocoa and cornstarch in a medium bowl. Whisk in the remaining ¾ cup milk until blended. Whisk the simmering milk mixture into the cocoa mixture. Pour the mixture back into the pan and bring to a simmer over medium heat, whisking constantly, until thickened and glossy, about 3 minutes. Remove from heat.

4. Whisk about 1 cup of the hot cocoa mixture into the beaten egg. Return the egg mixture to the pan and cook over medium-low heat, whisking constantly, until steaming and thickened, about 2 minutes. (Do not boil.) Whisk in vanilla. Serve warm.

MAKES 6 SERVINGS.

AMAZING NO-BUTTER APPLE CRANBERRY PIE

Most pie crusts use butter, shortening or lard to get a flaky texture—this one uses heart-healthy canola oil. We found that when we simply substitute oil for butter the texture suffers. The trick is to freeze the oil and a bit of flour together before incorporating it into the dough. The result is a flaky crust without all the saturated fat. This filling is on the tart side—experiment with less lemon juice or sweeter apples for a balance that's right for you.

CRUST

- ¼ **cup canola oil**
- 1¼ **cups all-purpose flour, divided**
- 2 **teaspoons granulated sugar**
- 1 **teaspoon baking powder**
- ½ **teaspoon salt**
- 4-5 **tablespoons low-fat milk**

TOPPING

- ⅓ **cup "quick" *or* regular rolled oats**
- ⅓ **cup all-purpose flour**
- ⅓ **cup packed light brown sugar**
- 1½ **tablespoons canola oil**
- ½ **tablespoon water**

FILLING

- ½ **cup granulated sugar**
- 3 **tablespoons all-purpose flour**
- 2 **pounds tart apples, such as Cortland *or* Granny Smith, peeled, cored and cut into chunks (about 6 cups)**
- 1 **cup dried cranberries**
  Grated zest and juice of 1 lemon

PER SERVING:

301 calories;

8 g fat (1 g sat, 5 g mono);

0 mg cholesterol; 57 g carbohydrate;

4 g protein; 3 g fiber; 176 mg sodium;

99 mg potassium.

NUTRITION BONUS: Vitamin C (18% DAILY VALUE).

ACTIVE TIME: 50 MINUTES

TOTAL: 2 HOURS 5 MINUTES

EQUIPMENT: 9-inch pie pan

1. TO PREPARE CRUST: Stir oil and ¼ cup flour in a small bowl until smooth; cover and chill in the freezer until partially frozen, about 40 minutes.

2. Whisk the remaining 1 cup flour, sugar, baking powder and salt in a mixing bowl. Using a pastry blender or 2 knives, cut the chilled oil-flour paste into the dry ingredients until crumbly. Stir in milk a tablespoon at a time just until a soft dough forms. Knead on a lightly floured surface 7 or 8 times. Press into a disk, wrap in plastic wrap and refrigerate.

3. Position rack in lower third of oven; preheat to 350°F. Coat a 9-inch pie pan with cooking spray.

4. TO PREPARE TOPPING: Work together oats, flour and brown sugar in a small bowl with a fork or your fingertips until there are no large lumps. Drizzle oil and water over the top and work together until the mixture forms small crumbs.

5. TO PREPARE FILLING & ASSEMBLE PIE: Combine sugar and flour in a small bowl. Toss apples and cranberries with lemon zest and juice in a mixing bowl. Sprinkle the sugar mixture over the apples and toss well.

6. Roll out the dough on a lightly floured surface into a 12-inch circle. Transfer to the prepared pie pan. Fold the edges under and crimp with a fork. Place the pan on a baking sheet. Mound the filling into the crust and cover with the topping.

7. Bake until the fruit is bubbling at the edges and is easily pierced with a skewer in the center, 55 to 70 minutes. Check toward the end of the baking time; if the crust or topping is becoming too dark, cover the pie loosely with foil.

MAKES ONE 9-INCH PIE, FOR 10 SERVINGS.

257 calories;

9 g fat (1 g sat, 4 g mono);

0 mg cholesterol; 46 g carbohydrate;

3 g protein; 5 g fiber; 7 mg sodium;

279 mg potassium.

High ⬆ Fiber

ACTIVE TIME: 25 MINUTES

TOTAL: 1½ HOURS

TO MAKE AHEAD: Prepare the topping (Step 2) and filling (Step 3), cover and refrigerate separately for up to 1 day. Bring to room temperature before assembling and baking.

♥ HEART-HEALTHY TIP

Oats: Oat bran and oatmeal are both high in soluble fiber, which helps lower cholesterol.

PEAR CRUMBLE

A dessert doesn't need to be complicated or fussy to be delicious. This easy, comfort classic is sure to please. Serve it as is or with low-fat ice cream or Vanilla Cream (eatingwell.com).

TOPPING
- 1½ **cups old-fashioned rolled oats**
- ½ **cup chopped walnuts**
- ½ **cup packed brown sugar**
- ⅓ **cup whole-wheat *or* all-purpose flour**
- ½ **teaspoon ground cinnamon**
- 5 **tablespoons canola oil**

FILLING
- 3½ **pounds ripe but firm Anjou pears, peeled and cut into ½-inch pieces**
- ½ **cup pure maple syrup**
- ½ **cup raisins**
- 2 **tablespoons all-purpose flour**
- 2 **tablespoons lemon juice**
- 2 **teaspoons minced crystallized ginger**

1. Preheat oven to 350°F.

2. TO PREPARE TOPPING: Combine oats, walnuts, brown sugar, flour and cinnamon in a medium bowl. Drizzle with oil and stir until evenly moist.

3. TO PREPARE FILLING: Combine pears, maple syrup, raisins, flour, lemon juice and ginger in a large bowl and mix well. Transfer the mixture to a 9-by-13-inch baking dish. Sprinkle the topping over the pears.

4. Bake the crumble until the pears are tender and the topping is golden, 45 to 50 minutes. Let stand for at least 10 minutes before serving.

MAKES 14 SERVINGS.

QUICK DESSERTS

BROILED MANGO

Healthy)(Weight   **Lower ⬇ Carbs**

Preheat broiler. Position rack in upper third of oven. Peel and slice 1 mango (*see Tip, page 244*). Arrange mango slices in a single layer in a broiler pan covered with foil. Broil until browned in spots, 8 to 10 minutes. Squeeze lime juice over the broiled mango and serve.

MAKES 2 SERVINGS.

PER SERVING: 69 calories; 0 g fat (0 g sat, 0 g mono); 0 mg cholesterol; 18 g carbohydrate; 1 g protein; 2 g fiber; 2 mg sodium; 167 mg potassium. **NUTRITION BONUS:** Vitamin C (50% DAILY VALUE), Vitamin A (15% DV).

CHERRIES WITH RICOTTA & TOASTED ALMONDS

Healthy)(Weight   **Lower ⬇ Carbs**

Heat ¾ cup frozen pitted cherries in the microwave until bubbling. Top cherries with 2 tablespoons nonfat ricotta and 1 tablespoon toasted slivered almonds.

MAKES 1 SERVING.

PER SERVING: 133 calories; 4 g fat (0 g sat, 2 g mono); 5 mg cholesterol; 21 g carbohydrate; 5 g protein; 3 g fiber; 33 mg sodium; 291 mg potassium. **NUTRITION BONUS:** Vitamin C (15% DAILY VALUE).

CHOCOLATE & NUT-BUTTER BITES

Top each of eight ¼-ounce squares of bittersweet chocolate with ½ teaspoon nut butter of your choice (almond, cashew, pistachio).

MAKES 4 SERVINGS.

PER SERVING: 79 calories; 6 g fat (2 g sat, 1 g mono); 0 mg cholesterol; 9 g carbohydrate; 1 g protein; 1 g fiber; 12 mg sodium; 20 mg potassium.

"COCOA-NUT" BANANAS

Place 4 teaspoons unsweetened cocoa powder and 4 teaspoons toasted unsweetened coconut on separate plates. Slice 2 small bananas on the bias, roll each slice in cocoa, shake off the excess, then dip in coconut.

MAKES 4 SERVINGS.

PER SERVING: 80 calories; 1 g fat (0 g sat, 0 g mono); 0 mg cholesterol; 19 g carbohydrate; 1 g protein; 2 g fiber; 5 mg sodium; 274 mg potassium.

NUTTY BAKED APPLES

Healthy)(Weight

Preheat oven to 350°F. Core 2 apples. Combine 4 teaspoons each chopped dried fruit and chopped toasted nuts (*see Tip, page 244*), 1 teaspoon honey and a pinch of cinnamon; spoon into the apples. Place the apples in a small baking dish and pour ½ cup apple cider around them. Cover with foil. Bake until tender, about 45 minutes. Serve topped with plain yogurt.

MAKES 2 SERVINGS.

PER SERVING: 165 calories; 4 g fat (0 g sat, 2 g mono); 0 mg cholesterol; 35 g carbohydrate; 1 g protein; 4 g fiber; 2 mg sodium; 215 mg potassium. **NUTRITION BONUS:** Fiber (16% DAILY VALUE).

STRAWBERRY-MANGO MARGARITA COMPOTE

Healthy)(Weight

Place 2 cups halved or quartered hulled strawberries, 2 cups diced mango (2 small or 1 large; *see Tip, page 244*), 2 tablespoons sugar, or to taste, 1 teaspoon freshly grated lime zest, 2 tablespoons lime juice, 1½ tablespoons tequila and 1½ tablespoons Triple Sec (or other orange liqueur) in a large bowl; toss gently to combine. (For a nonalcoholic or kid-friendly version, substitute fresh orange juice for the tequila and Triple Sec.) Let stand for 20 minutes for the flavors to meld. If desired, serve in margarita glasses: rub the rims with additional lime juice and dip in sugar, then spoon in the compote.

MAKES 4 SERVINGS.

PER SERVING: 134 calories; 0 g fat (0 g sat, 0 g mono); 0 mg cholesterol; 28 g carbohydrate; 1 g protein; 3 g fiber; 3 mg sodium; 231 mg potassium. **NUTRITION BONUS:** Vitamin C (110% DAILY VALUE).

STRAWBERRY-RASPBERRY SUNDAES

Healthy)(Weight

Puree 1 cup hulled strawberries and ½ cup raspberries with 2 tablespoons sugar and ½ teaspoon lemon juice in a blender. Serve over nonfat vanilla frozen yogurt (½ cup per serving) and top with sliced strawberries and raspberries, if desired.

MAKES 4 SERVINGS.

PER SERVING: 130 calories; 0 g fat (0 g sat, 0 g mono); 2 mg cholesterol; 28 g carbohydrate; 5 g protein; 2 g fiber; 65 mg sodium; 293 mg potassium. **NUTRITION BONUS:** Vitamin C (45% DAILY VALUE), Calcium (20% DV).

RESOURCES

KITCHEN TIPS:

No **buttermilk**? You can use buttermilk powder prepared according to package directions. Or make "sour milk": the ratio is 1 tablespoon lemon juice or vinegar to 1 cup milk.

To select **chicken breasts**: Our recommended serving size is 4-ounces (uncooked), so look for small breasts. If yours are closer to 5 ounces each, remove the tender (about 1 ounce) from the underside to get the correct portion size. Wrap and freeze the leftover tenders; when you have gathered enough, use them in a stir-fry, for chicken fingers or in soups.

To segment **citrus**: With a sharp knife, remove the skin and white pith from the fruit. Working over a bowl, cut the segments from their surrounding membranes. Squeeze juice into the bowl before discarding the membranes.

To remove **corn** from the cob: Stand an uncooked ear of corn on its stem end in a shallow bowl and slice the kernels off with a sharp, thin-bladed knife. This technique produces whole kernels that are good for adding to salads and salsas. If you want to use the corn kernels for soups, fritters or puddings, you can add another step to the process. After cutting the kernels off, reverse the knife and press the dull edge down the length of the ear to push out the rest of the corn and its milk.

To oil a **grill rack**: Oil a folded paper towel, hold it with tongs and rub it over the rack. (Don't use cooking spray on a hot grill.)

To cook **lentils**: Place in a saucepan, cover with water and bring to a boil. Reduce heat to a simmer and cook until just tender, about 20 minutes for green lentils and 30 minutes for brown. Drain and rinse under cold water.

To peel and cut a **mango**: Slice both ends off the mango, revealing the long, slender seed inside. Set the fruit upright on a work surface and remove the skin with a sharp knife. With the seed perpendicular to you, slice the fruit from both sides of the seed, yielding two large pieces. Turn the seed parallel to you and slice the two smaller pieces of fruit from each side. Cut the fruit into the desired shape.

To toast chopped **nuts**: Cook in a small dry skillet over medium-low heat, stirring constantly, until fragrant and lightly browned, 2 to 4 minutes.

To skin a **salmon** fillet: Place skin-side down. Starting at the tail end, slip a long knife between the fish flesh and the skin, holding down firmly with your other hand. Gently push the blade along at a 30° angle, separating the fillet from the skin without cutting through either.

To toast **sesame seeds**, heat a small dry skillet over low heat. Add seeds and stir constantly, until golden and fragrant, about 2 minutes. Transfer to a small bowl and let cool.

To make crispy **taco shells**: Working with 6 tortillas at a time, wrap in a barely damp cloth or paper towel and microwave on High until steamed, about 30 seconds. Lay the tortillas on a clean work surface and coat both sides with cooking spray. Then carefully drape each tortilla over two bars of the oven rack. Bake at 375°F until crispy, 7 to 10 minutes.

INGREDIENT NOTES:

Precooked **"baked tofu"** is firmer than water-packed tofu and comes in a wide variety of flavors. You might also like flavored baked tofu on a sandwich or in a stir-fry.

Fresh and dried **chiles** vary widely in spiciness depending on variety and seasonality. Smaller varieties are generally hotter. What makes chiles hot, capsaicin, is found in the inner membrane and seeds. Add chiles with caution when cooking, tasting as you go. **Chipotle peppers** are dried, smoked jalapeño peppers. **Ground chipotle** can be found in the specialty spice section of most supermarkets.

Often a blend of cinnamon, cloves, fennel seed, star anise and Szechuan peppercorns, **five-spice powder** was originally considered a cure-all miracle blend encompassing the five elements (sour, bitter, sweet, pungent, salty). Look for it in the supermarket spice section.

French green lentils are firmer than brown lentils and cook more quickly. They can be found in natural-foods stores and some supermarkets.

Green papaya is underripe papaya that is green and firm. Look for it in Asian markets. If you can't find one, a ripe papaya can be substituted in some recipes.

Hot **Madras curry powder**, located in the spice aisle of most supermarkets, adds a pleasant level of heat. Substitute regular curry powder for a milder flavor.

Pickled ginger is found at health-food stores, Asian markets and in the supermarket produce department.

Shao Hsing (or Shaoxing) is a seasoned rice wine. It is available in most Asian specialty markets and some larger supermarkets in the Asian section. An acceptable substitute is **dry sherry**, sold with other fortified wines in your wine or liquor store. (We prefer it to the "cooking sherry" sold in many supermarkets, which can be surprisingly high in sodium.)

Contrary to popular belief, **wheat berries** do not require an overnight soak before cooking. Simply boil them for 1 hour to soften the kernels, which will produce their characteristically chewy texture.

White whole-wheat flour, made from a special variety of white wheat, is light in color and flavor but has the same nutritional properties as regular whole-wheat flour. **Whole-wheat pastry flour** is milled from soft wheat. It contains less gluten forming potential than regular whole-wheat flour and helps ensure a tender result in delicate baked goods while providing the nutritional benefits of whole grains. Store in the freezer. **Sources:** Available in large supermarkets and in natural-foods stores, and from King Arthur Flour, (800) 827-6836, bakerscatalogue.com, and Bob's Red Mill, (800) 349-2173, bobsredmill.com.

Look for balls of **whole-wheat pizza dough**, fresh or frozen, at your supermarket. Choose a brand without hydrogenated oils.

REFERENCES:

American Heart Association: *americanheart.org*

BMI Calculator: *nhlbisupport.com/bmi/*

Calorie Counter/Nutrition Information: *nutritiondata.com*, *nal.usda.gov/fnic/foodcomp/search/*

DASH (NIH Dietary Approaches to Stop Hypertension): *nhlbi.nih.gov/hbp/prevent/h_eating/h_eating.htm*

EatingWell Diet: *eatingwell.com/diet*

Framingham Risk Calculator: *hp2010.nhlbihin.net/atpiii/calculator.asp?usertype=prof*

LEARN *Program for Weight Management 2000* (American Health Publishing Company, 2004)

Portfolio Eating Plan: *portfolioeatingplan.com*

Quitting Smoking Guide: *smokefree.gov/*

Weight Watchers: *weightwatchers.com*

FOR FURTHER STUDY:

Cardiac rehabilitation and secondary prevention of coronary heart disease. Ades PA. (*N Engl J Med.* 2001 Sep 20; 345(12):892-902.)

Comparison of the Atkins, Ornish, Weight Watchers, and Zone Diets for weight loss and heart disease risk reduction. Dansinger ML et al. (*JAMA.* 2005 Jan 5; 293(1):43-53.)

Comparison of the Atkins, Zone, Ornish, and LEARN diets for change in weight and related risk factors among overweight premenopausal women: the A TO Z Weight Loss Study: a randomized trial. Gardner CD et al. (*JAMA.* 2007 Mar 7;297(9):969-77.)

Diet Plan Ratings, *Consumer Reports*, June 2005: *consumerreports.org*

Effects of a dietary portfolio of cholesterol-lowering foods vs lovastatin on serum lipids and C-reactive protein. Jenkins DJ et al. (*JAMA.* 2003 Jul 23;290(4):502-10.)

Framingham Heart Study: *nhlbi.nih.gov/about/framingham/*

Mediterranean diet, traditional risk factors, and the rate of cardiovascular complications after myocardial infarction: final report of the Lyon Diet Heart Study. de Lorgeril M et al. (*Circulation.* 1999 Feb 16;99(6):779-85.)

Nurses' Health Study: *channing.harvard.edu/nhs/*

Physical activity in an Old Order Amish community. Bassett DR et al. (*Med Sci Sports Exerc.* 2004 Jan;36(1):79-85.)

Primary prevention of coronary heart disease in women through diet and lifestyle. Stampfer MJ et al. (*N Engl J Med.* 2000 Jul 6;343(1):16-22.)

Reduction in obesity and coronary risk factors after high caloric exercise training in overweight coronary patients. Savage PD, Brochu M, Poehlman ET, Ades PA. (*Am Heart J.* 2003 Aug;146(2):317-23.)

SUBJECT INDEX

Abdominal fat, 21, 23, 26
Ades-ocular test, 20
Alcohol, 15, 30, 32, 65–66
Almost-vegetarianism, 42–43
Aspirin, 46, 50, 65
Atherosclerosis, 9, 11, 34
Atkins Diet, 39–40, 41

Behavior modification, 39
Birth control pills, 16
Blood glucose levels, 23, 26, 48
Blood pressure
    aspirin and, 46
    coffee and, 66
    fish oil and, 46
    goals, 22, 24, 26
    high, health risks from, 22–24
    lifestyle approach to lowering, 34
    measuring, 24, 34
    in metabolic syndrome, 23
    potassium and, 63
    salt and, 51
    "white coat hypertension," 22–24
BMI (body mass index), 20–21, 26
Body fat distribution, 21

Calories
    in alcohol, 65
    burned during exercise, 54, 55, 56
    in dietary fats, 45
    food label listings, 61
    in nuts, 66
    for weight maintenance, 35
Carbohydrates
    complex versus refined, 47–48
    food label listings, 63
    glycemic index, 47–48
    high-fiber foods, 50
    low-carbohydrate diets, 39–41
    recommended intake, 48
    triglyceride levels and, 30
    whole grains, 47, 70
Cardiac risk factors. *See* risk factors for
    heart disease
Case histories, 19, 36, 53, 59, 67
CHD (coronary heart disease). *See also*
    risk factors for heart disease
    among women, 14, 15–16
    atherosclerosis and, 11
    prevalence of, 9–10, 14

Chocolate, 66
Cholesterol levels
    alcohol and, 65
    almost-vegetarian diets and, 42–43
    coffee and, 66–68
    dietary cholesterol and, 30
    dietary fats and, 45
    fish oil, triglyceride levels and, 46
    goals, 18–20, 26
    as heart disease risk factor, 18
    lifestyle approach to managing, 28–31
    measuring, 18
    medications and supplements for, 30,
        31–34
    in metabolic syndrome, 23
    niacin, HDL levels and, 32, 50
    omega-6 fatty acids, LDL levels and, 49
    Portfolio Eating Plan for, 42
    soluble fiber and, 48
    soy protein, LDL levels and, 50
    subclasses, 18
    tea and, 68
Coffee, 66–68
Coronary heart disease. *See* CHD
    (coronary heart disease)

Dairy products, 46, 64, 70
DASH eating plan, 34
Diabetes
    coffee and, 66
    complications associated with, 23, 24
    goals, 26
    as heart disease risk factor, 15–16, 24
    high-glycemic foods and, 48
    metabolic syndrome and, 23
    prevalence of, 12, 24
Diets and eating plans. *See also*
    EatingWell Healthy Heart Plan
    almost-vegetarian, 42–43
    DASH, 34
    healthy, cost of, 60–61
    LEARN, 38–39
    low-carbohydrate, 39–41
    macronutrient contents of, 41
    Mediterranean, 41–42, 51
    Portfolio, 42
    short-term effectiveness, 38
    VTrim, 37, 39
    Weight Watchers, 39
Drugs. *See* medications and supplements

The EatingWell Diet, 37
EatingWell Healthy Heart Plan
    alcohol, 65
    chocolate, 66
    coffee and tea, 66–68
    fats, 45–47
    ingredient substitutions, 64
    label reading, 61–64
    menus, 72
    nuts, 66
    pantry items, 60, 62
    principles of, 44
    recipe makeover strategies, 70
    restaurant meals, 64–65
    snacking, 64
Eggs, 46, 64
Exercise
    in daily routines, 57
    effect on LDL and triglyceride levels, 30
    exercise prescription, 56–57
    goal, 26
    lack of, as heart disease risk factor, 10, 22
    motivation, 57, 58
    number of heartbeats and, 57
    record keeping, 57
    regularity of, 22
    types, 54
    undertaking exercise program, 55–56
    walking, 35, 38, 55–56, 57, 58
    for weight control, 35, 38, 55, 57

Family history of heart disease, 8–9, 17
Fat distribution on body, 21
Fats and oils
    cholesterol levels and, 28–29, 46
    fish oil, 33–34, 46–47, 50
    food label listings, 61
    heart-healthy, 70
    omega-3 fatty acids, 33–34, 46–47, 49,
        50, 66
    types of, 45–47
Fiber
    benefits, 48
    in complex carbohydrates, 47–48
    food label listings, 63
    high-fiber foods, 50
    to increase in diet, 48
    recommended intake, 48, 63
    supplementation, 48, 50
    types, 48

Fish consumption, 47
Fish oil, 33–34, 46–47, 50
Food labels, 61–64
Framingham Risk Calculator, 17

Genetic factors, 8–9, 11, 22
Grains, 47, 70
Green tea, 50, 68

HDL cholesterol levels
    alcohol consumption and, 65
    dietary fats and, 45
    goals, 18–20, 26
    lifestyle approach to raising, 31
    in metabolic syndrome, 23
    niacin supplements for, 32, 50
Heart attack victims and survivors, 15, 34
Heart disease. *See* CHD (coronary heart
    disease)
Heart facts, 10
Herbal supplements. *See* medications and
    supplements
High blood pressure. *See* blood pressure
Hyperlipidemia. *See* cholesterol levels

Ingredient listings on food labels, 63
Ingredient substitutions, 64
Insulin resistance, 23, 24. *See also* diabetes

Label reading, 61–64
LDL cholesterol levels
    calculation of, 18
    dietary fats and, 45
    goals, 18–20, 26, 30
    lifestyle approach to lowering, 28–30
    medications and supplements for, 31–32
    omega-6 fatty acids and, 49
    soluble fiber and, 48
    soy protein and, 50
LEARN diet, 38–39
Lifestyle. *See also* EatingWell Healthy
    Heart Plan
    cholesterol levels and, 28–31
    healthy behaviors, 15–16
    heart disease and, 9–11
    integration of eating plan into, 38
    lifestyle exercise, 57
Lipids, blood. *See* cholesterol levels

Meats, 43, 46, 70
Medications and supplements
    aspirin, 46, 50, 65
    discontinuation of, with weight loss, 36
    for established heart disease, 16
    HDL-raising, 32, 50

herbal supplements, 33–34
    LDL-lowering, 30, 31–32
    for smoking cessation, 25
    triglyceride-lowering, 33–34
Mediterranean Diet, 41–42, 51
Menopause, 16
Menus, 72
Metabolic syndrome, 21, 23
Monounsaturated fats, 45

Niacin, 32, 50
Nuts, 29, 66

Obesity. *See* overweight and obesity
Oils. *See* fats and oils
Omega-3 fatty acids, 33–34, 46–47, 49, 50,
    66
Overweight and obesity. *See also* weight
    loss
    abdominal fat and waist circumference,
        21, 23, 26
    Ades-ocular test, 20
    BMI (body mass index), 20–21, 26
    diabetes and, 24
    as epidemic, 11–12, 20
    from excess dietary fat, 45
    as heart disease risk factor, 20–21
    from inactivity, 54
    in metabolic syndrome, 23
    triglyceride level and, 30

Pantry items, 60, 62
Physical activity. *See* exercise
Polyunsaturated fats, 45–46. *See also*
    omega-3 fatty acids
Portfolio Eating Plan, 42
Portion control, 37
Potassium, 63
Protein, 50

Red rice yeast supplements, 33, 50
Restaurant meals, 64–65
Risk factors for heart disease
    abdominal fat, 21, 23
    diabetes, 12, 24
    diet and lifestyle, 9–11
    family history, 8–9, 11
    Framingham Risk Calculator, 17
    high blood pressure, 22–24
    high cholesterol, 18–20
    metabolic syndrome, 21, 23
    multiple, 14, 16
    overall risk factor profile, 25–27
    overweight and obesity, 20–21
    physical inactivity, 22

rankings of, 16
    smoking, 24–25

Salt, 51, 61–63, 64, 70
Saturated fats, 29, 45, 46
Seeds, 66
Smoking, 16, 24–25
Snacks, 64
Sodium, 51, 61–63, 64, 70
South Beach Diet, 40–41, 41
Soy protein, 29, 50
Stanol and sterol spreads, 29
Statin drugs, 31–32
Stimulus control, 37, 60
Supplements. *See* medications and
    supplements

Tea, 50, 68
Trans fats, 28–29, 46, 63
Triglyceride levels
    alcohol consumption and, 65
    fish oil and, 46–47
    goals, 26
    lifestyle approach to lowering, 30
    medications and supplement for, 33–34
    metabolic problems associated with, 20
    in metabolic syndrome, 23

Vegetarian-influenced diet, 42–43
Vitamin supplementation, 50–52
VTrim Weight Loss Program, 37, 39

Waist circumference, 21, 23, 26
Walking
    in daily routines, 57
    versus running, 56
    step counters, 58
    undertaking as exercise program, 55
    for weight loss, 35, 38, 57
Weight loss. *See also* diets and eating plans
    benefits, 24, 34
    calories and, 34–35
    exercise for, 35, 38, 57
    impossibly rapid, 39
    maintenance of, 38
    obstacles, 35
    strategies and tips, 37–38, 40
Weight Watchers, 39, 41
Wine consumption, 65
Women, heart disease and, 14, 15–16

Zone Diet, 40–41

RECIPE INDEX

Our thanks to the fine cooks whose work has appeared in EATINGWELL Magazine. *Page numbers in italics indicate photographs.*

A

Almonds
  Cherries with Ricotta & Toasted Almonds, 243
  Chicken Mulligatawny, *114,* 120
  Creamy Wheat Berry Hot Cereal, *84,* 95
  Grilled Chicken Salad with Fresh Strawberry Dressing, *100,* 104
  Lentil & Almond Burgers, 151
  Scandinavian Muesli, *84,* 94
Amazing No-Butter Apple Cranberry Pie, 241
Anchovies, in Fresh Tomato & Herb Sauce, 229

Apples
  Amazing No-Butter Apple Cranberry Pie, 241
  Chicken Mulligatawny, *114,* 120
  Curried Waldorf Salad, 227
  Kale with Apples & Mustard, 231
  Nutty Baked Apples, 243
  Red & White Salad, 227
  Sweet Potato-Turkey Hash, 174
Apricot-Wheat Germ Muffins, 96, *97*
Artichokes: to cook, 234
  Snap Pea & Spring Herb Chicken, 164, *165*

Arugula
  Arugula & Strawberry Salad, 227
  Warm Bean & Arugula Salad, *100,* 110
  Warm Chicken Sausage & Potato Salad, 109
Asparagus: to cook, 234
  Egg Thread Soup with Asparagus, 124
  Grilled Chicken Salad with Fresh Strawberry Dressing, *100,* 104
  Roasted Asparagus with Caper Dressing, 230, *233*
  Shrimp & Pesto Pasta, 182
Athenian Pasta Primavera, 139

Avocados
  Avocado-Corn Salsa, 200
  Tilapia Ceviche, *198,* 199
  Zesty Wheat Berry-Black Bean Chili, 132, *133*

B

Baby Spinach Salad with Raspberry Vinaigrette, 227
Bacon
  Chard with Pancetta & Walnuts, 231
  Edamame Succotash with Shrimp, *178,* 179
  Garlic-Rosemary Mushrooms, 232, *233*
  Louisiana Red Beans & Rice, *202,* 223
  Roasted Snap Peas with Shallots, 232
Balsamic Roasted Chicken Breasts, 160
Bananas
  Banana-Berry Smoothie, 86
  Banana-Bran Muffins, *84,* 98
  Cantaloupe Smoothie, 87
  "Cocoa-Nut" Bananas, 243
Barbecued Pork Chops, Oven-, *214,* 215
Barbecue Sauce, Blueberry-Bourbon, 212, *213*
Barley, to cook, 236
Beans and legumes. *See also* Peas
  Caribbean Rice & Beans, 229
  Chile-Spiced Black Beans, 229
  Cucumber & Black-Eyed Pea Salad, *226,* 227
  Edamame Succotash with Shrimp, *178,* 179
  Egyptian Edamame Stew, 140, *141*
  Ginger Fried Rice, 145
  Green Bean & Cherry Tomato Sauté, 231
  green beans, to cook, 235
  Green Papaya Salad, *226,* 227
  Indian-Spiced Eggplant & Cauliflower Stew, *148,* 149
  Indian-Style Green Beans, 231
  Lemony Lentil & Salmon Salad, 193
  Lentil & Almond Burgers, 151
  Louisiana Red Beans & Rice, *202,* 223
  Middle Eastern Chickpea & Rice Stew, *114,* 119
  Paprika-Spiced Butter Beans & Polenta, 136, *137*
  Sichuan-Style Chicken with Peanuts, 166, *167*
  Smoked Salmon Salad Niçoise, *112,* 113
  Snap Pea Salad with Radish & Lime, 228

Snap Pea & Spring Herb Chicken, 164, *165*
Tilapia & Summer Vegetable Packets, 196, *197*
Warm Bean & Arugula Salad, *100,* 110
Wheat Berry-Lentil Soup, 118
Zesty Wheat Berry-Black Bean Chili, 132, *133*
Beef
  Bistro Beef Tenderloin, 211
  Blue Ribbon Meatloaf, *82,* 83
  Brazilian Grilled Flank Steak, 210
  EatingWell's Chicken-Fried Steak, *208,* 209
  EatingWell Taco, The, *206,* 207
  Filet Mignon with Blueberry-Bourbon Barbecue Sauce, 212, *213*
  Hamburger Buddy, *204,* 205
Beets, to cook, 234
Belgian endive, in Red & White Salad, 227
Berries
  Arugula & Strawberry Salad, 227
  Banana-Berry Smoothie, 86
  Chunky Blueberry Sauce, 93
  Filet Mignon with Blueberry-Bourbon Barbecue Sauce, 212, *213*
  Fresh Strawberry Dressing, *100,* 105
Bistro Beef Tenderloin, 211
Black Bean-Garlic Sauce, Roasted Savoy Cabbage with, 230
Black beans
  Caribbean Rice & Beans, 229
  Chile-Spiced Black Beans, 229
  Zesty Wheat Berry-Black Bean Chili, 132, *133*
Blackberries, in Banana-Berry Smoothie, 86
Black-Eyed Pea Salad, Cucumber &, *226,* 227
Blueberries
  Banana-Berry Smoothie, 86
  Chunky Blueberry Sauce, 93
  Filet Mignon with Blueberry-Bourbon Barbecue Sauce, 212, *213*
Blue Ribbon Meatloaf, *82,* 83
Bourbon-Blueberry Sauce, Filet Mignon with, 212, *213*
Bran-Banana Muffins, *84,* 98

Brazilian Grilled Flank Steak, 210
Breads
    Apricot-Wheat Germ Muffins, 96, *97*
    Banana-Bran Muffins, *84,* 98
    Buttermilk-Oatmeal Pancakes, 92
    EatingWell Waffles, *90,* 91
    Honey Oat Quick Bread, *84,* 99
Breakfasts
    Apricot-Wheat Germ Muffins, 96, *97*
    Banana-Berry Smoothie, 86
    Banana-Bran Muffins, *84,* 98
    Buttermilk-Oatmeal Pancakes, 92
    Cantaloupe Smoothie, 87
    Chunky Blueberry Sauce, 93
    Creamy Wheat Berry Hot Cereal, *84,* 95
    EatingWell Waffles, *90,* 91
    egg-white omelet technique and fillings, 89
    Honey Oat Quick Bread, *84,* 99
    Papaya Smoothie, 86
    Quick Breakfast Tacos, 88
    Scandinavian Muesli, *84,* 94
    Winter Fruit Salad, 87
Broccoli: to cook, 234
    Corn & Broccoli Calzones, *130,* 131
    Roasted Broccoli with Lemon, 230
Broiled Mango, 243
Brownies, Dark Fudgy, *237, 239*
Brown rice. *See* Rice
Brussels Sprouts with Walnut-Lemon
    Vinaigrette, *226,* 230
Bulgur, in Parsley Tabbouleh, 230
Burgers
    Lentil & Almond Burgers, 151
    Spicy Turkey Burgers with Pickled
    Onions, 172, *173*
Butter Beans & Polenta, Paprika-Spiced,
    136, *137*
Buttermilk-Oatmeal Pancakes, 92

C
Cabbage
    Crispy Fish Sandwich with Pineapple
    Slaw, *80, 81*
    Roasted Savoy Cabbage with Black
    Bean-Garlic Sauce, 230
    Savoy Cabbage Slaw, 228
Cajun Catfish, Quick, 201
Cake, Lemon Poppy-Seed, 238
Calzones, Corn & Broccoli, *130,* 131
Canadian bacon, in Louisiana Red Beans &
    Rice, *202,* 223
Cantaloupe Smoothie, 87

Capers
    Poached Salmon with Creamy Piccata
    Sauce, 189
    Roasted Asparagus with Caper Dressing,
    230, *233*
    Tilapia & Summer Vegetable Packets,
    196, *197*
Caribbean Rice & Beans, 229
Carrots: to cook, 234
    Garden Pasta Salad, *102, 103*
    Hamburger Buddy, *204, 205*
    Indian-Style Green Beans, 231
Catfish, Quick Cajun, 201
Cauliflower: to cook, 234
    Indian-Spiced Eggplant & Cauliflower
    Stew, *148,* 149
Champagne Vinaigrette, 228
Chard: to cook, 235
    Chard with Pancetta & Walnuts, 231
    Wheat Berry-Lentil Soup, 118
Cheddar cheese
    EatingWell Taco, The, *206,* 207
    Mini Chile Relleno Casseroles, *134,* 135
    Pureed Zucchini Soup, *114,* 126
    Quick Breakfast Tacos, 88
Cheese
    Arugula & Strawberry Salad, 227
    Athenian Pasta Primavera, 139
    Cherries with Ricotta & Toasted
    Almonds, 243
    Classic Lasagna, *73,* 74
    Corn & Broccoli Calzones, *130,* 131
    Creamy Squash Risotto, *128,* 138
    Cucumber & Black-Eyed Pea Salad,
    226, 227
    EatingWell's Pepperoni Pizza, *170,* 171
    EatingWell Taco, The, *206,* 207
    Gorgonzola & Prune Stuffed Chicken,
    162, 163
    Ham & Swiss Rösti, *224, 225*
    Mini Chile Relleno Casseroles, *134,* 135
    Paprika-Spiced Butter Beans & Polenta,
    136, *137*
    Pureed Zucchini Soup, *114,* 126
    Quick Breakfast Tacos, 88
    Rice & Peas with Feta, 230
Cherries
    Cherries with Ricotta & Toasted
    Almonds, 243
    Turkey Tenderloin with Whiskey-Cherry
    Sauce, *152,* 175
Chicken
    breast
        Balsamic Roasted Chicken Breasts,
        160

Chicken à la King, *78,* 79
Chicken Cutlets with Grape-Shallot
    Sauce, *152, 161*
Chicken Mulligatawny, *114,* 120
Five-Spice Chicken & Orange Salad,
    106, *107*
Gorgonzola & Prune Stuffed
    Chicken, *162,* 163
Grilled Chicken Salad with Fresh
    Strawberry Dressing, *100,* 104
Grilled Orange Chicken Fingers, 157
Lebanese Fattoush Salad with Grilled
    Chicken, 108
Pecan-Crusted Chicken, 158, *159*
Sichuan-Style Chicken with Peanuts,
    166, *167*
Snap Pea & Spring Herb Chicken,
    164, *165*
Sofia's Chicken Paprikash, 156
Sweet Potato-Chicken Hash
    (variation), 174
legs, thighs
    EatingWell's Oven-Fried Chicken, 76,
    77
    Old-Fashioned Chicken &
    Dumplings, *154,* 155
    Sichuan-Style Chicken with Peanuts,
    166, *167*
sausage
    Chicken Sausage & Potato Salad,
    Warm, 109
Chicken-Fried Steak, EatingWell's, *208,*
    209
Chickpeas
    Cucumber & Black-Eyed Pea Salad,
    226, 227
    Indian-Spiced Eggplant & Cauliflower
    Stew, *148,* 149
    Middle Eastern Chickpea & Rice Stew,
    114, 119
Chile-Mango Sauce, Salmon with, 192
Chile Relleno Casseroles, Mini, *134,* 135
Chili, Zesty Wheat Berry-Black Bean, 132,
    133
Chocolate
    Banana-Bran Muffins, *84,* 98
    Chocolate & Nut-Butter Bites, 243
    "Cocoa-Nut" Bananas, 243
    Dark Fudgy Brownies, *237, 239*
    Warm Chocolate Pudding, *237,* 240
Chowder, Manhattan Crab, *114, 121*
Classic Lasagna, *73,* 74
Coconut
    Chicken Mulligatawny, *114,* 120
    "Cocoa-Nut" Bananas, 243

Coconut Mashed Sweet Potatoes, 233
Scandinavian Muesli, *84,* 94
Corn: to cook, 234
    Avocado-Corn Salsa, 200
    Corn & Broccoli Calzones, *130,* 131
    Creamed Corn, *226,* 231
    Edamame Succotash with Shrimp, *178,*
      179
    Fresh Corn & Red Pepper Bisque, 116
    Mini Chile Relleno Casseroles, *134,* 135
Couscous, to cook, 236
Crab Chowder, Manhattan, *114,* 121
Cranberry Apple Pie, Amazing No-Butter,
    241
Creamed Corn, *226,* 231
Creamy Wheat Berry Hot Cereal, *84,* 95
Crispy Fish Sandwich with Pineapple Slaw,
    80, 81
Cucumbers
    Cucumber & Black-Eyed Pea Salad,
      226, 227
    Lebanese Fattoush Salad with Grilled
      Chicken, 108
    Lemony Lentil & Salmon Salad, 193
    Parsley Tabbouleh, 230
    Quinoa & Smoked Tofu Salad, 150
Curried Waldorf Salad, 227

D

Daikon, in Japanese Noodle & Shiitake
    Soup, 125
Dark Fudgy Brownies, *237,* 239
Desserts
    Amazing No-Butter Apple Cranberry
      Pie, 241
    Broiled Mango, 243
    Cherries with Ricotta & Toasted
      Almonds, 243
    Chocolate & Nut-Butter Bites, 243
    "Cocoa-Nut" Bananas, 243
    Dark Fudgy Brownies, *237,* 239
    Lemon Poppy-Seed Cake, 238
    Nutty Baked Apples, 243
    Pear Crumble, *237,* 242
    Strawberry-Mango Margarita Compote,
      243
    Strawberry-Raspberry Sundaes, *237,*
      243
    Warm Chocolate Pudding, *237,* 240
    Winter Fruit Salad, 87
Dressings. *See* Salad dressings
Duck Breasts, Five-Spice Roasted, 168
Dumplings, Old-Fashioned Chicken &,
    154, 155

E

EatingWell's Chicken-Fried Steak, *208,* 209
EatingWell's Oven-Fried Chicken, 77
EatingWell's Pepperoni Pizza, *170,* 171
EatingWell Taco, The, *206,* 207
Edamame
    Edamame Succotash with Shrimp, *178,*
      179
    Egyptian Edamame Stew, 140, *141*
Eggplant: to cook, 235
    Indian-Spiced Eggplant & Cauliflower
      Stew, *148,* 149
Eggs
    Egg Thread Soup with Asparagus, 124
    egg-white omelet technique and fillings,
      89
    Ginger Fried Rice, 145
    Ham & Swiss Rösti, *224,* 225
    Mini Chile Relleno Casseroles, *134,* 135
    Quick Breakfast Tacos, 88
Egyptian Edamame Stew, 140, *141*

F

Fattoush Salad with Grilled Chicken,
    Lebanese, 108
Fennel
    Manhattan Crab Chowder, *114,* 121
    Red & White Salad, 227
Feta cheese
    Athenian Pasta Primavera, 139
    Cucumber & Black-Eyed Pea Salad,
      226, 227
    Rice & Peas with Feta, 230
Filet Mignon with Blueberry-Bourbon
    Barbecue Sauce, 212, *213*
Filet of Sole with Spinach & Tomatoes, 195
Fish. *See also* Seafood
    Crispy Fish Sandwich with Pineapple
      Slaw, *80,* 81
    Easy Sautéed Fish Fillets, 200
    Filet of Sole with Spinach & Tomatoes,
      195
    Grilled Rosemary-Salmon Skewers, 188
    Grilled Salmon with Mustard & Herbs,
      190, *191*
    Grilled Tuna with Olive Relish, 194
    Honey-Soy Broiled Salmon, 186, *187*
    Lemony Lentil & Salmon Salad, 193
    Poached Salmon with Creamy Piccata
      Sauce, 189
    Quick Cajun Catfish, 201
    Salmon with Roasted Chile-Mango
      Sauce, 192
    Smoked Salmon Salad Niçoise, *112,* 113

Tilapia Ceviche, *198,* 199
Tilapia & Summer Vegetable Packets,
    196, *197*
Tomato, Tuna & Tarragon Salad, *100,*
    111
Five-Spice Chicken & Orange Salad, 106,
    107
Five-Spice Roasted Duck Breasts, 168
Flank Steak, Brazilian Grilled, 210
Flaxseeds, in Scandinavian Muesli, *84,* 94
Fresh Corn & Red Pepper Bisque, 116
Fresh Strawberry Dressing, 105
Fresh Tomato & Herb Sauce, 229
Fried Rice, Ginger, 145
Fruits. *See specific fruits*
Fruit Salad, Winter, 87

G

Garden Pasta Salad, *102,* 103
Garlic-Rosemary Mushrooms, 232, *233*
Ginger Fried Rice, 145
Ginger-Prune Sauce, Pork Medallions with,
    222
Gorgonzola & Prune Stuffed Chicken,
    162, 163
Grain-cooking guide, 236
Grains. *See specific types*
Grapefruit, in Winter Fruit Salad, 87
Grape-Shallot Sauce, Chicken Cutlets with,
    152, 161
Green beans: to cook, 235
    Green Bean & Cherry Tomato Sauté,
      231
    Indian-Style Green Beans, 231
    Smoked Salmon Salad Niçoise, *112,* 113
    Tilapia & Summer Vegetable Packets,
      196, *197*
Green Papaya Salad, *226,* 227
Greens. *See also* Salads
    Chard with Pancetta & Walnuts, 231
    Filet of Sole with Spinach & Tomatoes,
      195
    Japanese Noodle & Shiitake Soup, 125
    Kale with Apples & Mustard, 231
    Paprika-Spiced Butter Beans & Polenta,
      136, *137*
    Saag Tofu, 146, *147*
    spinach and chard, to cook, 235
    Wheat Berry-Lentil Soup, 118
Green Tea, Stir-Fried Noodles with, *142,*
    143
Grilled Chicken Salad with Fresh
    Strawberry Dressing, *100,* 104
Grilled Orange Chicken Fingers, 157

Grilled Rosemary-Salmon Skewers, 188
Grilled Salmon with Mustard & Herbs, 190, *191*
Grilled Tuna with Olive Relish, 194

H

Haddock
　　Crispy Fish Sandwich with Pineapple Slaw, *80*, 81
　　Easy Sautéed Fish Fillets, 200
Ham
　　Ham & Swiss Rösti, *224*, 225
　　Warm Bean & Arugula Salad, *100*, 110
Hamburger Buddy, *204*, 205
Hash, Sweet Potato-Turkey, 174
Hearts of palm
　　Brazilian Grilled Flank Steak, 210
　　Red & White Salad, 227
Homemade Buttermilk Mayonnaise, 228
Honey Oat Quick Bread, *84*, 99
Honey-Soy Broiled Salmon, 186, *187*

I

Indian-Spiced Eggplant & Cauliflower Stew, *148*, 149
Indian-Style Green Beans, 231
Ingredient notes, 244

J

Japanese Noodle & Shiitake Soup, 125
Jarlsberg cheese, in Ham & Swiss Rösti, *224*, 225

K

Kale with Apples & Mustard, 231
Kebabs
　　Grilled Rosemary-Salmon Skewers, 188
　　Shrimp & Plum Kebabs, 180, *181*
Kitchen tips, 244

L

Lasagna, Classic, *73*, 74
Lebanese Fattoush Salad with Grilled Chicken, 108
Lemon
　　Lemon Poppy-Seed Cake, 238
　　Lemon Soup, Yucatan, 122, *123*
　　Lemony Lentil & Salmon Salad, 193
Lentils
　　Lemony Lentil & Salmon Salad, 193
　　Lentil & Almond Burgers, 151
　　Wheat Berry-Lentil Soup, 118
Louisiana Red Beans & Rice, *202*, 223

M

Makeovers
　　Blue Ribbon Meatloaf, *82*, 83
　　Chicken à la King, *78*, 79
　　Classic Lasagna, *73*, 74
　　Crispy Fish Sandwich with Pineapple Slaw, *80*, 81
　　EatingWell's Chicken-Fried Steak, *208*, 209
　　EatingWell's Oven-Fried Chicken, *76*, 77
　　EatingWell's Pepperoni Pizza, *170*, 171
　　EatingWell Taco, The, *206*, 207
　　EatingWell Waffles, *90*, 91
　　Garden Pasta Salad, *102*, 103
　　Hamburger Buddy, *204*, 205
　　Old-Fashioned Chicken & Dumplings, *154*, 155
Manchego cheese, in Paprika-Spiced Butter Beans & Polenta, 136, *137*
Mangoes
　　Broiled Mango, 243
　　Salmon with Roasted Chile-Mango Sauce, 192
　　Strawberry-Mango Margarita Compote, 243
Manhattan Crab Chowder, *114*, 121
Maple-Mustard Pork Tenderloin, 218, *219*
Margarita Compote, Strawberry-Mango, 243
Mayonnaise, Homemade Buttermilk, 228
Meatloaf, Blue Ribbon, *82*, 83
Meats. *See* Beef; Pork
Mexican Sautéed Summer Squash, 232
Middle Eastern Chickpea & Rice Stew, *114*, 119
Mini Chile Relleno Casseroles, *134*, 135
Miso, in Japanese Noodle & Shiitake Soup, 125
Monterey Jack, in Paprika-Spiced Butter Beans & Polenta, 136, *137*
Mozzarella
　　Classic Lasagna, *73*, 74
　　Corn & Broccoli Calzones, *130*, 131
　　EatingWell's Pepperoni Pizza, *170*, 171
Muesli, Scandinavian, *84*, 94
Muffins
　　Apricot-Wheat Germ Muffins, 96, 97
　　Banana-Bran Muffins, *84*, 98
Mulligatawny, Chicken, *114*, 120
Mushrooms
　　Chicken à la King, *78*, 79
　　Classic Lasagna, *73*, 74
　　Creamy Squash Risotto, *128*, 138

Garlic-Rosemary Mushrooms, 232, *233*
　　Hamburger Buddy, *204*, 205
　　Japanese Noodle & Shiitake Soup, 125
　　Sesame-Roasted Mushrooms & Scallions, 232
Mussels, Spaghettini with Steamed, 183
Mustard & Herbs, Grilled Salmon with, 190, *191*
Mustard-Maple Pork Tenderloin, 218, *219*

N

Nectarines, in Baby Spinach Salad with Raspberry Vinaigrette, 227
New Potato & Pea Salad, 232
No-Butter Apple Cranberry Pie, Amazing, 241
Noodles
　　Japanese Noodle & Shiitake Soup, 125
　　Stir-Fried Noodles with Green Tea, *142*, 143
Nut-Butter & Chocolate Bites, 243
Nuts
　　Arugula & Strawberry Salad, 227
　　Banana-Bran Muffins, *84*, 98
　　Chard with Pancetta & Walnuts, 231
　　Cherries with Ricotta & Toasted Almonds, 243
　　Chicken Mulligatawny, *114*, 120
　　Creamy Wheat Berry Hot Cereal, *84*, 95
　　Curried Waldorf Salad, 227
　　Dark Fudgy Brownies, *237*, 239
　　Grilled Chicken Salad with Fresh Strawberry Dressing, *100*, 104
　　Lentil & Almond Burgers, 151
　　Nutty Baked Apples, 243
　　Pear Crumble, *237*, 242
　　Pecan-Crusted Chicken, 158, *159*
　　Scandinavian Muesli, *84*, 94

O

Oats
　　Amazing No-Butter Apple Cranberry Pie, 241
　　Buttermilk-Oatmeal Pancakes, 92
　　Creamy Wheat Berry Hot Cereal, *84*, 95
　　Honey Oat Quick Bread, *84*, 99
　　Pear Crumble, *237*, 242
　　Scandinavian Muesli, *84*, 94
Okra, in Sausage Gumbo, 169
Olives
　　Cucumber & Black-Eyed Pea Salad, *226*, 227
　　Garden Pasta Salad, *102*, 103
　　Grilled Tuna with Olive Relish, 194

Tilapia Ceviche, *198,* 199
Tilapia & Summer Vegetable Packets,
    196, *197*
Onions
    Roast Pork with Sweet Onion-Rhubarb
        Sauce, *220,* 221
    Spicy Turkey Burgers with Pickled
        Onions, 172, *173*
Orange Chicken Fingers, Grilled, 157
Oranges
    Curried Waldorf Salad, 227
    Five-Spice Chicken & Orange Salad,
        106, *107*
    Winter Fruit Salad, 87
Oven-Barbecued Pork Chops, *214,* 215
Oven-Fried Chicken, EatingWell's, *76,* 77
Oven-Fried Potatoes, 232
Oven-Fried Zucchini Sticks, 233

P
Pacific cod, in Crispy Fish Sandwich with
    Pineapple Slaw, *80,* 81
Pancakes, Buttermilk-Oatmeal, 92
Pancetta & Walnuts, Chard with, 231
Papaya
    Green Papaya Salad, *226,* 227
    Papaya Smoothie, 86
Paprika-Spiced Butter Beans & Polenta,
    136, *137*
Parmesan cheese
    Arugula & Strawberry Salad, 227
    Classic Lasagna, *73,* 74
    Creamy Squash Risotto, *128,* 138
    EatingWell's Pepperoni Pizza, *170,* 171
Parsley Tabbouleh, 230
Pasta
    Athenian Pasta Primavera, 139
    Classic Lasagna, *73,* 74
    Egg Thread Soup with Asparagus, 124
    Garden Pasta Salad, *102,* 103
    Japanese Noodle & Shiitake Soup, 125
    Shrimp & Pesto Pasta, 182
    Spaghettini with Steamed Mussels, 183
    Stir-Fried Noodles with Green Tea, *142,*
        143
    Tortellini & Zucchini Soup, 117
Peanuts, Sichuan-Style Chicken with, 166,
    167
Pear Crumble, *237,* 242
Peas: to cook, 235
    Athenian Pasta Primavera, 139
    Ginger Fried Rice, 145
    New Potato & Pea Salad, 232

Old-Fashioned Chicken & Dumplings,
    154, 155
Rice & Peas with Feta, 230
Scallops & Sweet Peas, *184,* 185
shoots
    Green Papaya Salad, *226,* 227
    Scallops & Sweet Peas, *184,* 185
Spring Pea & Scallion Soup, 127
sugar snap
    Grilled Chicken Salad with Fresh
        Strawberry Dressing, *100,* 104
    Roasted Snap Peas with Shallots, 232
    Snap Pea Salad with Radish & Lime,
        228
    Snap Pea & Spring Herb Chicken,
        164, 165
Pecan-Crusted Chicken, 158, *159*
Pepperoni Pizza, EatingWell's, *170,* 171
Peppers, bell
    Athenian Pasta Primavera, 139
    Baby Spinach Salad with Raspberry
        Vinaigrette, 227
    Caribbean Rice & Beans, 229
    Chicken à la King, *78,* 79
    Cucumber & Black-Eyed Pea Salad,
        226, 227
    Edamame Succotash with Shrimp, *178,*
        179
    Five-Spice Chicken & Orange Salad,
        106, *107*
    Fresh Corn & Red Pepper Bisque, 116
    Garden Pasta Salad, *102,* 103
    Paprika-Spiced Butter Beans & Polenta,
        136, *137*
    Quinoa & Smoked Tofu Salad, 150
    Sofia's Chicken Paprikash, 156
    Stir-Fried Noodles with Green Tea, *142,*
        143
    Sweet & Sour Tofu, 144
    Tangelo Pork Stir-Fry, 216, *217*
    Tilapia Ceviche, *198,* 199
    Zesty Wheat Berry-Black Bean Chili,
        132, 133
Pesto
    Roasted Zucchini & Pesto, 233
    Shrimp & Pesto Pasta, 182
Piccata Sauce, Poached Salmon with, 189
Pickled Ginger & Watercress Salad, 228
Pickled Onions, Spicy Turkey Burgers with,
    172, *173*
Pie, Amazing No-Butter Apple Cranberry,
    241
Pineapple
    Crispy Fish Sandwich with Pineapple
        Slaw, *80,* 81

Sweet & Sour Tofu, 144
Winter Fruit Salad, 87
Pizza, EatingWell's Pepperoni, *170,* 171
Plum Kebabs, Shrimp &, 180, *181*
Poached Salmon with Creamy Piccata
    Sauce, 189
Polenta, Paprika-Spiced Butter Beans &,
    136, *137*
Pomegranate, in Winter Fruit Salad, 87
Pork
    cured
        Chard with Pancetta & Walnuts, 231
        Edamame Succotash with Shrimp,
            178, 179
        Garlic-Rosemary Mushrooms, 232,
            233
        Ham & Swiss Rösti, *224,* 225
        Louisiana Red Beans & Rice, *202,*
            223
        Roasted Snap Peas with Shallots, 232
        Warm Bean & Arugula Salad, *100,*
            110
    fresh
        Maple-Mustard Pork Tenderloin, 218,
            219
        Oven-Barbecued Pork Chops, *214,*
            215
        Pork Medallions with Prune-Ginger
            Sauce, 222
        Roast Pork with Sweet Onion-
            Rhubarb Sauce, *220,* 221
        Tangelo Pork Stir-Fry, 216, *217*
Potatoes: to cook, 235
    Ham & Swiss Rösti, *224,* 225
    Manhattan Crab Chowder, *114,* 121
    New Potato & Pea Salad, 232
    Oven-Fried Potatoes, 232
    Smoked Salmon Salad Niçoise, *112,* 113
    Warm Chicken Sausage & Potato Salad,
        109
Poultry. *See* Chicken; Duck; Turkey
Prosciutto, in Warm Bean & Arugula Salad,
    100, 110
Prunes
    Gorgonzola & Prune Stuffed Chicken,
        162, 163
    Pork Medallions with Prune-Ginger
        Sauce, 222
Pudding, Warm Chocolate, *237,* 240
Pumpkin puree, in EatingWell's Pepperoni
    Pizza, *170,* 171

Q

Quinoa: to cook, 236
Quinoa & Smoked Tofu Salad, 150

R

Radicchio, in Red & White Salad, 227
Radishes
Japanese Noodle & Shiitake Soup, 125
Red & White Salad, 227
Snap Pea Salad with Radish & Lime, 228
Raspberries
Banana-Berry Smoothie, 86
Raspberry-Strawberry Sundaes, 243
Raspberry Vinaigrette, 228
Red Beans & Rice, Louisiana, *202,* 223
Red & White Salad, 227
Rhubarb-Sweet Onion Sauce, Roast Pork with, *220,* 221
Rice: to cook, 236
brown, to spice, 229
Caribbean Rice & Beans, 229
Creamy Squash Risotto, *128,* 138
Ginger Fried Rice, 145
Louisiana Red Beans & Rice, *202,* 223
Middle Eastern Chickpea & Rice Stew, *114,* 119
Rice & Peas with Feta, 230
Ricotta cheese
Cherries with Ricotta & Toasted Almonds, 243
Classic Lasagna, *73,* 74
Corn & Broccoli Calzones, *130,* 131
Roasted Asparagus with Caper Dressing, 230, *233*
Roasted Broccoli with Lemon, 230
Roasted Savoy Cabbage with Black Bean-Garlic Sauce, 230
Roasted Snap Peas with Shallots, 232
Roasted Zucchini & Pesto, 233
Roast Pork with Sweet Onion-Rhubarb Sauce, *220,* 221
Romaine & Fresh Herb Salad, 227
Rösti, Ham & Swiss, *224,* 225

S

Saag Tofu, 146, *147*
Salad dressings
Champagne Vinaigrette, 228
Fresh Strawberry Dressing, *100,* 105
Homemade Buttermilk Mayonnaise, 228
for New Potato & Pea Salad, 232
Raspberry Vinaigrette, 228
Walnut-Lemon Vinaigrette, *226,* 230

Salads
main dish
Five-Spice Chicken & Orange Salad, 106, *107*
Garden Pasta Salad, *102,* 103
Grilled Chicken Salad with Fresh Strawberry Dressing, *100,* 104
Lebanese Fattoush Salad with Grilled Chicken, 108
Lemony Lentil & Salmon Salad, 193
Quinoa & Smoked Tofu Salad, 150
Smoked Salmon Salad Niçoise, *112,* 113
Tomato, Tuna & Tarragon Salad, *100,* 111
Warm Bean & Arugula Salad, *100,* 110
Warm Chicken Sausage & Potato Salad, 109
side
Arugula & Strawberry Salad, 227
Baby Spinach Salad with Raspberry Vinaigrette, 227
Cucumber & Black-Eyed Pea Salad, *226,* 227
Curried Waldorf Salad, 227
Green Papaya Salad, *226,* 227
New Potato & Pea Salad, 232
Parsley Tabbouleh, 230
Red & White Salad, 227
Romaine & Fresh Herb Salad, 227
Savoy Cabbage Slaw, 228
Snap Pea Salad with Radish & Lime, 228
Watercress & Pickled Ginger Salad, 228
Winter Fruit Salad, 87
Salmon
Grilled Rosemary-Salmon Skewers, 188
Grilled Salmon with Mustard & Herbs, 190, *191*
Honey-Soy Broiled Salmon, 186, *187*
Lemony Lentil & Salmon Salad, 193
Poached Salmon with Creamy Piccata Sauce, 189
Salmon with Roasted Chile-Mango Sauce, 192
Smoked Salmon Salad Niçoise, *112,* 113
Salsas
Avocado-Corn Salsa, 200
for Brazilian Grilled Flank Steak, 210
Olive Relish, 194
Tomato Salsa, 229

Sandwich, Crispy Fish, with Pineapple Slaw, *80,* 81
Sauces. *See also* Salsas
Blueberry-Bourbon Barbecue Sauce, 212, *213*
Caper Dressing, 230, *233*
Chunky Blueberry Sauce, 93
Creamy Piccata Sauce, 189
Fresh Tomato & Herb Sauce, 229
Grape-Shallot Sauce, *152,* 161
Meat Sauce, 74
Prune-Ginger Sauce, 222
Roasted Chile-Mango Sauce, 192
Sichuan Sauce, 166, *167*
Sweet Onion-Rhubarb Sauce, *220,* 221
Whiskey-Cherry Sauce, *152,* 175
Sausage
Classic Lasagna, *73,* 74
EatingWell's Pepperoni Pizza, *170,* 171
Sausage Gumbo, 169
Warm Chicken Sausage & Potato Salad, 109
Scallions & Mushrooms, Sesame-Roasted, 232
Scallion & Spring Pea Soup, 127
Scallops & Sweet Peas, *184,* 185
Scandinavian Muesli, *84,* 94
Seafood. *See also* Fish
Edamame Succotash with Shrimp, *178,* 179
Manhattan Crab Chowder, *114,* 121
Scallops & Sweet Peas, *184,* 185
Shrimp & Pesto Pasta, 182
Shrimp & Plum Kebabs, 180, *181*
Spaghettini with Steamed Mussels, 183
Yucatan Lemon Soup, 122, *123*
Sesame-Roasted Mushrooms & Scallions, 232
Shallot-Grape Sauce, Chicken Cutlets with, *152,* 161
Shrimp
Edamame Succotash with Shrimp, *178,* 179
Shrimp & Pesto Pasta, 182
Shrimp & Plum Kebabs, 180, *181*
Yucatan Lemon Soup, 122, *123*
Sichuan-Style Chicken with Peanuts, 166, *167*
Slaw
Crispy Fish Sandwich with Pineapple Slaw, *80,* 81
Savoy Cabbage Slaw, 228

Smoked Salmon Salad Niçoise, *112,* 113
Smoked Tofu Salad, Quinoa &, 150
Smoothies
    Banana-Berry Smoothie, 86
    Cantaloupe Smoothie, 87
    Papaya Smoothie, 86
Snap peas
    Grilled Chicken Salad with Fresh
        Strawberry Dressing, *100,* 104
    Roasted Snap Peas with Shallots, 232
    Sichuan-Style Chicken with Peanuts,
        166, *167*
    Snap Pea Salad with Radish & Lime, 228
    Snap Pea & Spring Herb Chicken, 164,
        165
Snow peas, in Grilled Chicken Salad with
    Fresh Strawberry Dressing, *100,* 104
Sofia's Chicken Paprikash, 156
Sole
    Easy Sautéed Fish Fillets, 200
    Filet of Sole with Spinach & Tomatoes,
        195
Soups and stews
    Chicken Mulligatawny, *114,* 120
    Egg Thread Soup with Asparagus, 124
    Egyptian Edamame Stew, 140, *141*
    Fresh Corn & Red Pepper Bisque, 116
    Indian-Spiced Eggplant & Cauliflower
        Stew, *148,* 149
    Japanese Noodle & Shiitake Soup, 125
    Manhattan Crab Chowder, *114,* 121
    Middle Eastern Chickpea & Rice Stew,
        114, 119
    Pureed Zucchini Soup, *114,* 126
    Sausage Gumbo, 169
    Spring Pea & Scallion Soup, 127
    Tortellini & Zucchini Soup, 117
    Wheat Berry-Lentil Soup, 118
    Yucatan Lemon Soup, 122, *123*
    Zesty Wheat Berry-Black Bean Chili,
        132, *133*
Soy. *See* Edamame; Tofu
Spaghettini with Steamed Mussels, 183
Spicy Turkey Burgers with Pickled Onions,
    172, *173*
Spinach: to cook, 235
    Baby Spinach Salad with Raspberry
        Vinaigrette, 227
    Filet of Sole with Spinach & Tomatoes,
        195
    Japanese Noodle & Shiitake Soup, 125
    Paprika-Spiced Butter Beans & Polenta,
        136, *137*
    Saag Tofu, 146, *147*

Spring Pea & Scallion Soup, 127
Sprouts
    Ginger Fried Rice, 145
    Green Papaya Salad, *226,* 227
    Snap Pea & Spring Herb Chicken, 164,
        165
Squash
    summer: to cook, 235
        Athenian Pasta Primavera, 139
        Egyptian Edamame Stew, 140, *141*
        Mexican Sautéed Summer Squash,
            232
        Oven-Fried Zucchini Sticks, 233
        Pureed Zucchini Soup, *114,* 126
        Roasted Zucchini & Pesto, 233
        Tilapia & Summer Vegetable Packets,
            196, *197*
        Tortellini & Zucchini Soup, 117
    winter: to cook, 235
        Creamy Squash Risotto, *128,* 138
        EatingWell's Pepperoni Pizza, *170,*
            171
Star fruit, in Winter Fruit Salad, 87
Stews. *See* Soups and stews
Stir-fries
    Ginger Fried Rice, 145
    Sichuan-Style Chicken with Peanuts,
        166, *167*
    Stir-Fried Noodles with Green Tea, *142,*
        143
    Sweet & Sour Tofu, 144
    Tangelo Pork Stir-Fry, 216, *217*
Strawberries
    Arugula & Strawberry Salad, 227
    Grilled Chicken Salad with Fresh
        Strawberry Dressing, *100,* 104
    Strawberry-Mango Margarita Compote,
        243
    Strawberry-Raspberry Sundaes, *237,*
        243
substitutions, heart-healthy, 64
Succotash, Edamame, with Shrimp, *178,*
    179
Sugar snap peas. *See* Snap peas
Sumac, in Lebanese Fattoush Salad with
    Grilled Chicken, 108
Sundaes, Strawberry-Raspberry, *237,* 243
Sun dried tomatoes, in Classic Lasagna, *73,*
    74
Sweet potatoes: to cook, 236
    Coconut Mashed Sweet Potatoes, 233
    Middle Eastern Chickpea & Rice Stew,
        114, 119
    Sweet Potato-Turkey Hash, 174

Sweet & Sour Tofu, 144
Swiss & Ham Rösti, *224,* 225

T
Tabbouleh, Parsley, 230
Tacos
    EatingWell Taco, The, *206,* 207
    Quick Breakfast Tacos, 88
Tangelo Pork Stir-Fry, 216, *217*
Tarragon Salad, Tomato, Tuna &, *100,* 111
Tilapia
    Tilapia Ceviche, *198,* 199
    Tilapia & Summer Vegetable Packets,
        196, *197*
Tips, 244
Tofu
    Banana-Berry Smoothie, 86
    Quinoa & Smoked Tofu Salad, 150
    Saag Tofu, 146, *147*
    Stir-Fried Noodles with Green Tea, *142,*
        143
    Sweet & Sour Tofu, 144
Tomatoes
    Avocado-Corn Salsa, 200
    Brazilian Grilled Flank Steak, 210
    Classic Lasagna, *73,* 74
    Filet of Sole with Spinach & Tomatoes,
        195
    Fresh Tomato & Herb Sauce, 229
    Garden Pasta Salad, *102,* 103
    Green Bean & Cherry Tomato Sauté,
        231
    Grilled Rosemary-Salmon Skewers, 188
    Manhattan Crab Chowder, *114,* 121
    Parsley Tabbouleh, 230
    Quinoa & Smoked Tofu Salad, 150
    Tilapia & Summer Vegetable Packets,
        196, *197*
    Tomato, Tuna & Tarragon Salad, *100,*
        111
    Tomato Salsa, 229
Tortellini & Zucchini Soup, 117
Tuna
    Grilled Tuna with Olive Relish, 194
    Tomato, Tuna & Tarragon Salad, *100,*
        111
Turkey
    Blue Ribbon Meatloaf, *82,* 83
    EatingWell Taco, The, *206,* 207
    sausage
        Classic Lasagna, *73,* 74
        EatingWell's Pepperoni Pizza, *170,*
            171
        Sausage Gumbo, 169

EatingWell

FOR A
HEALTHY HEART
COOKBOOK

A Cardiologist's Guide to Adding Years to Your Life

REDUCE
Your Risk of
Heart Attack
by 50%

LOWER Blood
Pressure and
Cholesterol

EAT WELL with
150 Delicious,
Satisfying Recipes

By PHILIP A. ADES, M.D.
& the Editors of EATINGWELL

Foreword by Howard Dean, M.D., and Judith Steinberg, M.D.

The Countryman Press
Woodstock, Vermont

eatingwell.com
EatingWell
WHERE GOOD TASTE MEETS GOOD HEALTH

Spicy Turkey Burgers with Pickled Onions, 172, *173*
Sweet Potato-Turkey Hash, 174
Turkey Tenderloin with Whiskey-Cherry Sauce, *152,* 175

V

Vegetable cooking guide, 234
Vegetable dishes. *See also* Salads; *specific vegetables*
Brussels Sprouts with Walnut-Lemon Vinaigrette, *226,* 230
Chard with Pancetta & Walnuts, 231
Creamed Corn, *226,* 231
Garlic-Rosemary Mushrooms, 232, *233*
Green Bean & Cherry Tomato Sauté, 231
Indian-Style Green Beans, 231
Kale with Apples & Mustard, 231
Mexican Sautéed Summer Squash, 232
Oven-Fried Zucchini Sticks, 233
Roasted Asparagus with Caper Dressing, 230, *233*
Roasted Broccoli with Lemon, 230
Roasted Savoy Cabbage with Black Bean-Garlic Sauce, 230
Roasted Snap Peas with Shallots, 232
Roasted Zucchini & Pesto, 233
Sesame-Roasted Mushrooms & Scallions, 232

Vegetarian main dishes
Athenian Pasta Primavera, 139
Corn & Broccoli Calzones, *130,* 131
Creamy Squash Risotto, *128,* 138
Egyptian Edamame Stew, 140, *141*
Ginger Fried Rice, 145
Indian-Spiced Eggplant & Cauliflower Stew, *148,* 149
Lentil & Almond Burgers, 151
Mini Chile Relleno Casseroles, *134,* 135
Paprika-Spiced Butter Beans & Polenta, 136, *137*
Quinoa & Smoked Tofu Salad, 150
Saag Tofu, 146, *147*
Stir-Fried Noodles with Green Tea, *142,* 143
Sweet & Sour Tofu, 144
Zesty Wheat Berry-Black Bean Chili, 132, *133*

W

Waffles, EatingWell, *90,* 91
Waldorf Salad, Curried, 227
Walnut-Lemon Vinaigrette, Brussels Sprouts with, *226,* 230
Walnuts
Arugula & Strawberry Salad, 227
Banana-Bran Muffins, *84,* 98
Chard with Pancetta & Walnuts, 231
Curried Waldorf Salad, 227

Dark Fudgy Brownies, *237,* 239
Pear Crumble, *237,* 242
Watercress & Pickled Ginger Salad, 228
Wax beans, in Snap Pea Salad with Radish & Lime, 228
Wheat berries: to cook, 236
Creamy Wheat Berry Hot Cereal, *84,* 95
Wheat Berry-Lentil Soup, 118
Zesty Wheat Berry-Black Bean Chili, 132, *133*
Wheat Germ-Apricot Muffins, 96, *97*
Whiskey-Cherry Sauce, Turkey Tenderloin with, *152,* 175
White beans
Cucumber & Black-Eyed Pea Salad, *226,* 227
Warm Bean & Arugula Salad, *100,* 110
Winter Fruit Salad, 87

Y, Z

Yucatan Lemon Soup, 122, *123*

Zucchini: to cook, 235
Athenian Pasta Primavera, 139
Egyptian Edamame Stew, 140, *141*
Mexican Sautéed Summer Squash, 232
Oven-Fried Zucchini Sticks, 233
Pureed Zucchini Soup, *114,* 126
Roasted Zucchini & Pesto, 233
Tortellini & Zucchini Soup, 117

OTHER EATINGWELL BOOKS

(available at *www.eatingwell.com/shop*):

The Essential EatingWell Cookbook

(The Countryman Press, 2004)

ISBN-13: 978-0-88150-630-3 (hardcover)

ISBN-13: 978-0-88150-701-0 (softcover, 2005)

The EatingWell Diabetes Cookbook

(The Countryman Press, 2005)

ISBN-13: 978-0-88150-633-4 (hardcover)

ISBN-13: 978-0-88150-778-2 (softcover, 2007)

The EatingWell Healthy in a Hurry Cookbook

(The Countryman Press, 2006)

ISBN-13: 978-0-88150-687-7 (hardcover)

EatingWell Serves Two

(The Countryman Press, 2006)

ISBN-13: 978-0-88150-723-2 (hardcover)

The EatingWell Diet

(The Countryman Press, 2007)

ISBN-13: 978-0-88150-722-5 (hardcover)